NOBODY'S HOME

ESSAYS

DUBRAVKA UGRESIC

TRANSLATED
FROM
THE
CROATIAN
BY
ELLEN
ELIAS-BURSAĆ

OPEN LETTER
LITERARY TRANSLATIONS FROM THE UNIVERSITY OF ROCHESTER

Originally published in Croatian as *Nikog nema doma* (Devedeset Stupnjeva, 2005). Changes, additions, and revisions to the Croatian edition originate with the author.

Library of Congress Control Number: 2008926344
ISBN-13: 978-1-934824-00-9 / ISBN-10: 1-934824-00-3

Printed on acid-free paper in the United States of America.

Text set in Adobe Caslon, a family of serif typefaces based on the designs of William Caslon (1692–1766).

Design by N. J. Furl

Open Letter is the University of Rochester's nonprofit, literary translation press: Lattimore Hall 411, Box 270082, Rochester, NY 14627

www.openletterbooks.org

CONTENTS

NOBODY'S HOME

1.

1.
The Wall has fallen. It has fallen onto every single person, onto all of us . . .

—*anonymous commentator*

2.
"Falling off?" asked Ukhudshansky, poking his head and the newspaper out of the window.

"That's nothing!" said the photographer disdainfully. "You should have seen me fall off the spiral slide in the amusement park."[1]

—*Ilf & Petrov,* The Golden Calf

---

1. This and all later quotes from Ilf & Petrov's *The Golden Calf* are taken from the 1962 Random House edition, translated by John H. C. Richardson.

A GLOBAL VIEW OF THE WORLD

If I remember anything from a dream, it is usually a situation or a picture, but I seldom recall spoken words. My dreams are silent movies. Recently, however, someone in a dream tugged my sleeve and said, "Come, let me show you a global view of the world!" The promised view, regrettably, never materialized. I woke up. All that was left was the sentence and a mild twinge of disappointment at the unfulfilled promise.

What if I hadn't woken? What would I have seen? Images like the ones from sci-fi movies, where the earth looks like a fetching commercial for tourism? Video clips like CNN's ads for the world's best hotels? Would I be able to see a global view of the world if I were to look through a giant pair of binoculars, as Aelita, queen of Mars, does in Protazanov's old Soviet movie? Or would I get a global perspective by flying wrapped in Superman's powerful, safe embrace? That would suit me best, if I may say so.

What would I see? Would I see anything?

We live in a new, visual era, but the global view of the world is more opaque than ever. Many think, of course, that the earth has shrunk in this post-Utopian time, like a cotton towel in the laundry. Cyber-space surfers think they have the world in the palm of their hands. Business people, activists in the global circulation of capital, think they are carrying the earth in their pocket. For tourists, those industrious airline consumers, the earth has become disappointingly small. To migrants who excavate channels for crossing from places that are worse to places that are better, and to those who bear children in China and then ship them off like little airmail packages to Holland, the earth may seem like a wheel of Swiss cheese—full of holes. Even the inhabitants of Papua New Guinea watch CNN. So what could we possibly be missing?

We haven't got a global view! The sentence may have seeped into my dream from the general millennial malaise. But how is it showing? The term *la belle indifference* was used in old-fashioned psychiatric textbooks to describe one of the symptoms of hysteria. The absence of anxiety, a beautiful indifference, the attitude with which humankind awaited the end of the last millennium and the start of this one, may merely be a symptom of profound fear confounded by those pestering questions: who are we? what are we? where are we headed? Why had the hands of the great palm reader, foretelling the earth's future in ages past, spun it faster and with greater abandon back then?

Is it that the word *future* has been compromised? The costly fashion of having one's body frozen (hoping for another life in an uncertain future) has been replaced by the fad of launching one's ashes, post-cremation, into space. That is apparently how the latest in funeral rites are being advertised by a fancy American funeral home. The popular notion of buying tickets for the Moon, all the rage forty years ago, has been superseded by high-priced transatlantic cruises on modern replicas of the Titanic.

It is true that we all mull over the same images, information and virtuality, but each of us runs our own little life in our own way. There may be relief in those moments of exhaustion, melancholy, or passing dullness, when there is a brief lapse of the future projection or a refusal to think about it. Perhaps the unadapted heart of the world has been worn down by speed. The heart of the world is very old, while speed is new and young. Herein may lie the answer to the momentary global reluctance to be seen. Because mankind at this moment hasn't even set down the traffic rules for the future—whether we will be cycling, as the worried futurists warn us, or each riding our own rocket, as the less worried suggest, or something yet again.

I know nothing of global matters. If I had succeeded in finding something out, I'd tell you. I'm no miser. I wouldn't keep such important information to myself. Whatever the case, after those words in the dream—*Come, let me show you a global view of the world*—I have been trying to stay more alert in my sleep. Should the opportunity presents itself again, I don't want to miss the view.

FLEA MARKET

What is the purpose of your life? A passerby flung this question at me one morning on a street in Cambridge, Massachusetts. "This one has a screw loose," I thought and kept walking. Ever since, whenever anyone has stopped me on the street, I wince. I'm scared they will ask me that question again. I have no answer, yet.

I should go to flea markets more often. A flea market is a quick and telling lesson on the human condition. The flea market is a psycho-therapy session, a nightmare encounter with one's inner self. Plenty of people like poking around flea markets. Some are there for practical reasons; they need to find a little something, maybe an out-of-stock part for an ancient washing machine. Others treat flea markets as department stores for the unwashed. The third are collectors, people out to pluck pearls from the sea of trash, adventurers who haven't the cash for a proper adventure, people plagued by nostalgia, socialites from society's dregs. There are voyeurs, stopping by for a glimpse of their past, or their future.

Wealthy countries do what they can to eradicate these messy places, or at least to control the chaos. Flea markets are older and more vital than the municipality itself; they disappear in one place and crop up in another. The true strength of the flea market is not in its utility, but in its lack of utility. A flea market that is law-abiding and aboveboard is a surrogate and serves only tourism: the organized chaos of a flea market lends a city whimsy and color. A genuine flea market, however, is wild, semi-legal at best, never in the center of town, always on the outskirts, in neighborhoods where decent people seldom venture.

The flea market is a powerful metaphor for a world with no borders. People rub shoulders at flea markets who would have no occasion, otherwise, to meet. There are things at flea markets you'd otherwise rarely see: Chinese knock-off Nikes and Soviet military medals. And it is the Pakistanis selling the Soviet medals, while the Poles are hawking the Chinese Nikes. The flea market is a place of myth and a meeting point. Bosnian refugees used to converge at the Berlin flea market to share the latest news of far-flung refugee friends and compatriots.

The flea market is a place of disillusion, but also of solace, much like a cemetery: among the heaps of discarded books, photographs, family albums, old records, household objects, and moth-eaten clothing, you stumble on your own past, but you also see your future. Flea markets will, in short, be here when we are gone. Our possessions live longer than we do. Our things earn the right to an anonymous, ironic immortality.

Many years ago I visited the famous Moscow bird market. The Moscow bird market was a vibrant scene for the subversion of the otherwise totalitarian law and order. A metaphoric gesture of defiance to the grim, heartless communist system. A warm, contrary heart for the city.

A red-nosed fellow held a large, glass pickle jar and rocked it slowly back and forth. An indigo-colored fish swam around inside the jar.

"His name is Vasya," said the fellow.

Vasya's lady friend died recently, and Vasya had been swimming around ever since, inconsolable . . .

"Take him," pleaded the guy.

"What can I do with him? How will I be able take him out of the country with me?"

"Let Vasya live the good life since I can't," needled the man.

And so it was. I paid my dues. I was left holding the pickle jar in which Vasya the blue fish swam, while Vasya's former owner headed for the nearest bar.

I was in Moscow again not long ago, and went back to the bird market. Again I was astonished by its carnivalesque atmosphere. The air in the center of Moscow smells of money. At the bird market smelly animals and people are packed in together; you can hardly tell who is selling whom. While people downtown are out buying Gucci shoes, here they are buying all sorts of things. There are dealers who can find you crocodiles, boas, tigers, whatever you desire. Some sell falcons that are specially trained to chase pigeons away. The Kremlin buys them so that the domes will stay shiny and gold, and to keep Red Square clean. There is more. Small-time dealers catch swallows, shut them in cages and bring them to the bird market. For a price, their customers can release the swallows. This time I didn't buy a fish. I set several swallows free from captivity. The feeling of righteous satisfaction didn't cost much, just a few rubles.

A SUITCASE

There are authors who have penned marvelous pages on exile. They unwittingly polish the subject, and in doing so they give exile the glow of a romantic rebellion against the demands of everyday life, a rejection of home and homeland for the thrill of personal freedom. The people who have written these pages overlook the banalities: Walter Benjamin killed himself because he wasn't able to get his papers; everything might have turned out differently had that anonymous clerk stamped Benjamin's passport. But in myths, including myths about exile, everyone is inclined to forget the anonymous bureaucrat. And this is how dull, clerkish triviality, thanks to the author's, and the reader's, romantic expectations, becomes the face of cruel Destiny.

In many cases, people living in exile unwittingly embellish the story of their exile, or they acquiesce quietly as those around them glorify it. I know one guy who had no objections when the community where he found himself perceived his decision to live temporarily abroad as "the moral indignation of the intellectual against the rising tide of neo-fascism." My acquaintance was, in fact, eluding his wife rather than the rising tide of neo-fascism, but it was too late for him to say so. He could not bear to disappoint the expectations of his newly adopted community. Whatever the case, his moral compass was not far off: his escape from his wife made him an implicit combatant against fascism, which had, in the meanwhile, indeed surged to overflowing.

I know of an opposite case as well. One friend of mine did, indeed, leave his country in disgust at the incursion of fascism. And he made no bones about declaring this publicly. The country where he was offered political asylum allowed him to live cheerfully, without constraints, in a way he hadn't been able to live before: as a homosexual. The fascism no longer worried him so much.

Asylum seekers, emigrants, refugees, nomads, migrants, people who have been exiled and those seeking their papers—all of them annoy the communities where they end up. Civilized places never admit this, of course. They pound their chests with their multiculturalism, they work in earnest on projects for support and integration, develop caring institutions, foundations, bureaucratic networks and structures, they organize demonstrations for the support of This or That emigrant minority (whichever one is in the public eye just then). In a nutshell, good people perform their activism to exhaustion. All to keep from smashing their heads against the hard truth: newcomers annoy the local majority.

Literature tends to show the romantic side of exile. In reality, exiles live submerged in trauma. The image of exile suggests a rebellious fragmentation, but also a servile obedience to the process of acquiring a new home. The only way exiles are able to leave trauma behind is to not leave it behind at all, but to live it as a permanent state, to turn their waiting room into a cheery ideology of life, to live the schizophrenia of exile as the norm of normalcy and to revere only one god: the Suitcase!

The most intimate side of exile is tied to luggage. As I write these lines I am surrounded by a dozen kinds: bags, suitcases (with and without wheels), costly valises, and cheap duffels. I look at them fondly: they are my only true companions, witnesses to my wanderings. The suitcases travel, go across borders, move in, and move out with me.

If there is something I dream of, it is not a new home, but a new suitcase. I saw the suitcase of my dreams in a fancy London shop.

I will never forget it. It was almost as tall as I am. It opened like a wardrobe. It was finished in the finest hand-tooled leather. Inside it was outfitted more perfectly than the world's most beautiful wardrobe, with charming compartments to hold anything and everything from slender credit cards and toothbrushes to evening dresses, fur coats, and shoes. It cost 8,000 (eight thousand) pounds.

There you have it. If you know of a more expensive suitcase out there, let me know immediately, so that I am up to date. Because if I ever win big in the lottery, I know what I will buy first. East, West, home is best, most people would agree. But the majority is always wrong. East, West, suitcase is best!

THE BASEMENT

Who knows what sort of subversive activities people are undertaking against the regime of everyday life, without even realizing that they are subverting something? Because everyday life is a regime, unforgiving and rigorous, like army life. The repertoire of ways, however, to subvert, evade or deride the regime of everyday life is limited. All the grand ideologies—whether religious, communist or capitalist—support one another on this one point: work is our salvation. It is only thanks to hard work that we evolved from the ape, and only a person who works—and is not a loafer—can be a genuine human being. Alternative ideologies do not offer much comfort. The gurus of the modern age, the psychotherapists, the tutti-frutti ideologues, and our life coaches all subscribe to the communist-capitalist story.

Exile is an interesting condition for a number of reasons. A person usually flees a regime because of politics. After some time, if the urgency of those reasons fades, the person discovers that the regime of everyday life is more or less the same everywhere, and that countries are generally arranged in such a way that each one of us is subtly encouraged to become a productive cog in the bigger mechanism. Vacation, tourist travel, these are merely ritualized, structured, and socially acceptable ways of fleeing everyday life. But even vacation is not ideology-free (only a person who works has the right to a vacation), and this is poor consolation. There is no halfhearted way to sidestep the regime of everyday life. Doing this requires radical action.

I heard of the case of a Slovene who spent thirty years arriving at work on time. He was so prompt that others set their watches by him. Before he went into the building where he worked he would stop for a moment, take a deep breath, look up into the sky, exhale, and in he'd go. People knew him by the gesture—the breath in, the skyward glance, the breath out—he made when he entered the building. They say that one day the Slovene stopped as usual out in front, breathed in, gazed up at the sky, breathed out, and—sank to the ground, felled by a lethal heart attack.

My Russian friends the Punsheviches emigrated some twenty years ago to the United States. Whenever I am in the States I give them a call.

"So what are you doing?" I ask.

"*Valyaemsya . . .*"

The translation—nothing much, just lolling around—suggests a weekend-long lounge when you stay in bed or in your bathrobe and slippers all day, take your time with your coffee and stare at the television set. But the Punsheviches actually lived in bed: they dined in bed, read, talked, slept. I, too, was occasionally allowed a perch on the bed, as a Russian-speaking friend. The bed was their one and only solid ground, and getting up out of bed meant socializing, leaving the realm of freedom. The bed was an up-yours to America, to the ideology of work and success; the bed was their place of subversion, of desertion. The bed was a revolutionary cell bent on undermining the system, although the system was oblivious of their revolt.

But bed-bound life soon proved impracticable. Word got around. What are the Punsheviches up to? Lounging again. "I never supported communism with my work, and I will not support capitalism either," Punshevich announced firmly, and put a stop to every conversation about his getting a job. He stayed what he had always been, a Russian writer. Punshevichka, woman that she was, found a job, began paying taxes, and then, to reduce her taxes, she bought a house, an American house, with a garden (so they'd have somewhere to plant their little American flag, the symbol of their integration, or capitulation, depending on the perspective).

I visited them. Everything was where it was supposed to be: the TV, the fridge, the sofa, the cabinets, it was all here. And then they brought me, ceremoniously, downstairs to the basement. There was a huge bed down there, a library with the *right* books, a sound system with the *right* music. Downstairs their cheery up-yours to the system of everyday life was alive and well. The upstairs was an act of mimicry, a stage set, a Potemkin village for guests. Only the Punsheviches and their close friends were allowed down to the basement. The last time I was over we had a delicious time lolling around. True, it was a Sunday.

A RIGHT TO MISERY

People have come up with an impressive range of styles for verbal and non-verbal socialization. Italians kiss. Americans give that famous embrace, the bear hug, complete with the thump on the shoulder. The Dutch kiss three times when they meet. One Dutch fellow was nearly beaten up in Zagreb for that. They had assumed he was a Serb. Serbs kiss three times, but Croats only twice.

People use their mouth, hands, eyes, and sometimes nose (even toes, I've heard) to communicate non-verbally. Americans are the most polite verbal socializers: they are always *fine*, and their days are *nice*. The Dutch ask where your bicycle is, and if you don't have one, they advise you where to pick one up, because life can only be normal with a bike and anything short of that is misery. Easterners (Arabs, Indians, the Chinese) ask you straight away: are you married? do you have children? brothers and sisters? are your parents living? and so forth. It is family that interests Easterners. The best at *small talk* are the English, while the Russians are absolute champions at marathon conversations laced with smoke and alcoholic fumes.

People from my country, the ex-Yugoslavs, are the worst. You can spot them from afar on the streets of foreign cities. They scowl, their eyes dart right and left, they move cautiously, ready to stand their ground, as if they are in the middle of the jungle, as if the un-speakable lurks behind each and every bush. My compatriots like to complain. They are the people in the waiting room at the dentist's whose mouths gape as they show each other their cavities. They are the ones in hospital waiting areas who don't hesitate to bare their chest, pull their shirt up and pants down to show each other scars from operations, just to prove that theirs are worse. When you ask them how they are doing, my compatriots respond with, "Don't ask! You don't want to know." The best you can get out of them is: "So-so, could be better."

I often think that my countrymen are not people at all but cuttle-fish in human form: you have only to touch them, and they emit a black cloud. These are people who have been cultivating keeners since antiquity. Keeners are professionals with oversized tear ducts who mourn the deceased loudly at funerals. For a fee, of course. My countrymen are people who have been honing an instinct for misery. It is in their genes; tragedy has even crept into colloquial usage as a way of expressing joy. While other societies include in their ideological packaging the right of citizens to the pursuit of happiness, my former fellow citizens fight for (and have won) the opposite, the right to the pursuit of misery.

When summer comes I go off to the lovely, azure Adriatic. Instead of relaxing, I listen patiently to the regular reports of the ebb and flow of misery. Last summer, for instance, I rented a room on the island of Brač. My next-door neighbor, an illiterate laborer, had built a house of Brač marble with at least thirty rooms. I couldn't stop myself from saying how remarkable the building was. His first response was a bitter tirade against the communists under whom life had been unbearable (he built this modest home with his bare hands!), then a rant against the Serbs who had ruined tourism, and then invectives against today when a person can't do a room up properly. He had furnished only fifteen. The other fifteen were standing empty!

Every summer, as I said, I go off for my dose of misery. I have become an addict. I pay through the nose for those frozen mackerel with the local flies crawling on them and I sip the sour wine only so I can get my fill of the local grumbling.

On Saturdays I call my mother. Saturdays are a constant. The only difference is the city I see out the window as I make the call: New York, Amsterdam, Boston, Berlin . . .

"You'll never guess who died!" my mother says ever so brightly.

"Who?" I ask, just as brightly.

"Old lady Sušek . . . And have you heard how Perić had a stroke?"

"No, and where would I have heard such a thing?"

"He survived, but with terrible damage . . ."

By the time we get to Perić, I am at peace. Until next Saturday.

STEREOTYPES

They used to threaten me when I was little that if I wasn't good, they would give me to the *Gypsies* who stole little children. I was good, there was no reason for me to be stolen, though I was secretly intrigued by the idea. Today I know that the story of *Gypsies stealing little children* falls into the category of stubborn stereotypes about one of the most stigmatized populations in the world.

We grow up living in a world of stereotypes, we absorb them like a dry sponge soaks up water. Later, as adults who care about ourselves and our politically correct image, we pull the stereotypes off ourselves like burrs. This seems simple at first, but it soon turns out that stereotypes are the most tenacious type of mental weed: when you pull it out, it sprouts somewhere else. So most people give up, they live hand-in-hand with the stereotypes; what else can they do, life is always easier for two. We don't have to rely on the treacherous compass of our own heart when we have stereotypes. Stereotypes are a cozy system of signalization, something like highway signs: left, right, straight, slow down, curve ahead, stop. Who has ever seen someone driving a car by relying on their heart?!

I grew up in a country where *brotherhood* and *unity* were *the apple of your eye*, but at the same time the culture encouraged stereotypes about all the members of the brotherhood. I lived surrounded by Slovenes who were *penny pinchers*; Slovenian women, who, of all the women in our brotherhood, were the *easiest lays*; Montenegrins, who were *lazy*; Croats who were *fags* and *nitpickers*; Serbs, who were *yokels*; Macedonians who were *vegetable-growing hicks*; Bosnians, who were *dense*; Albanians, who somehow weren't even human; Muslims who instead of five had six toes; the minority Italians who ate cats; and the above mentioned Gypsies, who *stole little children*. All in all, it was a colorful community.

When I left the country I figured I had left these stereotypes behind. Was I wrong! The number of stereotypes around me only multiplied. Today I am surrounded not only by the stereotypes of the place where I live, but by the ones that the inhabitants of these environments harbor about—the Balkans. I am, after all, a Balkan woman. Out of fear of Balkanization, the European Union has produced an effective antidote: Brussel-ization. Within the walls surrounding Brussels everything teems with stereotypes, so I feel right *at home* in the United Europe. And what's more, stereotypes are the ideological and commercial staple of a United Europe.

In the souvenir shops of Brussels you can buy EU postcards, caricatures of *typical* representatives of the member countries. The cartoons show the characteristic features of the *lascivious* French, the *parsimonious* Dutch, the *stalwart* English. Another series of postcards advertises the sexual traits of EU members. The Portuguese, whether justifiably or not, are purported to be the worst lovers in the EU.

The people of the Balkans make their way around Europe like suitcases decked out with a host of destination stickers. Meanwhile, the Bulgarians, Romanians, Greeks, and others have done nothing to deserve the negative stereotypes they were saddled with by the ex-Yugoslavs during the recent war. The degree to which stereotypes are more powerful than legal procedure, or to which legal procedure is shaped by stereotypes, is something that every person from the Balkans knows: from the experience of his or her first crossing of the EU border.

As for me, I am not complaining. I do what I can to conform to the stereotypes people hold of me. I hope I won't disappoint them, or question the stereotypes of others; I know they are valuable household furnishings. It's true that my own masochistic nature lends itself to this. That is why I put up with it when people explain to me how to use an iron, or when waiters in restaurants deliberately avoid setting my place with a knife. That is why I usually write "cleaning lady" in the box under OCCUPATION; it's what is expected of me. Because my cosmopolitan countrywomen are known far and wide as excellent housekeepers in EU apartments, houses and public lavatories.

I put up with all of this calmly; I know that stereotypes are difficult to shed. I even think it isn't so much about us, good people, as it is about them, the indestructible stereotypes. Because stereotypes multiply and spread, mutate like viruses, and where there were older ones, new, unexpected ones sprout.

So it was one day that a Bosnian refugee child, a ten-year-old boy, having come home from his new Dutch school, asked his mother:
    "Mom, is it true that we Muslims are all lesbians?"

OSTALGIA

The business of remembering sometimes resembles a resistance movement, and those who do the remembering become like guerilla warriors. There is an official version of history, and official institutions and professional watch guards of history who attend to it. There is also a personal version of history: one that we see to ourselves. We catalogue our lives in family albums. But there is a third history, an alternative one, the intimate history of the everyday life we have lived. This one receives the least attention. The archeology of everyday life is the sort of thing that only oddballs care about. Yet it is the history of the commonplace which is the custodian of our most intimate recollection, more precise than official history, more exact and warm than the history bound up in those family albums. Because the secret of remembering is not conserved in a regional museum or a family album, but in that little cookie, the *madeleine*, that Proust knew so well.

With the breakdown of the system in the countries of Eastern Europe, the everyday life that the East Europeans had grown accustomed to without even realizing it is now gradually disappearing. Powerful western retail chains are moving slowly eastward. German yogurts, Dutch cheese, and British frozen pies are making their quiet, yet unstoppable, advance to the East. Western goods are slowly elbowing out the domestic products which used to frustrate the local consumers, but so amuse Western tourists and visitors with their communist design. And yet, (ah, ungrateful human nature!) it seems that the long desired sheen of western stores is tarnishing; the cravings for Dutch cheese, German yogurts and English pies are on

THE TAMILS

The Tamils are the most mysterious group that wends its way through European cities. They are seen only at night. They emerge from their secret dwellings at dusk and go from restaurant to restaurant holding bouquets of big roses. The Tamils are unusually quiet and polite, and their roses are always fresh. Yet no one buys them. I have sat in any number of restaurants, in this city or the next, but I can't remember ever seeing anyone purchase them. What do the Tamils do and how do they support themselves? This is the enigma. Are the Tamils a mysterious sect? Young, swarthy, handsome, grinning, roses in hand, they look like angels, they bear good tidings. The Tamils disappear quickly, as if borne by an invisible wind. And like angels they are mute. No, the Tamils are not of this world.

But this story is not about the Tamils. This is about Ivan Kostić. Ivan Kostić was there *before* the Tamils were.

"Ivan Kostić was there before the Tamils were, everyone in Berlin knows that," says Bosa, putting weight on the word "before." Bosa has been living in Berlin for thirty years or more. She knows: in Berlin, Bosa knows the most about *our* world.

A Gypsy, Ivan Kostić sold roses in the Berlin restaurants before the Tamils. He was a dashing man, with a long, black mustache, and he always wore a black hat. He would stride into the restaurant like a king. He'd toss the roses in a corner, fiddle importantly with his mustache, roll his eyes, let loose his hoarse voice, and sing a Gypsy song. The guests held their breath; the food cooled on the plates. Then, with the gesture of a poet who has thrown pearls before swine, he would stride toward the door.

"Kostić, come back, you've left your roses!" the restaurant patrons would shout after him, eagerly pulling out their wallets.

Kostić knew things. How to sell roses. How to fill out those nasty German forms. He wrote petitions, penned letters, and filled out forms for his fellow Gypsies. And never took a cent from them for it.

One day on a street in Berlin a car ran over Kostić. The Yugoslav Gypsies in Berlin collected 40,000 German marks and held a funeral that would be remembered. What can I say, Gypsy tears flooded Berlin.

A month after the burial, Kostić's wife began to complain that her husband was appearing to her at night, grumbling and muttering. Not only did his coffin chafe, he said, but everything was uncomfortable. And the Germans buried all around him were trying to get him to leave. "Go, back where you came from," the German dead harped. "Where do I have to go, all the way to Kruševac?" Kostić protested. "To Kruševac!" howled the hostile German deceased.

She was quite a woman, so Kostić's wife made up her mind. She went from one Berlin office to another, from offices for the dead to offices for the living, petitioning to move her late husband. "Crazy woman," they said, and they did not permit it. Kostić stopped paying his old lady those nightly visits.

"Ah, he's silent like a tomb. He's offended and that's why he doesn't come to visit me anymore," the Gypsy woman moaned.

And then, one night, Kostić appeared to her again. He was, he told her, in Kruševac. They didn't want him there, he said, either. "You can't get in without the right paperwork, you need the new passport, this is a new state, and there is no place here for Gypsies, even when they're dead. The people are all crazy, like dogs, the dead and the living, they have all become fucking fascists!" Kostić told his wife and vanished. His wife waited for him to get in touch with her again, and then, waiting no longer, she died.

Only then did the Tamils appear in Berlin. *After* Kostić and his wife disappeared. The Tamils go out only at night, they slip through the streets like shadows and offer their roses that nobody buys. They look like angels, they bear good tidings. They slip away quickly, as if borne by an invisible wind. And like angels, they are mute. They are mute because no one asks them anything. The real question would be whether they have met Kostić the Gypsy and his wife, and how the two of them are doing in the other world, have they settled down or have they gone somewhere new? If there is anyone who knows, it would surely be the Tamils.

BIRDHOUSE

Never buy a birdhouse if you have no tree to hang it from. I speak from experience. It happened to me. Long ago, in 1991, I bought a pretty little birdhouse at a store in New York. I have no idea why. I had no garden, and therefore no tree where I might hang it.

The war began that same year in my country. Who knows, perhaps this was my thinking: I'll come back, I'll get a garden, I'll plant a tree in the garden, and then I'll hang the birdhouse on that tree and—stop the war. I didn't take the birdhouse back with me. It was too heavy for the airplane ride. I left it at the apartment of some New York friends. The friends, meanwhile, moved to a new place. I no longer have their address.

I returned home from New York, but, instead of staying there, I moved away for good a month later. I have been on the road ever since, changing countries like shoes. It usually takes me about a year to wear out a pair of shoes. I leave the countries before I wear them out. It has turned out that the pointless purchase of the little birdhouse was a taste of the future. Without realizing it, I had been shopping for a poignant substitute for the home I would lose a month later.

Psychoanalysts know that a home (dwelling) is one of the strongest archetypal images we carry with us, from birth (womb) to death (grave). Ever since I left it, home has become my obsession. I have developed an unpleasant tic of grilling the people around me about their housing. I have another one: I can read other people's interiors the way some people read tea leaves. I have a third, the most awkward, which is that I can't resist giving people advice: how about moving that book case? why not hang the picture an inch or two lower? My Amsterdam friends, architects by trade, got so tired of my constant grumbling about how they absolutely had to get a sofa that they relinquished their minimalism and bought one. Whenever I visit them, I sink into it as if belongs to me.

Ever since I left home, the *whole world has become my home.* The trite appeal of that old Croatian pop song line has become my life. There is a secret geography of the things I leave behind me. I conduct a clandestine occupation, leave my mark, drop my secret anchor. My belongings—coffee pots, plates, bedspreads, shoes, sheets, sweaters— are scattered throughout European and American cities. Wherever I happen to be, I buy books compulsively, create little temporary libraries, and then, when I go, leave them behind. Luckily there are enough kind people in the world who are ready to give my orphans, my books, a home.

Some twenty years ago I spent the summer on an Adriatic island. I brought my typewriter with me, and since there was no carbon paper at the local store, I did my writing in only one copy. An old guy who ferried tourists to the mainland in a little skiff flung my bag up onto the roof of the cabin. The seas were rough, the boat tilted precariously, and the bag slid from side to side on the cabin roof. "It will fall off, tie it down," I said. "Oh, it won't fall off," he said. "I'm certain it will." "It won't," the old guy insisted. "But everything I own is in that bag," I said, meaning the manuscript that was there in single copy. "So what do you do?" asked the old guy. "I'm a writer," I answered. "Well you, of all people, should carry all you own up here!" he said, tapping his forehead.

The old guy's response, just like the purchase of that birdhouse, proved to be prophetic. Today I am forced to carry my things in my head. Using one's head as a suitcase is not the best solution. The capacity of the mind has its limits. Besides, the head is capricious: most often it carries things it no longer needs.

Yes, *the whole world is my home today.* The trite appeal of that old Croatian pop song line from long ago has become my life. Is this reality any better or worse than earlier ones? I don't know. I don't think about it. One thing I know for sure: I have been doing better at resisting the urge to buy pointless things. And the desire seizes me less often.

I recently turned up briefly in Berlin and called some friends.

"Hey, last time you left your hairdryer!" they said.

I asked, "Do you have my slippers?"

GARDENING

If you're going to dabble in gardening, you need a garden, or, better yet, a house with a garden. Gardening is not something for the poor, or for people on the move, because gardening means staying put. Gardening can be done with no garden, I suppose, but there is something a little bleak about it. People were made to tend their own gardens. Those with no garden satisfy their fancies with potted plants on a window sill, or by watching TV gardening programs, which are, I might add, my favorite form of recreation.

Communism was famous for the ascendance of one flower above all others. The carnation, usually red, blossomed in communism. A sad little bouquet of carnations in communist Moscow cost more than a bottle of vodka. Vodka was considered food, while flowers were a luxury. I knew a Russian who cultivated his floral passions in a tiny communist-era Moscow flat. He raised mushrooms, potted plants, trained vines to creep all over the place, and installed several aquariums with goldfish (as a substitute for garden ponds), until one day his whole 500 square foot jungle collapsed into the flat on the floor below.

As far as the former communist Yugoslavia is concerned, I would be lying if I were to say that my life had been less than floral. I would also be lying if I were to say that the floral circumstances changed for the better with the advent of democracy. Not at all. One plant is permanently linked in my memory to my former country. The ficus. Nowhere have I seen so many ficus plants as I saw in the store windows, offices, and apartments of my former country. I developed an aversion to them. Today the sight of these house plants with their fleshy, dark, dusty leaves makes my skin crawl.

I spent my childhood in a house with a garden. My mother raised daisies in the flower beds (out front). In the kitchen part of the garden (out back) there were fruit trees, lettuce, tomatoes, peppers, green beans, beans, zucchini and squash. Some of the flowers also belonged in the "kitchen" category. Elderberry flowers were batter-fried and dusted with confectioner's sugar, sweet acacia blossoms were nibbled raw, a kind of grass with little flowers, sorrel, had a nice taste and was the forerunner of chewing gum (which we hadn't discovered yet), and there was a kind of rose that was used for jam.

In my childhood the garden was also where little girls made improvised cosmetics. Rose petals were glued to fingernails as a substitute for fingernail polish. You could make daisy chains of small daisies for bracelets, necklaces, and hair ornaments. Cherries were fine for earrings, and the juice from sour cherries served as lipstick. My Arcadian childhood is forever lost, as it should be. I was definitively expelled from the garden of paradise to a more urban setting. Only once did I try to go back, by trying to turn my Zagreb terrace into the gardens of Babylon. The flowers could not be bothered. They preferred a voluntary death to growing on that terrace.

At this point I no longer want a garden. A garden is like a fingerprint, like the palm of a hand from which the soul of its owner can be divined. The garden is a relic of Arcadia for those of us who have been permanently expelled from paradise. Gardening is a way of evoking that paradise. It is a personal activity which exposes the owner's ideas of the beautiful, of art, of one's own status and place in this world. Why people seem so eager to show their gardens to others is beyond me. A garden says it all. You can read a person from his garden.

Everyone, of course, has his or her own idea about a garden. As far as I am concerned, I am content with plastic tulips. They are cheap, they don't weigh much, they are mobile, they take up no space, they are easily packed, and, most important, they require no care. From time to time you have to dust them, that's all.

MY HOMETOWN

If I were an American writer I could make money by writing stories about my hometown. Furthermore, I would be expected to. American literature and American movies have thrived, and still do, on this engaging theme. Indeed the finest writing in Croatian literature is about going back to where the protagonist is from, though these trips home tend to end badly: the heroes drink, go mad, kill themselves. In that sense there isn't much difference between a return to Smithsville or to Virovitica. The theme first wormed its way into Croatian literature in the late nineteenth century and reached its apotheosis with the masterpiece, Miroslav Krleža's novel *The Return of Philip Latinovicz*.

The image of my hometown fits snugly into the mythology produced by the American hometown movie. If I were to say there was no difference between the 1950s American films and Yugoslav life, it might sound surprising. But this is all about image manufacture, about mythology: one of these, the American image, has appeal, while the other, though just like it, has none. So it is unlikely I'll ever convince anyone that the differences between 1950s small-town life in America and small-town life in communist Yugoslavia were negligible. This is why, among other things, there is no money to be made.

The small town was and is called Kutina. It lies by what was the Zagreb-Belgrade highway, under construction for years but never finished, formerly known, in the Yugoslav days, as the highway of "Brotherhood and Unity." Kutina was a small town with some fifteen thousand inhabitants, capital of the Moslavina region, where the *world famous wines of Moslavina* were grown.

The Stružec petroleum field lay just outside of town. Kutina sat on top of petroleum and lived off of petroleum. There was also a factory called "Methane," which seemed mainly to produce soot and limestone. My father worked there. In my earliest childhood I learned all about petroleum, saw the wells and pumps, and the soot wafting in barely visible flakes over us every day. But Kutina looked nothing like those grimy English working towns. It was more like a small American town, in Texas.

My mother devoured American novels. Dad contributed a novel with the title *Oil!* to Mother's collection. The movies were American. There was only one movie theater in town. Mama and I went to the movies almost every day and we'd watch the same film several times over.

My teenage years were much like those of American teenagers, except they weren't American. The boys used to hang out, make a racket all day long in front of the local tavern and movie theater, or buzz around on scooters. Once a week we'd go to a dance (this was back in the time of the Twist and the Shake). The mammoth American series *Peyton Place* was on television. I had a hair cut like Jean Seberg in Godard's movie *Breathless*. And just like Jean Seberg, I wore a sailor blouse, pedal pushers that came down to just below the knee, and ballet flats. Except that I wasn't being Jean, I was being Allison MacKenzie, who was acted by that waif, Mia Farrow. The local boys were strong, short on words, and looked to the side the way James Dean did. The main street was called Railway Street and it ran from the little local train station to the center of town. The other street was called Church Street. That one ran from the center of town to the church up on a little hill. There was a view from that hill that overlooked the rolling hills of Moslavina.

My friends, unlike me, were worldly wise and full to bursting with amazing and useful knowledge. I learned from Almica that boys should not be *allowed below the waist*. From Lidija I learned that you should coat your lashes with cod liver oil and curl them with a kitchen knife. Štefica was the local Brigitte Bardot. She had that same haircut and those same naturally pouting lips. I learned from her that you can practice kissing on a mirror. Biba tried to teach me, to no avail, how to do cartwheels and handstands, but that was nowhere near as alluring as Almica's mysterious advice.

Boys were judged by how good they were at handball. Frga and Davor were the local handball stars. Lidija was dating Davor. Feelings were expressed indirectly. *Frga says hi*, Lidija told me. That meant Frga liked me. *Say hi to him*, I said. That meant that Frga and I would go see a movie. We did. Once or twice. They were American movies.

Aside from handball, the other local attraction was scooter racing. The racers were older kids and they didn't interest us. The racers carried out their stunts on the muddy hills and pits to the wild screams of their audience.

I left Kutina when I finished secondary school and went on to Zagreb University. Although my hometown was all of seventy-three kilometers from Zagreb, I returned only once: to my fifth high school reunion. Once I'd left it, my hometown became an indifferent blot on the map. I found Kansas, Kamchatka, and Katmandu—places I had never been—far more alluring than Kutina, where I'd spent eighteen years.

As for Štefica, the one who instructed me on kissing the mirror for practice, she took off for Germany after she earned her university degree. Lidija, who taught me how to oil my lashes and curl them with a kitchen knife, married, had two daughters, and lives with her husband in Kutina. Frga, the one who *said hi* once, became an alcoholic and died before he turned forty. Davor, the one who *dated* Lidija, became a teacher, and later a passionate nationalist, and he made it all the way to political honcho in the new democratic maelstrom. Almica got married and then divorced, and now she lives in Zagreb looking after her elderly father. Biba married, lost twins at childbirth, and works today as a visiting nurse.

The little town now produces artificial fertilizer. The industry they sank so much money into during the communist 1980s is collapsing today, or so they say. The grapes in the vineyards of Moslavina still ripen, however; the wine is just as sour as it always was.

OLD AGE—NEW CRAZE

Leon Štukelj died recently in Slovenia; he had been a Slovenian athlete and winner of Olympic medals back in the 1930s. Štukelj lived to a hundred, but not to a hundred and one. Just his luck, he died four days short of his one hundred and first birthday. A spry old fellow, Štukelj did one-handed push-ups for his hundredth. Leon Štukelj was a favorite of the Slovenian right wing, probably because he was living proof that Slovenians, too, might make it to a hundred. He was a favorite of many others as well: both the media (the malicious say he died before his time due to overexposure to the media) and the ordinary people. Štukelj is proof that life needn't be stripped of all its joy in old age. Indeed!

Štukelj is an example of a successful human struggle against the cruel laws of aging. Cher, who would have been described in the literature of the nineteenth century as an agile but elderly woman in her fifties, is a biological wonder. Tina Turner, who would have been sneered at a hundred years ago as a vulgar hag flaunting her legs in public, is a biological revolutionary in today's codes of values, and both grandchildren and grandmothers whistle at her with admiration.

If we say that our age is obsessed with youth, what we really mean is that it is obsessed with age. Age has been relegated to the lowest rung on the values ladder. Old age no longer means wisdom, experience, knowledge, or nobility. Old age is ugly, wrong, costly; old age is a necessary evil. The ancient eastern Serbian ritual of *lapot*—the ritual slaying of the elderly, when younger people drape a cloth over the head of an older person and then bash him or her to death with axes—may indeed sound gruesome. But the hypocrisy of civilized Western European society, in which people are willing to go to any length to avoid a symbolic *lapot*, is every bit as nasty. Dorian Gray's desire to stay young forever in Oscar Wilde's moralistic tale no longer sounds so bizarre. To stay as young as possible, for as long as possible, has become a priority all its own.

The powerful sway of American public opinion has succeeded in expunging the cigarette from American life over the twenty years that it has been focused on smoking. Cigarette smoke has been erased from American culture, from literature, from television, from the movies. The only function left today for the cigarette is that of a quick, convenient way to tag characters: in American movies today the only ones who light up are the bad boys. And the same, it seems, is true in life.

The American public opinion-makers are equally adept in the realm of young-old image manufacture. The traditional traits associated with age are vanishing, and new, euphemistic ones are on their way in. Fifty-year-olds are now in early middle age. The year of birth is gone from dust cover biographies, first from the bios of women authors and now for the men as well. One's birth date has become a closely held secret. I believe that even the police in the States are uncomfortable asking someone for their age. The industries—cosmetics, fashion, medicine, plastic surgery, fitness—are making huge profits by encouraging collective fantasies about eternal youth. It is media-unfriendly to be a poor, ailing, lonely, grumpy old man, and therefore this is the wrong image. Just as the image of a smoker is wrong, even if his name is Humphrey Bogart.

Fitness centers are cult spots in the battle against aging. People may hide their age, but they don't hide the number of cosmetic operations they have been through. No one seems disturbed by the fact that Cher has undergone so many procedures. In fact many admire her courage and persistence at staying young for so long. A Brazilian journalist in a documentary on cosmetic plastic surgery stated that she had liposuction done after every large meal. There is a lot of money to be made from the longing for an extended youth. And those who succeed in staying young-looking can also make money off it. The American woman who went through a series of cosmetic surgeries so that she would look like Barbie announced: "The Barbie look is my ticket to a better life."

The ancient Utopian dream of the happy Hyperboreans who lived in the extreme north and were immortal, just like the merry Ethiopians who lived in the south and ate roasted oxen and were nearly immortal, has never vanished from the horizon of human yearning. And just as Utopias are becoming less Utopian, so people have become less patient, and more shameless and aggressive in reaching for their dreams. Fear of aging and death are a moral justification for everything: for those poor souls who hope to extend their life by buying someone else's organs, and those cheery souls who watch a TV special on abandoned Romanian children while massaging their face with a face cream (produced illegally in Romania) made with a placenta additive that is supposed to make them look younger.

This is what things look like on the sunny side of the street. The old people on the sunny side are looking younger, while the kids are looking older. Teenage depression and suicide are on the rise. Things look different, meanwhile, on the shady side of the street. In Serbia, Croatia, and Bosnia old people are dying like flies. From old age and disease, to be sure, but by their own hand as well. What with their only prospects being a humiliating life of digging through trash cans, a cold apartment, unpaid bills, and loneliness, the elderly often choose—death. Do they catch sight of Cher in a video clip just as they are standing there with the noose around their neck, about to kick away the chair? I wouldn't know. I do know that this deal with death makes perfect sense.

AH, THAT RHETORIC!

An American friend of mine recently came across a potential partner over the Internet. The Internet interchange started with likenesses.

"People say I'm like Tom Hanks," the potential partner wrote. "And you? Who do you look like?" "I remind people of Dustin Hoffman," answered my acquaintance, who, by the way, was not far off.

After their first exchange on the Internet, they decided to meet.

"You look way nicer than Dustin Hoffman," remarked Tom Hanks.

There was no second date.

"He did not look a bit like Tom Hanks," my friend told me later. And he asked me, as an afterthought, "Do you really think I'm better looking than Dustin?"

"Definitely," I replied. "More like Banderas . . ."

Since we live in a market-based world, there is nothing left which exists for itself alone, not even at the level of private life. Everything has to be pegged to someone or something. There are two clothing stores on West Broadway in New York, one right next door to the other. One is called "Philosophy," and the other is called "Art, Science & Philosophy." Clothes are no longer being sold as apparel, but as "art, science, and philosophy." An amusing ad for a Mercedes shows animated portraits of Leonardo da Vinci, van Gogh, and Toulouse-Lautrec sitting in the car, grinning with glee. The car is no longer just a vehicle, it is a product of institutionalized higher culture being pegged to other products of institutionalized higher culture.

The world of market-based fickle triviality is happiest when it is draped in the apparel of known and tested values. Triviality leans heavily on the language of fine art (Jackie Collins advertises herself as "Hollywood's own Marcel Proust"), sophisticated medicine (laxatives are advertised by actors pretending to be famous doctors), serious knowledge, and culture, just to elevate the market value all the more.

My former country hardly manufactures or sells anything. The people there can barely make ends meet. Yet their ads and self-promotion are remarkably clever. Sometimes it seems as if the people who live in that country do nothing but talk through their hats and market hot air. In other places, people sell what they have. It turns out that Croats and Serbs are the absolute champions in selling morals. They are vending them to one another and to themselves. The Yugoslavia of the 1970s was less a "country of heroes" than a country "with the most beautiful sea coast in the world." The Yugoslav communist rhetoric of morals got more inept over the years until it burst into flames. Croatia (and Serbia, Macedonia, Montenegro, etc. are no better!) had, in the meanwhile, become the "most democratic country in the world," its first president "a giant of Croatian thought," and Zagreb, the Croatian capital, had advanced to become a "metropolis."

The opposition has recently taken up the same rhetoric as the government. As I write this essay, there are "fierce and unrelenting fighters for democracy" strolling around Croatia. All of this would be bearable if those petty vendors of hot air in the local political marketplace were able to admit that this is the language of advertising. They, however, believe in their own moral verticality. And, moreover, they are convinced that this verticality is lodged in their genes. Perhaps they aren't so far from the truth. Like the local joke, which goes like this:

"Hey there, you eagle, you," says the worm.

"Salutations, oh king of snakes," replies the chicken.

LITTLE DOG—BIG BARK

Now here's a paradox for you: not only do small people take up more space than large people do, they make more noise.

So I am getting on a plane. It's a long line, people are going into the aircraft one by one, slowly and quietly. A little guy is standing in front of me. *Tap!* The sound stirs me from my lethargy. *Tap! Tap!* The little guy in front of me is fidgeting; he is humiliated by the wait in the line, or maybe he's just bored. And what do you know, he has discovered that when he taps his shoe on the plastic flooring of the tube we are patiently waiting in it makes a loud noise. He tries it again. The travelers wince but no one turns. The feet of the small traveler become livelier and more assertive. *Tap-tap!*

I have never seen a big scooter rider. Scooter riders are diminutive men as a rule. And that is why they choose the vehicle that makes the most noise. *Brrrrrooom! Brrrrrooom!* There is no greater joy for a little guy than marking his territory with sound. A little guy sits on a scooter, at midnight, when everyone has gone to bed, and he kick-starts it—*brrrrrooom!* He is announcing his existence to the entire town. Why at night? Because sound travels farther at night. Little guys choose petite and light women for their partners, so there is room for them on the back seat. Have you ever seen a little guy who has a tall woman riding behind him on a scooter? Little guys choose compatible partners: women who fit on a scooter.

I have never seen a tall person fling firecrackers around in the days before Christmas. Usually it's children and teenagers. Occasionally among the kids and teenagers there are little guys. They do not move in packs, they'd be uncomfortable doing that, but they come out at night—and *boom!* They leave loud noises behind them.

Have you ever been elbowed by a large person on the street? I haven't. But little guys have often jabbed me in the ribs. They are the ones who conquer space and declare to everyone that they exist. They are the ones who whack you with their backpacks, who skin your shins, who bark into their mobile phones in public places. Have you ever seen an unusually large person barking into a mobile phone? I never have. Big people step out of the way, they tread cat-like so as not to disturb you, they pretend to be smaller than they are, quieter than they could be. As a rule the really big people do whatever they can to make themselves invisible.

"Little dog, big bark," my mother used to say. I will never forget the sound of the bold and self-confident tapping of that man's foot. The scene chilled me. The guy was no Fred Astaire. In that small, tense body and restless feet tapped the genes of a military leader, like leaders ever since the time of Attila the Hun.

I have observed a distinct preference among Americans for tall elected officials. As soon as they stray and choose someone shorter, the troubles begin. I have nothing against God's democracy and the fact that we are all just as God created us. But, in public service I would introduce a note of caution. If they are already skeptical about fat people—who have truly done harm to no one but themselves—I cannot see why they shouldn't exercise caution with little guys as well.

And what about nations? "Little nations make noise, while large nations make—sense," announced Goran. I am inclined to believe him. You see, he is from Macedonia.

TIME AND SPACE

Every time I call my mother from the United States (the New York side), she asks me first:

"What time is it where you are?"

"Noon."

"Well, here it is six in the evening," says my mother, sounding pleased for some reason.

Only after this exchange of information on the precise time *there* and *here* can we proceed with our conversation. My mother hasn't traveled much. It makes sense that she is interested in the difference in time. But even my more well-traveled friends invariably comment on the time difference.

The inhabitants of the former Yugoslavia were wanderers, vagabonds, tourists, and seafarers who plied the seven seas; they were migrant laborers, guest workers, emigrants, thugs, people who had geography at their fingertips. Something, however, is out of kilter when it comes to their sense of time. Besides time, there is another thing which bugs my fellow countrymen: their place in the world. Theirs is a specific sense of their own position in the world. When a fellow former Yugoslav calls me—no matter where I happen to be—he'll be sure to ask:

"Are they writing anything about us?"

They, in this case, are the inhabitants of the country I happen to be in at the time, and *we*, in this case, are ourselves.

"Nothing in particular," I say, cautiously.

At the other end of the line there is a silence which expresses both incredulity and disappointment.

The small nations in the Balkans have firmly embraced the belief that they play a remarkably vital geopolitical role. Many will agree to the fact that they are poor, that they are intolerant, and they will even concede (grudgingly) that the Adriatic Sea is perhaps not the most beautiful body of water in the world (though it is the cleanest), but they will never accept the notion that their geopolitical position is minor.

Why, they are the bulwark and the crossroads! Croatia has always envisioned itself as a bulwark. For awhile Croatia was the bulwark against the Turks (who would have taken Vienna had it not been for the Croats), then the bulwark against communism (those Serbs, as everyone knows, were all communists). The word "Balkan" means "Serbian," "Orthodox," "the Barbarian hordes." Croatia is renowned as a crossroads as well: a maritime crossroads but also a web of railway junctions and airline routes.

The bulwark and the crossroads are fantasies which have been disseminated with the same melodrama of patchy argumentation everywhere, particularly when one heads in an easterly direction from Croatia. Bosnia, too, is a bulwark and a crossroads, and Serbia is, too, of course. And don't forget Macedonia. A friend of mine who often travels to the southern states of the former Soviet Union has heard stories of the bulwark and the crossroads—told by Georgians, Azerbaijanis, Armenians, Uzbeks, the Turkmens, the Kyrgyz, Tajiks, and Buryats—that are identical in every detail.

There are moments when I feel genuinely sorry for us. It is not easy being a small nation and having no resources to speak of. It is also not easy being the member of a small nation. How does one even know where to begin? That must be why the first thing that occurs to him is to orient himself in time. Once he has been properly situated in time, the member of the small nation fixes his gaze on the imagined landscape. And behold! Along abandoned, weed-strewn train tracks speed gleaming trains, airplanes zoom like a swarm of mosquitoes overhead, and before his very eyes stretch expanses of sea over which ocean liners glide like a vast flock of ducks. And there, just beyond the impenetrable bulwark, you can hear the snorting of horses and the frustrated howls of the barbarians trying unsuccessfully to invade from the East.

THE NATIVES

Anthropology became an engaging discipline when it relinquished its objectivism. In its post-objectivist form, the new anthropology switches perspective between the described and the describer, and erodes the rhetorical forms of the old, colonial, authoritarian anthropology. One of the classic examples of the new anthropology is a text by Horace Miner, *Body Ritual Among the Nacirema*. The author uses the narrative strategy of "objective" description to de-familiarize the ritual of brushing teeth:

> The daily body ritual performed by everyone includes a mouth-rite. Despite the fact that these people are so punctilious about care of the mouth, this rite involves a practice which strikes the uninitiated stranger as revolting. It was reported to me that the ritual consists of inserting a small bundle of hog hairs into the mouth, along with certain magical powders, and then moving the bundle in a highly formalized series of gestures.

I perform the "group lunch" ritual with some American natives: my University colleagues from the Slavic Department. The natives bring their meal, which they call "lunch," in small plastic boxes. "Lunch" consists of several baby carrots, celery sticks, natural fiber cookies, or a grain bar. Some of them bring "lunch" in plastic boxes which imitate the appearance of certain food items: the "bagel" or the "oreo" (a dark brown cookie filled with white creme). The box has a small opening with a lid, through which the food drops out in limited amounts. I, too, have a "lunch" box in the shape of a hamburger. I usually bring a carrot in the box. While we nibble and chew, we talk about what is new in the department. No one shares the food items from their box.

We carefully pack up the leftovers and put them back in the box.

At home, while I chew on the vestigial nubbin of carrot lying on the bottom of the plastic hamburger, I recall the food rituals of my Balkan natives. I remember the New Year roast suckling pig (every house *had* to have its own piglet), the spring lamb turning on a spit, the autumn butchering rituals, the gorgeous chains of sausage links. I remember the putting up of preserves, the native pantries, rows of tall glass canning jars filled with jams, pickles and all sorts of other things. I remember the proud display of stores of ham and prosciutto, the sight-seeing tours of the rooms for drying meat, the cellars and attics, where every host would take their guests as an expression of intimacy and trust. I remember the Slavonian pastries spread out on platters on the double beds in village bedrooms, the favorite room for display (to show guests the total effect before bringing the feast to the table). I am overcome, from my current *low-fat* and *low-cholesterol* perspective, by a profound tribal compassion for that mute language of food. Food was a language for my natives, a system of signals that expressed a wide spectrum of things: love for a child, family, relative, guest. They knew no other language.

Food is both a mute language of love, and a gesture of personal freedom. Some twenty years ago a friend of mine, a Russian native, received his long-anticipated papers for America. He was halted abruptly at American customs. It was a police dog, in fact, which stopped him. He was carrying a sausage in his bag. My friend had purchased the sausage at the Munich airport, thrilled by how hefty and delicious it looked. He did what he could to save the sausage. The officials would not be placated. Then that native gave an emotional speech about how the freedoms of the West were a sham, and about his bitter disappointment with American democracy. The officials didn't blink. So the native sat down, right then and there, and devoured his sausage in a rage. And once he'd eaten it, he sauntered, full of importance, into America, where he lives to this day.

HISTORY AND CULTURE

I was recently on the phone with a European friend of mine. He happened to be in the States, as I was, for a year at an American university.

"You know," he said, "I like it here. I've always wanted a nice long stay in the States. But . . ."

"But what . . . ?"

"But I keep having the feeling that I'm missing something."

"What is it you're missing?"

"History!" blurted out my friend.

My friend knew, of course, that he was articulating the most common in a round of stereotypes on the theme of the differences between Europe and America. On the other hand, a foreigner from Europe does indeed have the feeling (rightly or no) that many things in the States don't have the weight they have in Europe, that they are only for a laugh: the politics, for instance, which will some day become history, and the history, which used to be mere entertainment. The American educational system is based on the belief that you learn faster when you're having a good time.

I was recently, for instance, in San Antonio, where I visited the famous site of the Alamo. At first I thought I was on a movie set. It turned out that this was a group of local people, volunteers, acting out the historical defense of the Alamo for the tourists. Despite the hands-on learning experience, I couldn't make heads or tails of what was going on. It only began to make sense when I got my hands on a tourist brochure. Then an American friend, a historian, explained that I had gotten it all wrong because I had consulted a propaganda version of events packaged for the tourists. This must be how Americans feel when they try to understand what has gone on in the Balkans. I was not involved, of course, in the defense of the Alamo. Luckily that wasn't required.

Europeans are always invoking their history. They've got history breathing down their necks; they are as intimate with history as they are with their cousins. Russians, for instance, call the former Soviet government Sonyka (little Miss Sonya), and they refer to Catherine the Great as Katya.

My countrymen, the former Yugoslavs, go after each other and shed each other's blood in the name of history. They defend the cradle of their civilization by expelling every cuckoo bird egg: the Serbs expel the Albanians from Kosovo, the Croats expel the Serbs from Krajina. And so it goes. The other word as sacred as "history" is "culture." Although many of its defenders were illiterate and hadn't had the opportunity to read even a single book, and could barely count the centuries, they were prepared to give their lives for culture. They were ready to destroy the lives of others, which they did with vigor. It turns out that the defenders of history and culture defend with the greatest ferocity the things they know the least, and care the least, about. The Croats tossed out piles of Serbian and other books from their libraries (while at war with the Serbs), and blew up the bridge in Mostar (while at war with the Bosnian Muslims). The Serbs shelled Dubrovnik, the National Library in Sarajevo, destroyed ancient Bosnian mosques, and turned Albanian culture in Kosovo into ashes. They did all of this in the name of defending their own history and culture. Yet when NATO bombs fell near the Serbian monastery of Gračanica it was an attack on "our most hallowed place of culture," and when the windows cracked at one of the Serbian universities in Kosovo it was NATO's attack on the "haven for the soul."

Things would be simpler if the people who did all this were willing to agree that they had been killing for the sake of killing, destroying for the sake of destroying, torching for the sake of torching. That, of course, will not happen. History and culture are the most reliable "banks" for laundering a dirty conscience. History and culture are part and parcel of what is known as the national cultural identity, though the national and the identity are only figments of the collective imagination. The collective, however, is to be believed. An individual killer would never be able to say: "I killed defending William Shakespeare because he is part of my cultural heritage." A collective, on the other hand, can. This is seen, indeed, as its right.

With this potential perspective in mind, how can any decent person aspire to being a builder, a composer, a painter, or a writer?

SHIT

My well-traveled friends insist that people are pretty much the same everywhere. In principle I agree. But nowhere have I heard so many lovely words uttered with such authentic, adrenaline-fired enthusiasm as I have in America (*Fantastic! Wonderful! Beautiful!*), and nowhere have I heard ugly words uttered with such undiluted loathing as I have among my own former Yugoslavs. In this regard they are all the same, the Croats, the Serbs, the Bosnians. In fact, they have replaced many of the ugly words with a single one: *shit*. My countrymen don't give much credence to the benefits of a larger vocabulary. Stingy people, stingy language. They invented minimalism in literature. Raymond Carver hadn't even been born yet.

I have never seen people express so much intimacy with the world as my countrymen do. In short, my countrymen are cosmopolitans. A conversation between literate people, easy to imagine in some Zagreb, Belgrade or Sarajevo café, might sound like this . . .

"Have you seen the new Altman movie?"

"Sure have! Shit!"

"And have you had a glance at the new Rushdie novel?"

"Shit. Every new novel of his is worse than the last."

"Seen the new Petrović play?"

"And why should I?! You know I never go to that local shit."

Thanks to their cosmopolitan views, my countrymen are inclined to claim that Holland is falling apart (it's a country which might find itself submerged any day); that Switzerland is no better than a hole in a hunk of Swiss cheese, a big zero (a country with nothing more to boast of than holding the money of foreigners in their banks); and that the French are unbearable, they stick their noses in the air (it must be that they find that their own cheeses stink). If it weren't for Thomas Mann and the BMW, the Germans wouldn't even merit a mention. The same can be said for the Italians because the Italians are out there only thanks to their gnocchi and good tenors, though some of them are blind as bats. The tenors, of course, not the gnocchi.

My countrymen did not acquire their cosmopolitanism by hot-footing it around the world; indeed, they stood stubbornly in one spot. The world had always come to them: as conquerors, colonizers, adventurers, tourists and—peace negotiators. For centuries they have sat on the bench in front of their house, watching, elbows on the window sill, rooted to the shore, waiting for the boats as they come in, chatting in the cafés and seeing the world go by. They sat there and commented, and the world went by.

If someone thinks my countrymen have it easy, they have another think coming. A superiority complex never comes alone. It goes in hand with self-pity. My countrymen maintain that they are victims. That is how they feel. They were born as the victims of the baser passions of lusting parents, of geography (if it wasn't for the peripheral position in Europe, why today they'd be—Germany!), of history (history never gave them a decent chance), of the economy (damned feudalism, communism and the transition), of politics (that stepmother—politics). They are victims of their own environment and the world. Locally and globally.

A normal person cannot help but wonder how—with the cards stacked against them—my countrymen have survived at all. Yet, survive they do. The only way this specimen of humankind manages is by turning its every defeat into a victory. My countrymen do that time and time again. They have no choice.

SOBS

Awakened by sudden cries one night in Antwerp, I went to the window to see what was going on. I was spending a couple of days in that marvelous, chocolate-hearted city. From the hotel window there was a view of a small square. The square was lit by street lamps, and a man and woman were standing there, out in the open, on a natural stage. The man ranted; the woman sobbed bitterly. I didn't understand what the man was saying, nor could I have. He was wound up tightly, like a flamenco dancer. It was as if he were using his voice to compensate for his tense body control. His voice cut like a seagull's scream. The woman whimpered limply, haltingly, like a child, as if she knew the man wouldn't hit her. But the man's voice lashed her as if with real blows, and the woman cringed in pain at each lashing with renewed tears.

This was a poignant altercation between lovers. I have not forgotten it. I was a chance witness of someone else's pain. We rarely witness the pain of others. Human pain reaches us through our television screens, filtered, most often for mass consumption, seldom in a personal form, and it leaves us indifferent. Once pain has been filtered through the media nothing is left of it but an image on the screen and news in the papers. We do not acknowledge this. We talk about how awful things are in the world, we express our sympathy aloud, we give a coin or two as a handout, we sign petitions, we have done what we could—yet we remain indifferent. We pinch our own heart, we picture how it would be if we were there with the Kosovo refugees, but our heart lacks imagination. The heart is a small machine, its only job is creating a regular rhythm.

So human pain is still a rare feeling. Societies are arranged like the human heart; their work is to create a regular rhythm. That is why pain is neatly shunted off into a diagnosis: depression, anxiety . . . The words serve to translate human pain into the language of disease. For disease can be treated, there are doctors for that, psychologists, psychotherapists, medicines, the *self-help* industry. An ideology of a world without pain supports the industry: the media, television with which we are entertaining ourselves to death, the cults of healthy mind and healthy body, the gurus who teach us how to listen to our *inner self*, how to make peace with the world, how to harmonize, how to finally embrace happiness as our fate. Ultimately, spiritual pain in the modern world has been reduced to an ailment that we should be able to overcome with a little good will, while physical pain can be dealt with through fashion (self-punishing earrings, piercings, tattoos), performance art, and images on a screen.

I recently moved to a new address in Amsterdam. The first morning I moved in to my new place, I went for a walk around the neighborhood. A woman came toward me along the street. She was a small woman. Her clothing was in disarray. She was teetering along on shoes with very high heels, her shoes appearing to be heavier than she was. The woman's face grimaced with pain. She was speaking. She looked as if she were about to choke on the words she was saying, and she sobbed. I was moved. The next morning I saw her again. She was, again, sobbing out loud.

This woman apparently was a neighborhood madwoman. But ever since that first encounter I have been thinking of her. I have been thinking that maybe this woman has been condemned to serve as the accountant for world pain. Maybe every night she registers in an invisible ledger all the pain that has happened in the world, and in the morning she publishes aloud all that she had written down. Maybe she is a crazy woman, nothing more, so she was able to take upon herself a job no one else would do. Perhaps the woman is some sort of divine emissary who appears in the form of a disheveled, mad woman. I also wonder what this book of hers would look like and what might be written in it. And then I think, maybe it would be wiser to move to another part of town.

THE HEART

There is a particular kind of canine parasite in North America—the heartworm. It invades the heart of a dog, and then multiplies until the heart finally explodes like a hand grenade. In the waiting room of a veterinary clinic I saw a model of an afflicted heart in a display case. It looked like a stuffed tomato with angel hair pasta sticking out every which way.

At this juncture it isn't just dogs' hearts that are at risk; there may be something essentially wrong with the heart of the whole world. If doctors were to listen to that gigantic organ, who knows what they would find? It seems to me that the heart of the world is enlarged, tired; its pulse is a touch arrhythmic. But I am no doctor. It is up to the experts to have their say.

We are living at the start of the third millennium, and if someone were to ask me what the global icon of the moment is, I would say without hesitation: the heart. The cultural obsession of our times with the heart prods me to caution: it must be that something is wrong with the heart of the world. The heart today has a grow-ing number of promoters, ardent supporters, eloquent priests, and devoted subjects.

The heart has affiliated itself recently with three princesses. First there was Princess Diana, who promoted the ordinary human heart as her royal emblem and stirred an unprecedented flood of ordinary human tears. Then there was Oprah, the good fairy with a global television audience, who used the heart as her emblem. Instead of the colloquial, *Break a leg!*, Oprah would finish her closing segment with the admonishment: *Break a heart!* At one point in her career, Madonna chose the heart as her new media aura. In the video "Frozen" (a variant of Andersen's "Snow Queen"), Madonna speaks openly of thawing someone's frozen heart (*You're frozen, when your heart's not open*), which might—why not?—be the global heart.

Other promoters of the philosophy of the heart attach themselves to superstars like Diana, Oprah, and Madonna. Paulo Coelho, a Brazilian writer with almost one-hundred million followers, is himself a media guru of the heart. In his books and interviews, Coelho openly pushes for the logic of the heart, instead of the reasoning of the mind. And it is worth mentioning that Oprah and Coelho, experts on the human heart, readily make use of the terminology and symbols of angels. Oprah founded the Angel Network to aid poor children with talent; the unceasing search in Coelho's books is for angels, the embodiment of spirituality.

The ideology of sincerity has attached itself to the current super metaphor of the heart. The brain does not require sincerity the way the heart does. We live in an age obsessed with sincerity. Both publishing (memoirs) and the television industry (TV confessionals, from Oprah to Springer) live off of sincerity. This is how sincerity has become an essential value of our time, and it is headed towards becoming a moral, an aesthetic, even a social, norm.

It seems that I, too, am having heart trouble. The doctors say I have a tired heart. Nothing terrible. The heart functions, they say; it is just a touch enlarged, sluggish. Obviously it has lost its youthful elasticity. I have noticed that I cry much more readily these days. Even the stupidest films—in which justice prevails in the end—reduce me to tears. I watch only old movies. Because only in the old movies does justice prevail.

This, it seems, is the source of the problem—a reversal of concepts. Without even realizing that the notion of old-fashioned justice has vanished from the stage of mass culture, and from everyday life, yet aware that something key is missing, people have replaced the more exacting and complex concept of justice with the easier, softer and more elastic concept of the heart. An exchange of vessels, an imperceptible, sneaky transaction with concepts, has given birth to a worldwide fraternity of angels, a global soap opera that has its producers, players, and consumers. And in the process it is no longer clear (and meanwhile it stopped mattering) what is real life, and what is a simulation. All in all, tears are shed, the world is awash in soap suds, and it is perfect, of course, as it has always been.

IDENTITY

These last few years whenever I hear the word "identity" I am over-come by a powerful allergic reaction. I hear this word everywhere, all the time, these days. My life is not easy. It is not easy to live plagued by allergy, especially an allergy like this. Other people can control their allergies. If they are allergic to milk, they don't drink it; if they are allergic to pollen, they wait for the flowering season to pass. For me, it is as if I am allergic to bees, but live in a beehive the size of the planet. I have no idea how I picked up this allergy. I must have been over-exposed to identity.

They constantly assaulted me with that word in my former homeland. They beat at my eardrums to the point of exhaustion, and beat me with that word as if it were a stick. No wonder I developed a chronic aversion. My former countrymen howled and moaned; they wailed and pleaded. Defending their identity, both personally and collec-tively, they barked and snarled, gnashing their canine teeth and flash-ing their dog collars. I couldn't help but hear. At first I thought: *Oh, let them be, people must need their national, ethnic, state identity. Let them have it. What could possibly be bad in that?* I was all about being politi-cally correct; I respected their urge for identity. I myself didn't have it, nor did I miss it. But then, in the name of defending their identities, they lit into one another like mad dogs. And, while they were at it, they lit into me. "How can you live with no identity," they snarled. "Thanks, I don't need one, you go on without me. I'm allergic, you know," I'd answer politely. It didn't help. They turned on me. They tried to snap a dog collar around my neck too, but somehow, thank God, I managed to elude them. At least that was what I thought.

It turned out that, if I was to elude them, I would have to show a dog collar of my own: my passport. Without it you can't budge. Any time you cross a border they ask you to show it. Every form I fill out requires that I enter my "identity." By occupation I am a writer. Nobody's perfect. Everyone has to earn their bread and butter. But, what do you know, it turned out that the things I wrote weren't written by any old writer, but by a *Croatian* writer. Ah, identity!

I changed my place of residence, and that helped some, but not much. I continue to inhale identity like pollen; that word keeps resounding around me like a mantra. I'm constantly sneezing, and tears well in my eyes. Recently, for instance, I was watching an American television show. A young woman decided she wanted to open a men's salon where, she said, she will cut hair in the nude. Why shouldn't the woman be naked while she cuts their hair, I thought. What is so bad about that? I was prepared to offer her my silent support until the woman suddenly erupted with: "This is the identity I have been looking for, and now I've found it!"

Sometimes I think all this is Madonna's fault. After she broadcast her rhythmic thought to the world—*Express yourself!*—the whole world rushed to express its repressed identity. Yes, the word is a sacred mantra. Not a day goes by that I don't hear: "This is my identity!" OK, don't you have anything else in your repertoire? I think, but don't say anything. I continue to respect the identities of others. What can I do? I'm polite. Sometimes I pity them. Sometimes the ones who thump their chests the most with their identities are the ones who have nothing else.

I felt a little better when I came across the sentence "Come, let me introduce you to my mother, who used to be my father!" in a Japanese bestseller. The sentence appealed to me enormously. In an American television ad, the beautiful Linda Evangelista announces: "I have no identity!" It turns out that *Identity* was the name of a new kind of credit card. That appealed to me, too. For the first time it occurred to me why people hold on to this identity of theirs so fiercely—precisely because they know that identities can be changed. That is why a new word should be circulated: integrity. Because even people with no identity, like myself, for instance, can have integrity. Identities are interchangeable, like passports. Integrities are not. And now, am I not right, doctor? Say so yourself.

PAVLIK MOROZOV

The world is populated today by adolescents, kids. It isn't true that the world is getting older. Every day it is getting younger. Children used to imitate the world of adults and hurry to grow up as soon as possible. Today children are refusing to grow up. And adults try to stay young as long as possible.

Recently I have been taking special care when I walk down city streets. I get into trams cautiously, like someone who has been condemned. Because there is a danger that any minute someone might whack me on the back, ribs or head. The people who have provoked this caution wear backpacks. Their packs have become joined to them like a hump. They sweep the area around them with the hump innocently. The backpack and little bottle of water are the trademarks of these new human specimens. Adolescents embraced the fashion in order to draw a line between themselves and the world of adults, but the adults are joining them. More and more I run into mature women who can't be separated from their little bottles, which they take swigs from with a semi-pornographic, yet meditative, expression. And it bears saying that the owners of the backpacks and little bottles do not communicate with others. It seems that each of them is walking through the world alone.

"I am just a kid," is the phrase I hear most often. "I am just a kid" is a magic formula which removes all responsibility from the person who utters it. In 1989, a group of adolescents in an American town called Glen Ridge raped a seventeen-year-old retarded girl with a baseball bat. The entire town did what it could to conceal the crime, because those were our good boys who did that, our kids. America was recently alarmed by a case where young parents killed their own newborn baby, wrapping it in a plastic bag and dumping it in the garbage. Many tried to justify these cases by saying, "They were just kids!" The child murderers were each about nineteen.

Paula Jones is a woman whose name traversed the world media thanks to a detail. Some years ago a governor's, and future president's, trousers dropped before her, which later deeply insulted and traumatized her for life. Defending her innocence and naiveté, Paula Jones said, in the voice of a fifteen-year-old girl: "I am just a country girl." In other words, "I am just a kid."

The model of the authoritarian parent, father or mother, which was the foundation of modern psychoanalysis and which nourished it for decades, has gradually mutated, pathologically, into the model of a parent-pedophile. The collective obsession with that culturally adapted traumatic model is at its peak today. There are few public figures in the American entertainment industry who have not publicly acknowledged that they were sexually molested by their parents in childhood. Hundreds of thousands of anonymous people have subsequently disclosed their repressed sexual trauma to their psychotherapists. Pavlik Morozov—a boy famous for denouncing his father to Stalin's secret police—has risen from the grave and arrived in America.

The world is populated today by adolescents, children. I am doing what I can to adjust. I have purchased my backpack and my little water bottle. I observe these evolved specimens of the human race. With wan faces—which give no clue as to age, thought, feeling or life experience—we move lightly through the world, and all of us diligently suck on our little bottles. We take swigs of purified water, nursing at this substitute for the long lost nipple, a substitute of a substitute.

HAPPINESS

Once when I was in New York I met a young American who, it turned out, was a second-generation Croat. He told me that his parents had moved to the United States in the early 1960s in their search for happiness. "How did your parents picture their happiness?" I asked. "Like in the movies of Doris Day," the young man replied. His parents live in New Jersey now. His mother has her hair bleached with peroxide once a month and wears old-fashioned suits, just like Doris Day. "And those high-heeled slippers with the pom-pom," said a housepainter in Zagreb several months later who was there to paint my apartment. It turned out that the painter (what a coincidence!) was a brother of the mother who had adored Doris Day. He, too, spent some time in the United States. "And?" I asked. And nothing. He spent five years painting the Brooklyn Bridge. He finished painting it and went back to Croatia. He didn't like America much. The former Brooklyn Bridge painter said it shook him up too much.

I am not a historian of ideas, so I can't actually say how personal happiness has rated at other times. The history of the idea is a long one: *eudaimonia* was a preoccupation of the Greeks; Aristotle interpreted happiness as the realization of human potential. The "pursuit of happiness" shows up in the American Declaration of Independence. Before their right to pursue happiness was legitimatized, people were caught up in meeting their obligations, their duties to God and people, for centuries. The question of happiness was something left to the elite: the gods, philosophers, poets and sovereigns.

Happiness, it seems, began its advance on the masses at the moment God died (when Friedrich Nietzsche published God's clinical death), and the market, then still in its infancy, understood that there is money to be made in the production of a substitute. That is why this last century—the century of the global marketplace, information, the mass media, human rights, cheap transportation, vacations, tourism, sexual and other freedoms, movies, television and entertainment—managed to produce human happiness on a massive scale. There were also two world wars and acts of genocide, and we discovered the efficacy of the atomic bomb.

The articulation of the notion of human happiness belongs to those who have the most powerful media and the strongest market. Happiness is, in that sense, an American product. There is no country in which the word "happiness" is used more frequently in everyday life than the United States. Many languages don't even have a word that covers the range of the notion of happiness. Yes, in this century happiness is definitely an American product.

In the country in which people do not even allow you to feel sad because of your own death (a recent fashion is encouraging patients on their death bed to try "laughter therapy"), in which burial insurance is advertised just as cheerfully and brightly as Coca Cola is, there is also a resistance movement. It's numerically insignificant, but it does exist. *Happiness*, a movie by Todd Solondz, is a dark and startlingly harsh portrayal of the search for personal happiness. The members of the Jordan family—from New Jersey—who display the gruesome essence of their personal happiness for movie viewers, end the film with their glasses raised, stubbornly toasting: "To happiness!"

Forty years ago the image of familial happiness—new kitchens, fridges, cars, houses and lawns with neatly mowed grass—was powerful enough to draw a woman from Zagreb to New Jersey. Today the Fifties look like an irretrievably lost Utopia, and the rebellious sixties, with flower children in search of an Arcadian happiness, seem outdated. We view the happiness of the orgasm, unfettered at last, with a tinge of boredom. The wall came down and the communist masses were freed in the 1990s, but this did not, it seems, bring the expected happiness for the unhappy on that side of the wall, or the happy on this side.

In an environment like this, the only thing I can offer from my repertoire is an old Russian saying: "Happy people do not look at their watches." Sure. Especially those who wear a Rolex.

CELEBS

Celebrity is a phenomenon that has flourished hand in hand with the media, as its offspring. It used to be that people were famous for what they had accomplished. Occasionally there was a biography that became an accomplishment in its own right, but the person described in the biography had had to work for his or her fame. Heroes, artists, explorers, doctors, inventors, actors, courtesans, spies, dukes, murderers and saints—all of them earned their personal glory, dark or light, with hard work.

Celebrities, or celebs for short, are stars who belong to entirely different orbits and another (capricious) law and order. "I am not an actress. I can't dance or sing. I am not a superstar. I am a personality. Maybe I'm selling me," declared Ivana Trump, struggling for a moment with her own definition of herself. A celeb is an empty screen onto which the rest of the world projects its meaning. The celeb is a cultural text, an artifact of mass culture.

Monica Lewinsky was an ordinary American girl—not especially smart or especially stupid, competent or incompetent, beautiful or ugly. Monica Lewinsky did nothing remarkable (her sexual adventure was characterized by its lack of adventure), except that the "nothing" she did was with the President of the United States. Lewinsky became a product of the culture and the media precisely because she lacked any significance of her own, and this made her an ideal screen onto which to project meaning. Her name raised the adrenaline level of Americans and the rest of the world. Lewinsky's circumstances provided an impulse that provoked debate on a wide range of themes.

Her name fed an industry: books flooded the market, including her own, there were videos, illustrated porn parodies, Internet jokes, TV shows, newspaper cover pages and articles, souvenirs. The replica of a baseball cap that Monica Lewinsky once wore, which advertised a small radio station, sold millions and brought the radio station vast profit. Celebrity is not a value in and of itself. It generates value. Monica Lewinsky's figure prompted the arbiters of style and fashion to re-think the standards of female beauty to include a "pleasantly plump" woman. Her announcement that she was going to see a psychotherapist gave credence to psychotherapeutic services, which had otherwise been going out of fashion. The intellectual gurus of popular culture, always starved for cultural material, performed their art of interpretation on the case of Monica Lewinsky.

Komar & Melamid, the authors of psychoanalytic fantasy paintings on the theme of totalitarianism and sex, painted a girl pioneer, a Soviet Lolita, with her knees spread apart ambiguously and a large portrait of Stalin in the background. Monica Lewinsky was the American Lolita, a girl scout in love with her President. Political psychoanalysts profited from Monica's case, feminist critics took their slice of the pie, while those in favor of popular culture, who see in its forms a resistance to the power elite, took theirs. For Monica's ". . . eyes are not windows but mirrors, and what we see in them is awful," as David Remnick of *The New Yorker* remarked in his column.

The phenomenon of celebs is a perpetuation of the old Russian fairy tale about Ivan the Fool. Ivan the Fool is a boy with a simple mind who wins happiness and wealth with nothing but magic and helpers. So, parents, when your children ask you what they should do to become famous, tell them: Nothing. We must not forget that many an unfortunate soul has been misled by the lure of fame. A serial killer once commented bitterly: "How many times do I have to kill before my name appears in print?!"

RISE UP, YE PROLETARIANS!

I was getting onto the #15 bus the other day in Amsterdam. I snapped open my purse, dug around for a few minutes for my wallet, and finally fished the fare out for the driver.

"Two zones, please," I stammered in my clumsy Dutch.

"Are you one of 'us'?" the driver asked me in Serbo-Croatian, with a knowing look.

"Yes, I am," I said.

"From where?" he asked and firmly returned my bus fare.

"From Zagreb," I said. He was Macedonian. He had been living in Holland for twenty years. He'd married a Dutch woman, they had three children.

My stop was coming up.

"Whenever I am on this route, you'll have a free ride. OK?" he called after me.

"Sure!"

I was staying at a Boston hotel. The hotel room was for non-smokers, as is all of America. The maid came into the room. She said, "Good morning," and apologized for disturbing me. Her accent rubbed up against my ear, so I went over and looked at the name tag on her uniform. Ferida.

"Are you one of 'us'?"

"I'm from Travnik. What about you?"

"I'm from Zagreb."

She had already been in the States for a few years, having arrived with her husband and two children shortly after the war started in Bosnia. They liked it in the States. They had recently bought themselves an apartment. No, she wouldn't be going back to Bosnia, no way . . . There were other people from there at the hotel. The guy at the reception desk was from Zadar, and a woman who worked in the administration was from Karlovac. A guy in the kitchen was from Požarevac. The hotel was like a whole little Yugoslavia . . .

"Is it really forbidden to smoke in the rooms?" I asked.

She gave me a knowing look and grinned. She went over to the windows and showed me how to crack them open . . .

"Don't you worry about a thing! While I'm in charge of the twelfth floor, you are free to smoke here . . ."

She stepped out for a moment and came back with a spray can.

"Look, there are these Arabs who send their kids to Harvard and stay here when they visit. Who has heard of Arabs without tobacco? And how would Americans dare to forbid their wealthy Arab visitors from smoking! When you've finished your cigarette, you just spray around the room with this . . ."

In Germany, while I was on a long trip, I stopped at a motel somewhere near Frankfurt. I went to the bathroom. I put a fifty-cent piece in the little basket by the entrance to the lady's room. The boy sitting by the table with the basket said thank you in Polish.

"Are you a Pole?"

"A Russian," he said.

"Did you think I was Polish?" I asked, in Russian.

"I did. Where are you from?"

"From the former . . . Yugoslavia."

"How come you know Russian?" he asked, as if he had never until that moment met anyone who spoke Russian.

"It's a long story . . ."

"Don't pay . . ." he said, returning my money and grinning broadly.

"Oh, no, you mustn't . . ." I put the coin back into the basket. I was confused, thinking that I really ought to be leaving him two or three euros.

"Good luck . . ." said the young man in English, awkwardly, as if only in English did "luck" have a chance.

"Good luck," I said to him.

I don't know why, but after encounters such as these—and there have been many—I feel like the protagonist in a fairy tale. In fairy tales there are always figures who offer assistance. The Macedonian man treated me to a ride on bus #15, the Bosnian woman offered me the right to smoke, and the Russian gave me free use of the lady's room. And suddenly it hit me: there is a global brotherhood after all! That is what we are, the proletarian class. We recognize each other in an instant, test each other with words, treat each other to little favors like kids, we release one another from a heavy, invisible burden, and push onward. I, for my part, will repay my debt. The money I earn by writing these lines will end up in the hands of a Bulgarian woman in charge of a toilet somewhere, a Romanian window washer working for cash, a Russian street musician who holds a degree from the Academy of Music, a woman from Moldova, who asks me for a smoke on the street . . .

So rise up, ye proletarians; there is hope for us yet!

BEAUTY KILLED THE BEAST

I should hate to see our country endangered by my underwear.
—*"Ninotchka"*

In this weary post-Utopian time it seems as if the human body is the only place left where Utopia is thriving. All the major Utopian ideas have fractured; there are minor ones which have survived, but they are suffering from chronic fatigue syndrome. The stock market of ideas is collapsing; the stock market of money is volatile; our petroleum-based civilization is, they say, in its death throes; pensions no longer secure the future, nor will the future secure pensions; laws on labor and other relations mutate by the minute, all to the detriment of the employed. Sometimes it seems as if all of Western civilization is returning to the brutal law of the jungle. The only thing we all still have as a stronghold is our own body. The body is the realm of the individual: our freedom, control and manipulation, our pleasures, and our future. The consumer ideology of our age has succeeded in convincing us of this, spurring our self-confidence.

What is this "liberated" human body for? Aside from serving as a source of pleasure when coupling with other bodies (or with itself), the human body serves as an organ bank. There aren't any clones yet to serve as a living bank of organs, but compensation for this is a dynamic market. One body sells its organs to other bodies—kidneys, livers, hearts and eyes travel the world. The demand is among the rich, while the supply is from the poor parts of the world.

Some human bodies serve to produce offspring for other human bodies. There are sperm providers, providers of eggs and carriers of fertilized eggs, all for sale. Some well-paid carriers go through the nine-month job several times in the course of a lifetime.

There are bodies that are paid couriers for delivering drugs across borders. Male bodies carry the drugs in their intestines and rectums, female bodies insert them into their breasts. Breast implants are packed with drugs. Later, more solvent human noses snort the contraband.

There are bodies of female children which serve adult male bodies for healing, or so those seeking the services believe. In Bombay there are many children—aged 5 to 10—whose undeveloped sexual organs provide mystical cleansing for adult men who have been afflicted by the AIDS virus. The female children's bodies, immediately infected with AIDS, die much faster than the male infected bodies will.

There are bodies whose crazy minds are convinced that there ought to be less of them: these are people who suffer from a strange self-amputation craze, obsessed with the idea that they must rid themselves of an arm or leg to be happy. Since there are no legal services which will oblige, these poor people must seek help illegally, often from professional butchers. Once they have had the objectionable leg or arm amputated, they say they feel enormous relief.

There are bodies which, according to the thinking of others, are too small. A pathological male minority—known as *feeders*—who find satisfaction in force-feeding fat women has recently been described. Feeders often marry the female objects of their dark desires, and feed their five-hundred-pound darlings until the women die.

The human body also serves for self-punishment, which brings with it an aesthetic satisfaction. People get tattoos, piercings on various parts of their bodies, they insert implants under the skin, most often on the head, write messages, images, drawings in their own skin, tattoo their body as if it were an artwork. The body can, indeed, become a source of constant physical pleasure if balls, piercings, needles, and implants are inserted in the right places.

The body serves for self-sculpting (to which gymnastics, body-building and other sports contribute). The body can be made smaller or larger (diets), and can be shaped by artificial means (liposuction, stomach stapling, insert silicon implants to the cheeks, lips, breasts, transplantation of hair, teeth, and so forth). The body can change the color of its skin (bleaching) and other racial traits. Chinese and Japanese people straighten and widen their eyes, and more and more are submitting themselves to grueling hip operations—to give themselves longer legs, so they will be able to stand taller and, thereby, be more suited to the business world.

The body can change its sex: male to female or vice versa. The human face can change its racial, sexual and gender features, and it can also change its human features, thanks to cosmetic surgery, to look more animal-like. As far as transplanting faces is concerned, surgeons claim this will be a routine procedure in the future. If that happens, there will be a legalized hunt for freshly killed young bodies and undamaged faces. Not to speak of the illegal hunt that will spring up.

The dream of metamorphosis is the most ancient, profound and persistent human dream. The dream of turning a frog into a princess has caught the personal and collective imagination, it nourishes the most profitable industries in the world (such as the diet industry), starts revolutions, brings down systems and changes worlds. The Utopian projections of personal and collective transformation were the foundation of both the fascist and the communist ideologies. The fascist version collapsed after they killed millions of people, including six million Jews. The communist version collapsed from the victims of their own death camps and the deficit of—underwear.[1]

The big ideologies have vanished, but their "atomic" nucleus remains: an archetypical dream of metamorphosis, a dream of a superhuman, of a superwoman and a superman, which is being realized at this point in a protean body which is devouring itself and stretching itself out like chewing gum.

The world right now is crazy about butts. The key word is: the butt. J. Lo deserves the credit for promoting the round, Latino butt. Music videos with Afro-American, Brazilian and other female butts doing all sorts of exciting shaking have set in motion a new dream about transformation, and have inspired the cosmetic industry to new endeavors: inserting silicon implants into women's bottoms.

Since the only revolutions that happen today are on the human body, serious medicine is working on pumping up the brain's potential. So the question remains: what will this head, with its expanded brain power, see when it looks into the mirror? Its butt?!

---

1. *Ninotchka*, the famous film by Ernst Lubitsch, is a story about communism collapsing over the question of underwear and fancy hats. It was made in 1939, but the story on the fall of communism was reinforced later on several occasions, until it really did collapse. Before the Italian elections of 1947 and 1948 the Americans were quite worried about the possibility that communists might win. They had a special copy of *Ninotchka* made and showed it in Italy. Although the communists did all they could to prevent the showing of the film, some five million Italians managed to watch it. One pro-communist worker commented: "What licked us was *Ninotchka!*" The worker was paraphrasing a famous line from another film: "It wasn't the planes that got him, it was Beauty killed the Beast." That movie was called *King Kong*.

2.

"To hell with it!" cried Bender in a sudden fit of viciousness. "It's all made up. There isn't any Rio de Janeiro, or any America or Europe, or anything else. The last town is Shepetovka, and the Atlantic waves lap against its shore."

—*Ilf & Petrov*, The Golden Calf

EUROPE, EUROPE

"So what does Europe mean to you?" I ask my colleague, a Czech writer.
"Who knows. Right now I've got goulash on my mind . . ."

How to send a postcard

I may not know how to tickle the fancy of people elsewhere, but I do know how to warm the hearts of my Dutch friends. It is a little thing, really: a postcard. There is no one as happy to send and receive postcards as the Dutch.

On my way back from my trip around Europe I called a friend.

"Well, thanks for the postcards!" she said with ironic emphasis on the word "thanks." "Why did you bother? Why even send them? A disgrace for a woman who makes her living as a writer! And the dates . . ." she grumbled.

"What dates?"

"Precisely! There were no dates! A postcard of Lisbon sent from Madrid, and a postcard of Madrid from Paris!"

I confess that I never got the knack of writing postcards. As if my ways were set permanently by the unimaginative sentence I once wrote on my first card: *Warmest regards from the beautiful blue Adriatic, from . . .* When I write out postcards I feel handicapped. I'm best at the cards where the message is only: *Love . . .* When I write that, *love* is my excuse for the absence of any other text.

Everywhere in Europe the postcard sender is faced with an absurdity: postcards and stamps are invariably purchased in separate places. The postcards are sold at a newspaper kiosk or souvenir stand, and the stamps usually at a post office or tobacco shop. The postcard sender has to invest major effort to please their friends; first, buy the cards, then locate the stamps, and then find the place to send them from. If your stay in some city is brief, as was ours, the sender quickly becomes a strategist. After all that, there is no oomph left to stick on the stamps, let alone write anything.

I speak from experience. I traveled from Lisbon to Madrid, then on to Bordeaux, Paris, Lille, Brussels, Dortmund, Hanover, Malbork, Kaliningrad, Vilnius, Riga, Tallinn, St. Petersburg, Moscow, Minsk, Warsaw and, finally, Berlin. Eighteen European cities. Ten times eighteen postcards.

In Moscow there was a savvy woman who ran a kiosk right next to the Hotel Rossiya. She was the only one in all of Europe who came up with the brilliant idea of bringing together two things that were meant for each other: the postcard and the stamp. For that reason I am using this opportunity to send the nice lady who ran the kiosk in Moscow my very warmest regards.

Nenad, a writer from Sarajevo, is a genuine postcard artist. With awe I watched him buy postcards, then slowly—like a perfect lover, who knows the secret language of touch—glue on the stamps. Then he swept a space in front of him clean (the breakfast table in the hotel restaurant), pushing aside the coffee cups, smoothing the surface of the table before he lay the picture side of the postcard down on it, took out his fountain pen, and neatly wrote the address. Then he would painstakingly write something out.

"May I read it?" I asked.

"Sure," he said, and passed me the card.

Instead of a message, there was a jumble of numbers and letters. Nenad had written his card out in code. And then he would send another postcard from another town, explaining to his addressee how to read the code on the first card.

With this intimate game, my colleague was constructing a metaphor for the lost cause of the literary genre known as—travel writing. It is a waste of time to write about travel. That is why tourists would rather have a tour guide—with shiny photographs and drawings that elbow out the text—than read the impressions of a traveling writer. When a writer keeps a travel diary, it, too, is in code. Only when the addressee (the reader) has the chance to compare what the writer wrote with the reality of the place is he able to see what was meant, but by then the text is gone. The same sort of thing happens with the sender of the text, the writer, who can no longer decipher what he wrote during the trip. What he remembers no longer corresponds to what he jotted down as a reminder for later. So the travel writer has no choice but to fabricate reality. If the writer is good, the fabrications generally overlap with reality. We should add that reality itself isn't so stable. It, too, travels.

A journey as retro-utopia

Literaturexpress Europa 2000 was a journey in which a hundred writers from some forty-three countries covered seven-thousand kilometers and visited eighteen European cities. It was the collective experience of a retro-Utopia. There have been similar train-metaphors which have crisscrossed Europe in the past.

I can remember the *brotherhood and unity* trains that chugged along Yugoslav railway lines, and the youth brigades who rebuilt the tracks that had been destroyed in Yugoslavia during World War II.

The train was part and parcel of the early communist propaganda iconography and the clearest and most vital representation of the implacable march into a "brighter day." The symbolism of cheery trains forging ever onward concealed something that needed to be forgotten: the image of trains crisscrossing Europe as they transported Jews to concentration camps.

Veljko Bulajić's movie *Train Without a Timetable* was etched in the Yugoslav collective memory. It is about a trip from Herzegovina to Vojvodina, post-war colonization, and the migration of whole villages to a new place for a better life.

The post-war fascination with trains soon waned. Work began on building roads, among others, the "Brotherhood and Unity" highway which was to connect Zagreb and Belgrade. The trains were given names to emulate a fashionable, European, mood. The "Matoš" (named after a Croatian writer) ran from Zagreb to Belgrade, and the "Mimara" (after a dubious Croatian art collector) between Zagreb and Munich.

The train made a comeback in the 1980s. The "Blue Train" was the last uniting symbol of Yugoslavia, but also a preview of its demise. This was the train that bore the body of the late Yugoslav President Tito. On the route from Ljubljana to Belgrade the train passed by thousands of mourning Yugoslavs.

About ten years after the passage of the "Blue Train," Krajina Serbs in Croatia obstructed the passage of trains on the Zagreb-Split line by felling logs and laying them across the tracks. They continued to obstruct the passage of trains for the next several years. This symbolic act served as a prelude to war, and meant the vanishing of Yugoslavia, and with it, the Yugoslav State Railway.

Several years later the "Freedom Train" carried the Croatian political elite on the Zagreb-Split railway line. In practical terms, *freedom* meant that more than a hundred thousand Croatian Serbs were finally forced to leave Croatia. The greatest performance of *freedom* would be staged at the train station in Knin, the *cradle of Croatdom*. A few days later that same "Freedom Train" would bring in the looters who set out to ransack Serbian property in Knin.

The Literaturexpress 2000 was a summary of sorts of an entire century of European train history that had symbolically connected places and people, the postmodern quotation of the pioneering, victorious, boisterous Utopia of the twentieth century.

For us, the travelers on the train, the retro-Utopia began in its most literal sense when we moved onto one which had been outfitted for us, the German "Gorlitz VT 18.16.07," a technical marvel of the 1950s.

Our retro-Utopia continued as we traveled on a Latvian train which had been at the beck and call of the President of the Latvian Republic during communist times. The train had a *presidential* car with a lavish broad bed, a bathroom, and compartments designed to accommodate staff. The lavish *presidential* compartment was not occupied by the French writer, who, despite her venerable age, rubbed shoulders in an ordinary compartment. Instead, the *presidential* compartment was taken over by the young organizer, guided by his sense of natural privilege. He was a chef by training. Tito, after all, had been a locksmith. Thanks to an attack of boldness, the "Balkan" group (Nenad, Maja, and I) managed to occupy the smaller *staff* compartment for several hours.

"This makes us feel almost like Tito!" Nenad said, having made his peace.

We were back in the retro-Utopia in Kaliningrad, which had, apparently, bought the idea that our train was bringing with it European unification, and that the Literaturexpress Europa 2000 was magically going to zip up the rift that had been yawning for years, so unfairly.

In his words of welcome, the mayor of Kaliningrad euphorically declared, "I wish many expresses to everything in the future: expresses carrying artists, musicians, yes, particularly musical expresses, many, many various expresses . . ."

And a child, Aleksandar Moskalev, a fourteen-year-old high school student from Kaliningrad, quoted Dostoevsky in his composition "Memory Train" and there was a line about how only *beauty can save the world*. The boy voiced his sincere hope that we would do this, we, the writers traveling on the Literaturexpress 2000.

And speaking of Dostoevsky, a few days later I found myself in the Dostoevsky Bar in St. Petersburg, where I stared in astonishment at the boisterous crowd of New Russians who were having a fine time salsa dancing.

"Poor choice!" a Russian-American friend of mine remarked in an email. "You should have gone to Café Idiot."

In every traveler there crouches a colonizer
"In each and every traveler there crouches a colonizer. Just look at our colleague talking to that waiter! Something has got into me,

too. This trip is tugging at the hidden trigger in all of us for colonial superiority. I was appalled at myself when I noticed the ease with which I judge whole cities and countries, how I embrace them or shrug them off. If I had another month of travel, I'd soon be Alexander the Great!" a fellow writer confessed.

The passenger of a literary train: travel as a literary quote

The train is one of the most quoted themes of the twentieth century. The history of cinematography began with the shot of a racing train, and the train is the beginning, focus and topos of filmmaking. All of Russian literature rides on trains. Along with the soul, the train is one of the most frequent topi of Russian literature, from Dostoevsky to Venedikt Erofeev and his wonderful little novel *Moscow to the End of the Line.*

Along with terrifying revolutionary trains that transported the frenzied mob, there were agitprop trains that chugged back and forth across Russia, convincing people that the empire of equality was just around the corner and that there would be justice here on earth. In *The Golden Calf* there is a description of one such train, which was heading off to the Far East. There are foreign and domestic journalists on board, writers, shock workers, and, of course, the smooth operator, Ostap Bender. One of the travelers announces:

"I know all about these trips . . . I've been on them myself. I know what's going to happen to you. There are about a hundred of you here. You'll be traveling for about a month in all. A couple of you will get left behind on some small out-of-the-way station without any money or papers and won't catch up with the others for maybe a week, arriving tired and in rags. Somebody's suitcase is bound to be pinched. And the victim will moan the whole way and keep borrowing his neighbor's shaving brush. He'll give the shaving brush back unwashed and lose the mug. One passenger will die, of course, and his friends, instead of going to the joining-up ceremony, will be forced to bring his dearly beloved ashes back here to Moscow. Carrying ashes is a terrible bore and nasty, to boot. In addition to all that, people will start bickering on the way. Believe me! Someone, whether it's Palamidov or Ukhudshansky, will do something antisocial. And for a long time you'll all sadly take him to task, while he screeches and moans that it wasn't his fault. I know all about it. You're going off in caps and hats, but you'll come back in Oriental skullcaps. The biggest fool among you will buy a full set of armor from a Bukhara Jew—a velvet cap edged with jackal fur and a thick padded blanket made in the style of a gown. And it goes without saying that you'll be singing '*Stenka Razin*.' Not only that, the foreigners will sing 'Down Mother Volga; *Sur Notre Mère Volga.*'"

How did our group measure up to the Ilf & Petrov standard?

1. The writers who got off the train were, as far as I know: a Greek writer who had gotten on in Paris and off in Hanover, a Croatian writer who got off in Hanover, another Croatian writer who got off in Malbork and back on in Warsaw, and a Bulgarian writer who got off in Moscow though he threatened in Lisbon that he'd get off in Paris.

2. A Slovak writer's bag—with his computer and documents—was already stolen in Madrid. From that moment forward, a writer had something pinched in almost every city, including the very last day in Berlin, when $1000 disappeared from the inside pocket of a Serbian writer.

3. At the Unter den Linden Hotel in Berlin I lent my hair dryer to an Italian writer. He returned it immediately.

4. No one died, although several of the travelers nearly drank themselves to death.

5. Some of the writers exhibited *anti-social behavior*, but my collegial feelings prevent me from going into details.

6. I bought a colorful Estonian embroidered sweater, the Slovenian poet Aleš bought himself a colorful, embroidered Lithuanian sweater, and the Bulgarian poet Virginia bought herself a colorful, embroidered Latvian sweater. At the Petersburg flea market, Nenad, the Bosnian writer, bought himself sailor undershirts (five of them) and a blue Soviet Navy jacket. The same writer had someone take a

picture of him wearing a Soviet pilot's cap at the same market, but he didn't buy it. Virginia, the Bulgarian poet, bought a Latvian embroidered cap and a pound of dried sardines at the Riga open market. She nibbled on the sardines from Riga to St. Petersburg. I bought a *matryoshka* in Moscow. Tolstoy was inside of Pushkin, Dostoevsky inside of Tolstoy, and Chekhov inside of Dostoevsky, while inside Chekhov there was a tiny Gogol.

7. I sang *Stenka Razin* and some other songs, joining in with some Russian writers who organized a little get-together with a bottle of vodka and sandwiches made of leftovers from the hotel breakfast.

To this report on the similarities between literature and life I can add that the menu in the restaurant car described in that same Ilf & Petrov episode corresponds perfectly to the reality of the menu in our restaurant cars (Vilnius-Tallinn; Tallinn-St. Petersburg; St. Petersburg-Moscow; Moscow-Minsk) though the novel *The Golden Calf* was published in long ago 1931. Except for the fact that the vodka was not as cold in our case, nor was the caviar quite so fresh.

The stop named "Nostalgia."

After muggy Hanover, a visit to EXPO, and a Disneyified projection of the global future, we arrived in cool Poland. We traveled for hours through a corridor of green fields and summer rain that streamed down the windows of the train until we finally arrived in gloomy Malbork. Our luggage was unloaded by NATO soldiers. The train station was empty; it was the only station where there was no official welcome. For a moment I felt as if we'd come to a war zone. And then, in my room at the Sbyszko Hotel, the seismograph of my heart (the power of banality lies in its precision!) recorded the first tremor.

I am at a loss to explain precisely what caused the earthquake. I cannot say whether it was the Trilux-brand television set; the floral bedding, threadbare from laundering and ironing; the naked lady in the picture over my head; or the stuffy, unaired smell. That same tremor of excitement woke me up at about four o'clock in the morning. I went out barefoot into the hallway and sat in the smokers' corner. That is at least what the sign said—*Tu wolno palić!* (Here you are free to smoke!)—and there was a metal ashtray. Surrounded by the dusty hotel foliage—ficuses mostly—I rubbed my bare feet on the coarse dark red carpeting and sleepily sniffed at the air around me. There was a reproduction of van Gogh's *Sunflowers* on the wall, and the chair was draped with a linen dish towel with a floral design. In the sleepy early morning moment I began to feel as if I had arrived at some sort of a beginning: I smoothed the linen dish towel (my mother had had one just like it) and realized I'd come home. Sitting in that corner, I was overcome by a feeling of dense, warm reconciliation with my own biography, with *them*, with the *Easterners*—liars, smart alecks, tricksters, losers, matchbox swindlers, sleaze-balls, thieves, petty and big-time operators, survivors (because there was never time left over for living life, but only for survival), re-sellers (*Poles*, from whom my mother could buy that cheap *Polish* dish towel at the Zagreb flea market, although the *Croatian* dish towels looked just the same)—with people who are clandestinely laying the paths to a future, united Europe.

Malbork, which exists thanks to the largest medieval castle in Europe, works hard at reviving its chivalric past (those shabby productions of chivalric games which we were to watch thereafter in city after city). Somehow it turns out that the Middle Ages (the age when all we Europeans were, supposedly, equal, is that it?) were not only for tourists; they were an ideological, romantic handkerchief which Eastern Europe drops flirtatiously for Western Europe (*Look at me, we two have always been a couple*).

The chivalric games didn't hold my attention. The early morning flutter in my heart had turned me into a junkie for Eastern European sentiment. I became a bloodhound. I sniffed around town until, in a half-empty store window, I saw them: "Bobi pretzel sticks." (*For your hobby, pretzel sticks Bobi! Paluszki. Legendarny smak. Cheesz paluszki?*)

The slender, salt-studded snacks elbowed their way into everyday Yugoslav life in the 1960s, along with the first television sets (manufactured in a factory in Niš). Guests would come over, perch on our first armchairs and sofas, and gather around the television set, while the hostess would serve drinks and Bobi Pretzel Sticks, invariably asking: "How about a Bobi Pretzel?" as if with that sentence she was heralding a better and brighter future. *Cheesz paluszki?* Television and Bobi Pretzel Sticks were a clear introduction to a better life.

That evening we sat with Dragana and Vlado at the Hotel restaurant. There was nowhere else to go. The restaurant was empty. We sat at the table, surrounded by a dusty jungle of ficus ("communist flora"), as if we were in a museum. The waitress was serious, as if she was the museum curator. There were no desserts on the menu (it seems as if Eastern Europe begins where desserts disappear from restaurant menus). I had three packages of Bobi Pretzel Sticks in my purse. We ordered martinis. The sweet taste of the martini and the salt-studded Bobi Pretzel Sticks took me back for a moment to those first teenage parties, school tea parties and small town dances. Dragana, who could easily have been my daughter, savored some future nostalgia of her own along with her martini.

In the morning, as I left the hotel room, I took a sheet of paper from the metal chain on the toilet tank in the bathroom as a souvenir. On it was the handwritten message: *Prosze lekko pociegać za sznurek. Dziekuje!* (Please pull the toilet chain gently. Thank you!). The message pierced me to the quick, as if I had read a brochure from a member of an underground movement in an occupied zone. The words touched me: for a moment it seemed much easier to read Europe from the Prado or the Louvre than it was to read the message on the yellowed piece of paper hanging off the toilet tank in an East European toilet. I was encouraged by the fact that the "occupation" of this place had not yet begun. Only a little later, in the stores in Petersburg, I found I was being followed by Dannon products; I saw an advertisement for Ariel detergent on Moscow television—the actor was German, speaking Russian with a heavy German accent; I watched *Star Trek* on Belarusian television dubbed in Italian; and everywhere I was surrounded by the revolutionary predecessor to globalization: American sitcoms and Mexican soap operas.

By the way, how big is Europe and where is it?

No one knows the answers to that question, though many pretend to. Our organizers told us we covered 7000 kilometers going from South to North. Our route around Europe was shaped like a lasso. The lasso-like contours stirred the imagination and suggested that the travelers had embarked on a hunt. For what?

There are many ways to measure Europe. For example, how many times the travelers had their hair cut during the trip and how many times they clipped their nails. It turned out that finger and toenails grow faster on a trip than the traveler expects. That must be why the little things for snipping nails, those clippers, cost so much. I bought myself clippers in Hanover (29.90 German marks), although I have several at home. According to my calculations, finger and toenails need clipping by the time you reach Hanover from Lisbon. Some writers, such as Herkus, a Lithuanian, got onto the train smooth-shaven in Lisbon and had a beard by the time we arrived in Berlin. Nicola, an Italian, measured Europe by the number of socks he changed. Some of the writers traveling through Europe got thinner, others gained weight.

Answers to the question of where West and East lie in Europe are much less clear and more flexible than answers to the question of where the North and South are.

In Kaliningrad I stopped in front of some women who were selling homemade cakes. One of them was selling something reminiscent of a muffin on a small improvised stand. Below the little lumps of dough was a sign: *Keks zapadnyji*, western cookie.

"Why western?"

"Because we are the West!" she said, sounding like a member of the European Parliament and flashing the golden crown on her tooth at me.

As we left the Belarusian border at Brest behind us, many travelers on the train felt like they were crossing the border between East and West. The Poles were relieved to hear this. The Belarusians were saddened.

The problem of orientation in Europe comes from the fantasies its inhabitants have about themselves and others. The dusty rhetoric in tourist guides tries to convince us that these countries, regions, or cities have served through their whole history as a *bulwark* against the Other—the Other coming invariably, of course, from the East. It turns out that all the inhabitants of Europe would rather see themselves as part of its western than its eastern end. Being on the western end gives Europeans the feeling that they are on the right side of life.

The other key word of national fantasies is *crossroads*. If they have nothing else, at least these peoples, countries and cities experience themselves as being at crucial junctions.

The bulwark and the crossroads are the most widely held fantasies small peoples use to construct a positive image of themselves.

So it turned out that Warsaw is significant because twenty-one meridians pass through it! And it turned out that Vilnius is the *geographic center of Europe*, whatever that means. There are more cafés and restaurants with Europe in their name in St. Petersburg than anywhere in Europe because St. Petersburg so longs to inscribe itself on the European map. In a Belarusian tourist brochure, in the column under the heading "*Kto est kot v Belarusi?*" ("Who's who in Belarus?") a whole page was dedicated to the Belarusian president Lukashenko. Judging by the brochure, Lukashenko has the status of a geographic feature, an essential meridian, or the like.

Symbols

If they have nothing else, small European peoples have an abundance of symbols. So it turns out that Estonia chose the cornflower as its national symbol because, as the Estonian tourist brochure explains, the *cornflower has grown on Estonian soil for thousands of years*. Apparently the cornflower is an exclusively Estonian flower, because it generally grows in corn fields, *creating a strong association in the minds of Estonians between the blossom and the daily bread.* Furthermore, the cornflower in Estonia is a powerful symbol of the resistance movement because its blue color was banned in the red Soviet period. At celebrations, apparently, all the cornflowers had to be painted red so that they might mimic the (communist) carnation. The other important national symbol was the swallow, while one of the unofficial symbols is the oak tree. For, the brochure instructs, *Estonia is rich in national symbols, official and unofficial, which are dear to its people.*

Precisely as is the case with the European song contest, every European country is happiest singing its own state hymn. *Mu isamaa, mu onn ja room . . .*

An exercise in homelessness

"This trip of ours is an exercise in homelessness. All you do is travel, you don't think about a thing. You don't tie yourself down to anything. If a feeling floats up now and then and threatens to nibble at the heart, I crush it with lightning speed, like a worm," a fellow writer says to me.

"I know what you mean," I tell her.

Fantasies

I didn't hear any of the writers complain about the bad hotels in Madrid or Brussels (though they were bad), but I did hear many of them complain about bad hotels in Malbork and St. Petersburg. I didn't hear anyone complain about the rude waiters or awful coffee in Paris (although they were rude and the coffee was awful), but I did hear complaints about the same in Moscow.

I sat at a table in a restaurant in Minsk with a colleague from Western Europe who was appalled when the waiter brought her chilled red wine. Another insisted that a waiter show her the whole bottle of mineral water—she was certain he'd brought her tap water rather than the bottled water she'd asked for. And the water in Minsk comes straight from Chernobyl, right?

All the Literaturexpress travelers were given yellow and black travel bags in Moscow. While we were waiting for the bus, I watched several of my colleagues bet that if they left their bag out in plain sight, the first passerby would snatch it. No one took the bag.

I am sure that many of my fellow West European writers felt uncomfortable during the trip, or even felt scorn for the East which is not the West, for the East aspiring to be the West, and for the East which is like the West. I believe that many writers brought a significant overweight of stereotypes about Eastern Europe in their mental luggage, but they paid no mental fine for that. The regulations in the mental customs zones are the most flexible of all.

Many of the Western European writers did not, for example, notice that we were surrounded during our three-day stay in Moscow by some fifty soft-spoken colleagues, Russian writers. They had traveled to Moscow from Murmansk, Vladivostok, and a number of other places, to spend three days with us. That they were fellow writers became apparent only at the last moment, when, as we were leaving Moscow, they gave us copies of their books, with dedications. None of them got a single book from us.

What about the Easterners? Do they harbor fantasies of their own about the West? Indeed they do. Many of them want to be West because many of them are ashamed that they are East. Most of the Western fantasies about the East come from an unarticulated feeling of superiority, just as most of the Eastern fantasies about the West spring from an articulated sense of inferiority.

What is self-confidence based on? Little things. Like that we have learned that the civilized world drinks its red wine at room temperature. We are just like all *other normal people* and that is the first reason that we feel good. A fear of being shut out from the community is one of the most virulent of human fears, and the subtext for the heights and the depths in the history of the human race. Fear of exclusion from the community is at the root of all fascisms. In this consumer age of ours there is profit to be made from this fear. We come together through Coca-Cola, Nike, Oprah Winfrey, we come together through information, ethnicity, the state, symbols, the community of equals. Each of us takes care of the individual nuances on our own.

Lamerica, the film by Gianni Amelio, is one of the best analyses of the slippery topic of the European East and West. The plot develops the idea that ethnic, national, racial and social identity, and with them personal self-confidence, are essentially quite fragile. It is enough to find ourselves somewhere else (in the film it's an Italian who turns up in post-communist Albania). It is enough for someone to steal your Ray-Ban sunglasses, slash the tires on your car, steal your wallet, your credit cards. All it takes is a few days spent in jail, your passport confiscated—and suddenly your sacred, personal identity vanishes as if you'd never had one. You become simply a human being.

Other people
A fellow writer, a Slovak, explained to me that he was glad he had never been in Eastern Europe before (he meant Russia and Belarus), and now that he had been forced, essentially, to travel there, he was surer than ever that there was no reason to go *there* again.

"Why?"

"Because it is a whole other world! They are entirely different people!" the Slovak declared, confidently.

What I meant to write, but didn't, on the postcards I sent
From Lisbon. The color of Lisbon. The Cais de Sodre marketplace. A dome with a balcony where the flower vendors peer down, angel-like, from above. About the Portuguese who are kind, yet restrained, as if they live in a place where foreigners visit but never linger. About having coffee with David, an Armenian, who, when savoring a *pastel de nata*, a Portuguese pastry, announced, "Kak ekler no vkusnee!" (Like an eclair, only tastier!)

From Madrid. About billboards with the slogan "Momento de Inspiracion" (an ad for Ballantine's), chirping traffic lights, a rain of blossoms (the air was filled with wafting poplar fronds). About the way I sit on a bench in a park as if hypnotized, listening to the metallic chirp of the traffic lights and watching the passersby. There is a pervasive softness, fogginess and fullness in the air which makes the passersby appear to float.

From Bordeaux. About the city which looks like Proust's aunt. And what did Proust's aunt look like? Bordeaux.

From Paris. About the tourists climbing the Eiffel Tower and flashing in the sun like ants.

From Lille. About how I never saw Lille because I slept the whole afternoon, and played "le souffleur" with the waitress that evening at the hotel restaurant.

From Brussels. About the view from the window of Hotel Saint Nicolas. About two nights spent at the front: the smell of beer, urine and sweat, the male fraternity of sports fans, the center of the city packed with men who announced their existence in the world with a roar. About a visit to the European Parliament and writers made to write postcards to the invisible authority, as if they were writing to Santa Claus. And then about how the postcards were drawn from a hat and the authors were made to read one out loud, though there was no addressee to hear what they had written.

From Dortmund. About an abandoned industrial facility that had been made into a gallery. Vision. Ruhr. About how in the abandoned halls life (an electric spark, the holographic image of a face, a mechanical movement, a sound) begins with the pressure of a visitor's finger on a key. About how the visitor to the exhibit feels like God. *Heute ist morgen!*—announces the brochure. If that is so, then virtual reality is our future.

From Hanover. About the EXPO. About *Heute ist morgen*, presumably.

From Kaliningrad. *Heute is gestern.* About Kurskaja Pitch, the dunes, wild strawberries and birds. About how I ringed a bird. About how the *lakirovka*—the way Soviets used to disguise reality, lacquering it over, in order to make it appear better than it was—was gradually becoming authentic. About a Serbian joke. A Gypsy says to a Serbian policeman: "Hey, Serbs, who would there be to love you if it weren't for us Gypsies!" Western Europe, who would there be to love you if it weren't for us here in Kaliningrad!

From Vilnius. About Lietova Hotel, prostitution, the European trade in human flesh. About *sovietshchina*, the Soviet mind-set, which, paradoxically, has been the most tenacious where the attempts to expunge it are the most dogged. About the poignant little paper napkins in the hotel restaurant that were folded into tidy twists and arranged in each glass. Soviet style. About inferiority complexes: about erasing Cyrillic letters. About erasing the past.

From Riga. About lands of linen, amber and *pelymeni*, Russian dumplings. About a conversation with a taxi-driver, a Russian. About discrimination against Russians. About the Riga food market.

From Tallinn. About casinos. The whole town has become a casino. About prostitution again and how tourism invigorates the organism. Swedes, Finns, Norwegians.

From St. Petersburg. About Hotel Oktyabrskaya. About a nocturnal stroll, about a boat ride along the Neva and our tour guide: an eye doctor who, after a hard day's work at the hospital, earns money on the side as a tour guide. About a taxi driver, an Afghanistan war veteran (*Voina, eto gryaz!*—The war is dirt!). About cafés with no bathrooms. About strolling around Vasilyevski Island, one of St. Petersburg's neighborhoods, and old newspaper stands there, where you can still buy "*Belomorskiy kanal*" branded *papirosy* cigarettes, undrinkable *kvas*, inedible *bubliki*, and quite edible sweets: *pryaniki*, *pechenye ovsyanoe*, *vatryushki*. About nostalgic flirtation with Soviet cakes—that are still made in Soviet cake factories (*Praga* tortes still exist!)—through a glass display case.

From Moscow. About Moscow (*Moskva kupecheskaya*, city of merchants). About a tourist guide using the newly coined phrase: *Stalin-style*. About a writer from Murmansk and his living hero, who murdered his unfaithful wife with a dagger concealed in a bouquet of flowers and his cry: *Oh, suka, a ya tebya tak lyubil!* (Ah, you bitch, I loved you so!) About the bird market where I purchased the release of several swallows for 25 rubles. About cafés with no bathrooms. About Moscow, the Emerald City.

From Minsk. About Belarusian landscapes, little village houses and fences that flit by, one by one, like a moving gallery. About the Museum of Janka Kupala and the rhetoric of those who have nothing. About the aesthetics of poverty.

From Brest. About a ceremonial reception and faith in the train-metaphor. Train, meaning *vlak*, meaning *voz*, meaning *poezd*, meaning *zug* . . . About the *vlakirovka* (*lakirovka–vlakirovka!*). About miniature swans made of sweetened meringue floating in baskets of puff pastry.

From Warsaw. About metaphysics. About how we always lose umbrellas, but never come across any.

From Berlin. About how, strangely, I'm home.

The new age: the European bazaar

Europe is tired. During the twentieth century, Europe has spent itself on wars, ideologies, and Utopias. Right now, Europe is doing what people are always happiest doing. Europe is looking more and more like an open market, a *yarmarka*, a fair, a bazaar. Money is the lingua franca of Europe and European unification. Money is the most natural of languages. There is a seller for everything, just as for everything there are buyers. And while ideologists of European unification are still tearing their hair out over a European identity (forgetting that identity is always articulated by contrast to an Other, which Europe has done with enthusiasm throughout its history), the European-ness of Europe is being determined by life itself. The Chinese are settling Eastern Europe (Budapest has a China Town even though it hasn't been given the name officially), and Germans are buying summer houses in Sweden and Portugal. The Dutch are snapping up apartments in Moscow, the Serbs are buying in Budapest, the Italians in Croatia, the Muscovites in Italy . . . The migrations are not only moving North to South and East to West, as the demographers had feared they would, but also West to East, and South to North, and round and round in circles. Dutch tomatoes, German yogurt, French cosmetics, Italian shoes. Who could keep track of all that has occupied Eastern Europe? The occupation is sensual, exciting and pleasurable; if it hadn't been, someone would have objected already. Invisible money rustles, clinks, and pours from pocket to pocket. While Europe's thinkers are searching for a harmonious formula for a new European-ness, America has virtually occupied Europe, promptly unifying the European *East* and the European *West*. There is no difference between the Portuguese fish vendor and the Petersburg barmaid at the little upstairs bar at Hotel Oktyabrskaya. Both watch the same American sitcoms and soap operas with bated breath, and when they speak they know what they are talking about. The old idea of Europe as the cradle of civilization, art, and culture has survived only in Kaliningrad (where the citizens of Kaliningrad tormented the literary representatives of Europe with an overdose of European culture) or Murmansk (from which a local writer traveled as far as Moscow to see the "European" writers). The idea of "culture against money" is essentially religious. Culture is about money just as religion is, after all. My fellow travelers from the Literaturexpress Europa 2000 did not fail to understand this. Grumbling about their joint public statements, about every manipulation of political engagement, about acting as a group, they gave the upper hand to the words: image, publicity, network, lobby, management, and at the end of the trip they made a joint public statement after all. It was essentially a statement about the practical nature of a writer's work, about future transactions from one language into another, packaged in the *unity through diversity* Brussels ideology.

Ostap Bender, the smooth operator, who did not succeed in realizing his dream of going to Rio de Janeiro, ends his picaresque with the words: "You don't need to applaud! I didn't make a Monte Cristo. I'll have to change my profession to apartment-block superintendent."

All that is left is for me to note, discreetly, that the current equivalent of "apartment-block superintendent" would be: manager.

August 2000

AMSTERDAM, AMSTERDAM

Cities are like coats

Cities are like coats. I turned up in New York ten years ago, in late October, with no luggage and no coat, so I bought myself a duffle coat. I still wear it today. The edges are frayed, and I look like a fifty-year-old teenager when I wear it, but I won't abandon it. That would be tantamount to abandoning a crucial episode of my own biography, all in all, a story that's too long to go into just now. Another coat, this one cashmere, in which I looked the way my mother felt a woman who cares what she looks like ought to look, I only wore once. Then, without any regrets, I gave it to an old lady, though it had cost three of my paychecks.

Cities wear like coats.

Some cities are boring, a real travail for their inhabitants, a blotch on the map, a hole in a hunk of Swiss cheese.

The relationship between a coat and its owner is a personal one; the same can be said of the relationship between a city and its inhabitants. So when someone says, "I love London," or, "I love Paris," these are serious statements, every bit as serious as any public declaration of religious, ethnic, sexual, or fashion commitment. When someone says, "I love both Paris and London, every city is beautiful in its own way," you'll know you are dealing with a liar.

There are cities where I feel compelled to intervene. In these cities some devilish voice is constantly nudging me: I'd move this, smooth over that. In cities like that I feel like a self-appointed mayor.

There are cities whose former beauty brings tears to my eyes. St. Petersburg is one such city. There are cities which galvanize me, raise the level of adrenaline in my bloodstream and blur my vision. New York is a city like that.

There are cities held together by a river. Take away the river, and the city turns into an amorphous smudge. Belgrade is one such city. There are cities whose beauty lies in the promise of sea and shore. Take away the promise, and all that is left is a mega-oasis. Los Angeles is a city like that. There are cities which bring together essentially incompatible things such as power and melancholy. Berlin is that sort of city. There are cities which would need nothing more than a facelift to place them among the most beautiful cities in the world. Budapest is one such city.

The beauty of a city is in the eye of the beholder. The more beholders, the more visions of beauty.

The first taste of beauty

What looks beautiful to a child? I don't remember much from my own childhood, but I have a precise recollection of the things that dazzled me.

A cardboard picture, the size of a child's palm, in the shape of a flower basket and frosted with glitter is etched in my memory as the first, dizzying image of *absolute* beauty. I remember how I drank in every detail, even the most minute, for hours on end, every petal, every line on the flowers, each curve of the basket. I must have been about four. "Auntie" Tinka, a student of literature who had volunteered as a helper at the nursery school, gave me the little basket, taking it from her own modest collection of glittery trinkets.

Toys were scarce back then. The children who had been born before the war, or those born only a year or two after me, didn't suffer from the awful vacuum. My first doll came too late. Maybe that is why the flower basket—a Victorian motif stamped on flimsy cardboard—stirred something so like intoxication, and with it the suggestion that there were other, more wonderful worlds.

We used candies—long and thin, hard, inedible—as ornaments

on our New Year's trees. The candies had two wrappers. The first was made of white paper and its twisted ends protruded like little tails, while the outside wrapper was a kind of foil. After the New Year's holidays we would take the foil wrappers off the candies and carefully iron them out with our fingernails until they were completely smooth. The thin, shiny squares of foil, most often gold colored, were a real treasure. That is what we called them, *my treasure*. We would study each others' foil collections (*Show me your treasure!*) and trade them back and forth. Handling the leaves of foil was indescribably thrilling. In a childhood stripped of toys, to own a bundle of leaves of foil was like owning a handful of shooting stars.

Just before I turned seven, I discovered an object that left me breathless. It was a pillow my Grandma had made, a creation that she had embroidered with colored threads. There were big red strawberries dangling from the pillow, some of them hidden behind green leaves. I remember gazing at that pillow for hours, lifting the green thread leaves, fingering the red thread strawberries. I was little then, and the pillow was big. I have no idea where that pillow went. Perhaps it didn't go anywhere, perhaps it stayed there on Grandma's bed but I stopped noticing it after a while.

Then there was a glass ball with a miniature city that slumbered under the glass. When the ball was shaken, snow would fall. For a long time, the glass ball was the subject of my deepest fantasy, real beauty that took the breath away.

These beauty fetishes—the flower basket, the strawberries made of thread, the bundle of foil sheets and the glass ball—were the treasures of my earliest childhood. I remember the objects, but the fascination they stirred in me is as incomprehensible today as the contents of a crow's nest.

Descending into Amsterdam's airport at night, a traveler looking out of the plane can see golden squares in the darkness. Holland seems paved with golden squares. These are greenhouses: while the Dutch sleep, flowers have been tricked into blooming under an artificial sun.

By day the traveler can see the patches of purple, red, yellow, and blue fields of flowers.

Those golden and colored squares remind me of the sheets of foil, the gilt of my childhood.

Where do the grownups live?

When I was first in Amsterdam (I went there much later than I went to some of the other world cities), it took my breath away, dazzled me with the sight of a beauty such as I had *never seen*. I say *never seen* because I had already been to other cities people described as beautiful. I had been in Venice and St. Petersburg, Paris, Florence and Verona, Dubrovnik, New York, San Francisco, and Chicago . . . But Amsterdam stirred an unconditional delight in me. It was the same sort of hypnotic fascination that had kept me staring for hours at Grandma's pillow and that glass ball.

I once sat down on a bench in an Amsterdam park next to a shabby old man who was taking bits of crusty bread out of a filthy little sack and feeding them to invisible ducks.

"You live in Amsterdam?" mumbled the old man.

"I do, yes . . ." I said.

"Grown-ups don't live in Amsterdam . . ."

"Where do grown-ups live?" I asked.

"Somewhere else . . ." mumbled the old man, shooting me a blurred glance. "Rotterdam . . ." he added, and grinned.

I wondered whether my unreliable recollections of a child's notion of beauty and a chance conversation with a senile old man in a park said more about the city, or about me, about the visitor.

Body and space

I have always been fascinated by how a body perceives the area around it. There are people who walk down a street as if it belongs to them alone. They are natural conquerors. They force other passersby to make way with the strength of their inner conviction. There are people who take a seat on a tram as if it is theirs, their private possession. They comport themselves freely, and are ready to pray on a tram, eat a sandwich, chat noisily on the phone, pick their nose, or put their feet up on the seat across from them for a rest. There are young people who clear away the space around them with bulky backpacks, whacking whatever is in their way, and then calmly, as if nothing had happened, they take a long sip from their handy water bottles. Large women have the most delicate relationship to public space. They have a constant sense of guilt; they are plagued by the feeling that they take up too much room. Thinner and shorter people feel that they must keep inscribing themselves on public maps, that there is never enough of them, physically.

Amsterdam, in a spatial sense, is an unusual place. To say that Amsterdam is a city built to human proportions, which I have heard said any number of times, is not quite right, but it is also not altogether wrong. This all depends on the proportions and the human. I, myself, often get lost in Amsterdam, which has never happened to me in other cities. I often lose my way in the small city of Amsterdam, which is only one more proof that a person can drown in a glass of water. Amsterdam has the structure of a dream; the heart of the city is a densely interwoven spider's web.

I own a collection of maps of Amsterdam and a child's compass. The maps have never helped me figure out where I am. They are useless. Maps and compasses don't help a dreamer wend his way through dreams.

Amsterdam is perhaps most itself when a dense fog rolls in. Then the walker has no need of a map. The fog seems to the walker to have been spun by those countless, stray Amsterdam cats who are always out creeping around on the facades, watching passersby with their grey-green eyes from the windows of houses, dozing in store windows, snaking between the feet of the patrons in pubs, and prowling through gardens and over roofs. When it is foggy, the city seems in the thrall of these cats, silent mistresses of the city. When the fog licks the city the way a cat licks its paws, Amsterdam becomes a city for dreamers. The dreamer follows the map of his dreams as he walks, and the city extends a helping hand.

Perhaps all these confusions of space come from the firm conviction the Dutch hold—that they live in a small country. "We are a small country" is a sentence that a foreigner often hears. There are many countries smaller than the Netherlands, but the inhabitants of those countries do not feel that they live in a small country the way the Dutch do. "We are a small country" serves as an excuse for all sorts of things. If you mention that the eggs seem a little small when you are buying them at the marketplace, you may well get the response:

"Well, we live in a small country, you know . . ."

Rhetoric

"A house within a house, the dollhouse not only presents the house's articulation of the tension between inner and outer spheres, of exteriority and interiority—it also represents the tension between two modes of interiority. Occupying a space within an enclosed space, the dollhouse's aptest analogy is the locket or the secret recesses of the heart: center within center, within within within."[1]

Amsterdam is a dollhouse. An old Dutch dollhouse, one of those ones from the seventeenth century, a precise reproduction of the owner's house. They were to look at, not for playing with. Amsterdam is a perfect, precious dollhouse.

Where does the Dutch people's obsessive need for making things ever smaller come from? The Dutch language is rife with diminutives. The daily exchange of diminutives must be equal to the daily flow of money on the Dutch stock exchange. The Russian language, which is renowned for its affinity for diminutives, is far outstripped by the Dutch language.

You can see the smallest public sculptures in the world in Amsterdam. There are Lilliputian nudes of women, the statue of a potato,

---

1. Susan Stewart, *On Longing, Narratives of the Miniature, the Gigantic, the Souvenir, the Collection.* Duke University Press 1993, p. 61.

miniature sculptures of characters from classical Dutch literature, small busts planted among the grass around which, when it rains, a ring of water pools, making the heads look as if they are afloat in puddles. There are small reptiles discreetly slithering along Leidseplein.

Diminutives are the language of Amsterdam. Diminutives are like the flags displayed in the windows of Amsterdam houses: you can see miniature Amsterdam houses on them. The dollhouse inside a dollhouse signals a secret, the metaphor of the onion with its heart wrapped in layers, the metaphor of the Russian *matryoshka*. Sometimes it occurs to a person walking around Amsterdam that its inhabitants belong to a secret sect engaged in white magic; the diminutives protect the natives from evil.

The people of Amsterdam have definitely outgrown their city. Dutch women sometimes reach Amazon-like heights of six feet or more; white Dutch women are often taller then African-American men. Who knows, maybe the diminutives are an apology for the growing disproportion between the city and its inhabitants. Perhaps the point of all those diminutives, linguistic and otherwise, is to appease the environment, a need stemming from the fear that the environment might squeeze them even more.

The Amsterdammers are the natives of Europe. Their obsessive miniaturizing may be a subconscious ritual to appease the gods. If they, the water gods, were angered, Amsterdam might vanish. Perhaps the diminutives are an indirect apology for the intrusion into nature that Dutch hands have engineered, an apology for the decision to live on land that had not been meant for two-legged mammals. True, the gods looked the other way during the intervention itself, but one can never tell whether they have forgotten it.

In contrast to the Amsterdammers, many of my former countrymen rely on the augmentative when they talk. *Ljudina* (a bruiser of a guy), *ženetina* (a woman of generous proportions), *ručerda* (a meaty hand), *kućerina* (a vast house), *tjelesina* (a massive body), *vojničina* (one hell of a soldier). Linguistic gigantism helps my countrymen feel bigger. As *large* people, my countrymen experience their surroundings as unpleasant, hostile. Diminutives help the Amsterdammers feel smaller. As *small* people the Amsterdammers describe their surroundings as *lekker* (nice), *mooi* (lovely), and *gezellig* (charming). It is as if the Dutch are living life in a Bollywood film where, as we all know, everything moves toward a happy ending, well marinated in song and dance.

"Whereas the miniature represents closure, interiority, the domestic, and the overly cultural, the gigantic represents infinity, exteriority, the public, and the overly natural,"[2] writes Stewart. The rhetoric of the miniature is a rhetoric of mystery. The need to miniaturize is an expression of a need to build secrets into the surroundings. The great artist of micro-miniatures, Hagop Sandaldjian, who wrote messages on a strand of hair, built a sculpture of Napoleon into the eye of a needle, and etched Mount Ararat on a grain of rice, was an Armenian living in the United States. I have a feeling, however, that a Dutch heart beat in Hagop Sandaldjian.

A dream of flying
In contrast to the old Dutch dollhouses, the bicycle is not for looking at but for playing with. This toy is the trademark of the city of Amsterdam. While Amsterdam stands still, its most popular tourist attraction is on the move. The bicycle, furthermore, is more popular as an attraction than Rembrandt or van Gogh. Perhaps because the beauty of Rembrandt and van Gogh is beyond question, while every Amsterdammer is eager—when it is in question—to enter the bicycle into the list of essential life values.

As you are standing at the door, saying good-bye to your Amsterdam host, he will ask you, "Where did you leave your bike?"

He will ask this as a matter of course, just as he might inquire whether you have an umbrella if it's raining.

"I haven't got one . . ."

---

2. Ibid, p.70.

"You came without your bicycle?"

"Well, actually I don't own one."

"You don't own a bike?!"

Your host will be genuinely shocked. An inhabitant of Amsterdam who does not use a bicycle is a rare human specimen indeed. Even saying that you're a tourist won't lessen the astonishment. When they travel, the Dutch actually pack their bicycle in their personal luggage, with the blessings of KLM. I once met a Dutch woman who went to New York when she was eight months pregnant. Instead of taking a cab into town, she opened up her luggage, assembled her bicycle, and cycled off toward Manhattan.

I have always been leery of constructs like *national* identity or *national* character, but I do believe in a deep symbiosis between the Dutch and the bicycle. I am surprised that the Dutch flag doesn't have a bicycle on it. I am vexed by the fact that there isn't a verse in the Dutch national anthem on the bicycle, though this could be remedied at any time.

From an ecological perspective, the bicycle is undoubtedly the finest possible way to travel. From a rational perspective, the bicycle is the cheapest and most practical form of transportation. As far as health benefits are concerned, the bicycle is certainly the healthiest way to travel. Psychologically speaking, the bicycle is the cheeriest form of transportation. There is nothing more fun than pushing the pedals. So why do I grumble about the bicycle? It is not the bicycle I am grumbling about, but—cyclists.

Amsterdam is a city made for pedestrians. It is a city that lives off of the interaction between the admiration of pedestrians and its beautiful landmarks. The pedestrian needs to stop every few minutes, take a deep breath, and gaze at the facades of houses and their reflection in the canals. Pedestrians are sensible adults. These sensible adults are forced to lurch through Amsterdam in terror. They can be seen flattened against the walls of buildings, or clutching at the facade with both hands, as if trying to prevent the building from collapsing, while madly looking in all directions like actors in a silent movie.

Because they, the terrible cyclists, are zipping by in all directions.

The cyclists are a majority mobile population which respects no traffic rules. And besides—with the exception of foreigners, tourists, and the occasional anti-cyclist—everyone is a cyclist. It is enough to stand still and watch elderly tourists crossing the street. Once I watched a group of them. They waited at a crosswalk, and the light changed from green to red, then to green, then to red again . . . Finally they took each others' hands, a small, valiant troop, and plunged out into the street. A maniac on a bicycle smashed into their formation with glee, and the poor tourists scampered, defeated, back to the sidewalk. Now and then there is a cyclist who, after chasing your heart into your throat, will cheerfully chortle, "Sorry!" with that characteristically innocent intonation with which the grown-up children of Amsterdam beg your pardon. Amsterdam cyclists look like copies of the Miss Gulch who rides a bicycle through the air in Dorothy's nightmare: the same Miss Gulch who later becomes the Wicked Witch of the West and rides a broomstick.

The Amsterdammers tote television sets on their bicycles, they carry bureaus, bookshelves, their children, wives, friends. Amsterdammers carry their old, young, fat, thin, tall, and short bodies. Watching them, the onlooker feels some ambivalence. The Amsterdammers look like incorrigible exhibitionists. On the other hand, the bicycle, to them, seems like the extreme point for realizing a person's personal freedom. There is no scene more erotic than a young woman wearing a skirt with high slits climbing onto her bicycle, settling her attractive bottom on the seat, straightening her back and slowly moving the pedals while the slits in her skirt show her long, slender thighs. Women carry their future babies on their bicycles, even when they are nine months pregnant. As soon as it is born, their baby is on the bike, as are their older children, their hats, their flirtatious bicycle baskets (with flowers), their lovers, their pets. Men carry their bodies, their possessions, their progeny. While riding, many read the newspaper, eat a sandwich, swig coffee from a thermos. I have seen cyclists singing at the top of their lungs. I have seen two people on a bike, one cycling, and the other looming over the first, surveying the city like a conquering general.

I have wondered whether there is something beyond the merely physical, something metaphysical in the fatal attraction between Amsterdammers and the bicycle. Unconsciously, every Dutch person has a finger in the dyke at all times. That much we all know. If we follow the logic of collective trauma, it is possible, then, that the Dutch are stubbornly pumping the pedals on their bicycles in the hope that they will pull their country out from beneath the surface of the sea through their common efforts. Moreover, that by dint of their stubborn pedaling they will one day stir up a typhoon which will catapult the Netherlands to a place where the land is spacious and dry.

When I watch cyclists on the Amsterdam streets from behind the window of a sandwich joint, the bicycle begins to look like a substitute for some powerful, obsessive collective dream of flight. In the most glorious part of their past, the Dutch were people with seven-league boots, seafarers, mapmakers, explorers, merchants, people who, long before globalization, held the whole world in the palm of their hand.

I finally understood, however, when a flash of insight came to me. We were beginning our descent into Schiphol. The day was sunny, the sea, a radiant green. Looking at the land through the airplane window I was struck by the fragility of the Netherlands; it's thin like the thinnest Swedish wafer. I was choked by a profound sense of sadness. Ever since that moment I have been tiptoeing around on the Amsterdam streets as if I was walking on eggs. Since then I have understood that riding on slender bicycles is the best way to get around on such crust-like ground. That is when I decided to buy a bicycle. Furthermore, I decided to lose weight. Even Miss Gulch no longer seems as overbearing as she used to.

Osmosis
The desk in my temporary Amsterdam apartment stands by a picture window. The window looks out over a park. Sometimes the best way

a person can learn something about life in a city is by settling down in a good spot and watching, encouraging one's voyeuristic nature, turning the fun into work, into people-watching.

Strollers, with dogs or children, meander through the park; so do the loners, the joggers, the drug addicts, the homeless. On Sunday morning, the Muslim formations move slowly by: the men lead the way, and behind them pad the women, swathed from head to toe. Early in the morning, in the semi-darkness, a plump young Muslim woman goes out for a jog in sweats and a head scarf. Drums can be heard from the park, usually on Sundays. Joggers readily adjust their running to the rhythm. On Queen's Day, when all of the Netherlands is decked out in orange, an elderly gentleman from India strides through the park with dignity, sporting an orange turban.

On the street where I live there is an place called The Laughing Institute. The man who teaches laughing displays his publications, and a poster with his photograph, in the window. The picture of the teacher—a man from India with plump cheeks, a weak smile, and sad eyes—watches me from the display when I pass by on the street. Sometimes I catch myself in front of the bathroom mirror, astonished: that smiling face, with the plump cheeks and the sad eyes, is looking back at me! Anxiously, I wonder if this is a case of a gradual magical osmosis. Is it possible that the face of my neighbor, the teacher, has copied itself onto my own? And if this is what has happened, which, then, was my first face, the *western* one, or the *eastern* one?

The cities of Western Europe are thronging with *Easterners*: London with Indians and Pakistanis; Amsterdam with the Surinamese and Moroccans; Paris with the Algerians; Berlin with the Turks, Greeks, Yugoslavs, and, more recently, the Russians; Budapest with a growing number of Chinese. The East is on its way West; the pending migration has already begun.

The *Easterners* are coming and bringing their flutes, tamburitzas and harmonicas, their unusual voices. The Russians and Mongols recently replaced the Chileans—who for years held a monopoly on the streets of Western cities with their diligent renditions of "El Condor Pasa." The *Easterners* are coming and bringing their messy consolations, their melancholic philosophy of the soul, their fortune-telling with tarot cards, their reading of palms. *"Waarom Ongelukkig Zijn?"* asked a little leaflet I picked up from some Amsterdam *Easterner*. Mr. Fadjal, Professor Banjian, Professor Moustapha, Professor Gadiry (who can keep all these Eastern names straight!) promise me that they will transform me into a harmonious person (how did they know I was in chaos?).

The *Easterners* are coming and offering their former communist and anti-communist bodies for sale. Russian, Ukrainian and Polish women, Croatian women, Serbian women, Moldavian and Thai women, young Bosnian, Albanian, Macedonian men—all of them are the sexual proletariat inundating the West like rising ground water. The *Easterners* are coming and bringing their dances: their circle dances, their belly dances, their tango, their salsa, their trouncing and shaking. The *Easterners* are shaking up the drowsy West with their rapid rhythms. The *Easterners* are coming and bringing their mobile *bazaars*, their trinkets, souvenirs, their heavy spices and even heavier fragrances. The *Easterners* are coming and bringing their beggars' hats: Rome, for instance, is overcome with Czechs and Romanians. Whatever possessed them to occupy the cradle of civilization? The *Easterners* are coming and doing all sorts of odd jobs: they are smuggling parrots, washing the dead. The *Easterners* are coming and bringing computer viruses. The Bulgarians (ah, those Bulgarians!), the Poles (look who's here!), the Russians (of course, the Russians are coming!) . . . The *Easterners*, it seems, have nothing better to do than the dirty work.

Has the West, in fact, conquered the East, or has it been the other way around? Is it possible to tug at a loose end, is it possible to let the security wall that kept the East and West apart for so many years crumble and think that there will be no consequences? Have the seismographers been keeping something under wraps? Didn't anyone notice the cracks spreading? Doesn't anyone see that what we are being faced with is a secret process of global osmosis? What is happening to me? Does that innocent Laughing Institute have something to do with this secret process? Who is laughing at whom here? Can someone explain to me how it could be that—having come to the West from the South of Europe, from the former Yugoslavia— I look more and more, with every new day, like—a woman from India?!

Columbus's gaffe is proliferating. I went westward and turned up in the East. Moving from East Amsterdam to West Amsterdam didn't help either: in doing so I found myself even further eastward.

A petrol station and a mosque

That iconography—the petrol station and the mosque—precisely encapsulates the essence of life in the grey urban ring that encircles the museum heart of Amsterdam. These residential areas—strung like keys along the metro line that circles the city—all look more or less the same. The famous Dutch architects apparently signed some sort of clandestine agreement that they would never build anything to compete with the beauty of the center. All the satellite neighborhoods are designed for the newcomer: the supermarket called Albert Heijn, a driving school (newcomers need to learn how to drive), a dry cleaner, sometimes a store selling technical goods (newcomers buy video recorders, refrigerators and television sets), and fruit stores, mostly run by Turks.

There are also framing shops (usually run by newcomers so that other newcomers can frame their pictures; having pictures means being at home), hairdressers, and often hardware stores selling house paint and hand tools (newcomers paint walls, mount Venetian blinds, fiddle with nails, hammers and the like). Neighborhoods like these have a little park, a playground for the children, benches that the newly arrived women can sit on and chat while they keep an eye on their kids, and a bar for the men. Sometimes there is a remarkably bad sculpture produced by socialist art in the arrangement, a fountain which is supposed to be equally accessible and beautiful to all. And that's it.

Life in these neighborhoods couldn't be termed provincial. Provincial life has its habits, quality, and color. Life in the peripheral Amsterdam neighborhoods is tinged by the melancholy of the absence of color, the melancholy of a megafailure. Built in the 1960s, the neighborhoods, and their socialist orientation, promised a sunny, clean, spacious, and comfortable place to live which would be accessible to everyone, but today they are immigrant ghettoes. In their search for a better life, Moroccans, Turks, and Surinamese are getting a taste of the urban retro-Utopia. Life in these neighborhoods is irreparably newcomer-based, it is as it was, in those same places, some eight centuries ago, or so they say.

Life on the edge of Amsterdam could be anywhere. The observer is haunted by the feeling that the residents might roll up their tents tomorrow, put out the fire, smooth the sand after them, and set off for somewhere else. The oasis with the petrol station and the mosque will be there to greet the next strangers who happen through. When a brisk wind blows and flaps the long dresses of the Moroccan women and men, when the observer snags a grain of sand in his teeth, this fancy starts turning real.

The Voltaire metaphor

Subversion flourishes in those places where the bans are the strongest. A right to privacy, which the Dutch proudly set forth, along with tolerance and democracy, as a fundamental principle of their society has nowhere been so subverted as it has in Amsterdam. The curtains in Amsterdam houses are never drawn. Any passerby can freely give in to the passions of voyeurism. Those with a proclivity for staring at naked flesh can satisfy their longings with a stroll through the red light district. Prostitutes are on show behind glass, just as the quiet book reader is on show in his or her apartment. Furthermore, prostitutes may be seen, dressed from head to toe, engrossed in a book while waiting for their clients. Amsterdammers often display a collection of objects in their windows and on their balconies which give voice to their aesthetic, ideological, and other preferences. Toys, teddy bears, ornaments, posters, slogans, drawings, figurines, sculptures, and masks stare at passersby from the windows and balconies of the houses of Amsterdam. World-wide television, *Big Brother* entertainment, which, by the way, was an innovation not of the Americans but of the Dutch, is only the logical conclusion of the gradual process of the erosion of the civil right of privacy. Today, one no longer needs the display window or the window with the curtains pulled back. All a person has to do is sit on any tram, from Oostdorp to Leidseplein, and learn from one of the many freaks with cell phones everything there is to learn about them. Buñuel's inverted movie scene—in which people sit talking at the table on toilet seats, and then run off to a concealed place where they eat something—has lost its absurdity entirely.

The only thing left is the garden. The people of Amsterdam seem to have taken Voltaire's idea literally: after everything else, a person can still hoe his or her own garden. Each garden, like each person, is different. They are socially marked, just as people are. There are gardens with green plastic grass and miniature plastic lakes in which plastic frogs swim. And, of course, there are garden dwarfs, who are threatening to overrun, demographically speaking, their owners. The owners of both the gardens and the dwarfs. The dwarfs are being manufactured larger and larger, but, nevertheless, garden dwarfs are yet another implicit message to the world that Holland is a tiny country.

Whoever doesn't have a garden can always lease one. Hence those little plots that surround Amsterdam, with miniature wooden huts, benches in front of the huts, miniature flowers, vegetables, and, sometimes, a tiny tree.

Lomanstraat

Lomanstraat is the loveliest street in Amsterdam. It is the loveliest street in Amsterdam because the trees of Lomanstraat voted it so in a secret ballot. Joining forces, the trees of Lomanstraat showed that a) it is possible for them to grow up to be large trees in that light and airy soil; b) that they can grow without keeping to any rules and regulations; and c) that the power of a tree is in its crown, not its roots.

The jaunty sycamores along Lomanstraat grow down both sides of the street. They do not grow straight, but at a slant, the crown of each tree arching to brush the roof across the street. Some of the sycamores' crowns merge, forming a lavish vault. Measured in footsteps, Lomanstraat is 553 steps long. Measured in minutes, Lomanstraat is about fourteen minutes long. The time depends on the walker: whether he looks straight ahead as he walks, or if he stares upward at the treetops.

Lomanstraat is my favorite street. Whenever I look at that green vault, so much like the vaulted arch of a cathedral, my back begins itching, right between my shoulder blades, and I raise both my arms slowly like wings. And then, with my arms raised, I lift my gaze up to the green heavens. And I am not alone. Once I saw a man, his arms raised and his head flung back, his gaze fixed upwards, staggering awkwardly towards me.

Carnival

The moment when intimacy sparks between a city and a visitor depends on the visitor. Zoran, a countryman of mine, ended up in Amsterdam, as a refugee. He says that Amsterdam became *his* city only the moment when he began to recognize litter on the city streets. Reading litter—an empty Mars wrapper wafting through the air, or a crumpled milk carton with the word "Melk" on it leaning against a wall, or a little plastic bottle with "Spa" on the label bobbing in the canal—was an introduction to reading the city. As he read it, Amsterdam began its intimate relationship with Zoran.

So a visitor reads Amsterdam as if it were a book. A book that is thrilling and enjoyable, but the reader feels stabs of a fleeting discomfort. It seems to him that he has read this book somewhere before, but he can't remember where or when, it seems so familiar and yet so strange. He is confused that the borders between the two worlds, the one that is make believe and the one that is real, keep slipping out of his grasp. For a moment the reader shuts the book. Then he plays the scenes that he has seen on the Amsterdam streets again on an imaginary screen . . .

The fire swallowers on Leidseplein. The street musicians: Mongols, Russians and Chileans. Cyclists spin across the screen perched on tall unicycles. The gay parade, a floating carnival. Boats slip by with transvestites, sailors in sailor's caps with their thighs bared, male strippers. Scots on the Dam playing the bagpipe. The Dutch Santa Claus, Sinterklaas, the patron saint of retailers, sailors and small children, mounts a white horse and flings a rain of small, round ginger snaps behind him. Suddenly, look, everything is orange, even the water that bubbles up in the fountains is orange. People clutch orange balloons, wear orange top hats, and breathe deeply of air redolent of beer and urine. Police saunter by on their horses. A funeral passes, black coaches with black coachmen and black horses, and the onlooker can't be sure whether this is a funeral or a black carnival. Prostitutes, scantily clad, in shop windows. Erotic "paraphernalia" is scattered around the display case: rubber penises in all shapes and sizes, erotic trinkets. Large plastic mushrooms in front of small shops announce that they sell hash cakes. The Amsterdam parks. One, at Slotermeer, is called the Rabbit Park. Rabbits freely live out their rabbit lives there. An army of Amsterdam mice chase the rabbits, and lazy Amsterdam cats slink after them. One of them is called Dinah. A rabbit runs close by and mutters to itself: *Oh dear, Oh dear! I shall be too late.* And, can you believe it, takes a watch out of its pocket, and then pops down a rabbit hole . . . If the visitor trots after the rabbit, she'll journey into another, parallel Amsterdam, into a city within a city, which is reflected like a hologram on the face of the first Amsterdam. No one knows for sure how many parallel cities there are hidden inside Amsterdam. No one, apparently, has counted.

A my name is Albert

I love visiting the open market. The market is a spiritual (ah, what a revolting word!) place. In other words, what places of worship are for many people, the marketplace is for me.

The purchasing of fresh fish, vegetables, and fruit is merely a good excuse for the less obvious allure that the open market has for me. The marketplace I head for is wrapped in a fog of pollen which, with the strong fragrances of exotic spices, cinnamon, cloves, nutmeg, mingling with the fragrance of wind and salt, brings on a fever in me. The air shimmers with the gleam of lush bolts of silk and velvet, jewels from across the sea, silver, pearls, a mother of pearl shell (parted lasciviously), and the silvery scales of the fresh fish. The apples at my open market gleam with a golden glow, the grapes shine as if there are tiny lanterns in each one, and the cheese and milk are creamy and white like the skin on the women in Vermeer's paintings. The open market where I go belongs to a time when whales used to flounder on the Dutch shores, and when the tall, fair women, drunken with beer, used to founder in the Dutch bars.

And then, as I walk around the market, my hedonistic fantasies go sour and a feeling of murky discomfort gradually swells in me like yeast. Dead fish lie there on the scales, their sheen dulls; yes, the apples are red, the lettuce is green, but the gleam is gone. The sleazy salesmen stand under tent flaps selling sleazy clothing made of mildly galvanized synthetic and nylon. The hawkers of trinkets stand there. No one knows the proper names for what they sell: nail clippers, slicers, dicers, dust wipes, plastic combs and brushes, synthetic hair pieces in all colors, back-scratchers with a little plastic hand at one end. The merchants of soaps, shampoos, creams, cheap purses, artificial flowers, shoulder pads, elbow patches, needles and thread, pillows and bedspreads, frames and pictures, nails and hammers, sausages and cheeses, chickens and pheasants, clothing that falls apart at a touch . . .

The "Zuid" butcher shop is there, where people from the ex-Yugoslavia can sate their gastronomical nostalgia. Pig feet, lamb,

Macedonian "ajvar" relish, Serbian sausages, Croatian olive oil, "Plasma" cookies, whole heads of soured cabbage for New Year's "sarma," and that all-uniting Yugoslav "Minas" coffee, which is produced in Turkey. They even have the candy of my childhood: "Negro" (*The chimney sweep of your throat*).

The feeling of discomfort grows to mild nausea. The open market is where grown-ups buy food, but also toys. Many of the shoppers have paid a high price for their place in the so-called better world, they have found their so-called human dignity, they have made good on their right to a so-called decent life, the right to buy sausages, synthetic hair pieces, and back-scratchers with a little plastic hand at one end.

I go back along Albert Cuypstraat and hail a cab at the taxi stand on Ferdinand Bol street. In the taxi I indulge my fantasies about the marketplace for a few more minutes. I am not sorry at how much the taxi costs, but I allow myself that little luxury; the cab is the fastest way for me to get back to my shelter, to get home.

Where does the discomfort come from? What is it I'm after? Because the alternative I have is the other Albert, *Albert Heijn*, a chain of supermarkets which have spread around like a vine and which have set the standards—more than the language, state apparatus, flag and national anthem—in Holland. *Albert Heijn* does not hesitate to attach itself to the Stedelijk Museum, to become an indivisible part of it. Having seen the Maleviches, the museumgoer goes to the museum cafeteria where he sees the blue letters AH, for *Albert Heijn*. Foreigners learn the Dutch words for things in their textbooks. In the book, a baker is a baker, a butcher is a butcher, and a cheese vendor is a cheese vendor, but the Dutch word for supermarket is *Albert Heijn*. Often the *Albert Heijn* is the one and only store in Amsterdam's urban ghettoes, it is the single public space. And people frequent it. What else can they do? They post little ads on the bulletin board at the *Albert Heijn*, they run into each other at the *Albert Heijn*, children spend their school recess at *Albert Heijn* picking up something sweet for a snack, and in the process they learn the skills of grown-up life. How to slip the coin into the slot and free the shopping cart, how to pay at the cash register, how to return the shopping cart and retrieve the coin . . .

As I ride in the cab I think back to my early *socialist* childhood, in which all cheese was called "trappist." It was the only kind of hard cheese you could buy. Even after other kinds appeared, the name held on. All hard cheeses were called "trappist" at one point. In poverty, one thing stands in for all else. And in affluence one thing often stands in for all else. The difference is only in the illusion.

Bridges
If one face of Amsterdam is carnival, and carnival-esque, then the other is contemplative.

Amsterdam is a contemplation all its own, a kind of puzzle that needs to be solved. Amsterdam is a city with canals that create a fine spider's web. If person A is standing in front of the Rijksmuseum and is supposed to meet with person B, who is waiting in front of the Ouderkerk, how long will person A need to find person B? Which canals and bridges will he have to cross? The question is only theoretical at first glance. A proper walk through Amsterdam is a kind of mental filigree. Because a city like this is the work of filigree masters.

There are more than four hundred bridges in Amsterdam. Crossing a bridge is a contemplative moment. The pedestrian looks right, then left, then straight ahead at the point toward which he is headed, and then he turns to see the point from where he has come. The very act of crossing from one shore to another, no matter how short the journey, is, in essence, a serious, contemplative act.

Among the four hundred bridges there are drawbridges, which are often raised to let boats pass through. At that point, the pedestrian, cyclist, or automobile has no choice but to wait. And waiting is a brief daily situation which forces us to think, to slow our movements because of a greater force. Forced waiting is an invitation to humility, to cooperation and tolerance, because we need to stop in order to let someone else pass. While waiting, the person looks at the boats, which when rushing by he wouldn't even notice, the faces of the other people waiting, which he would never, otherwise, look at, the surrounding buildings, the sky, a duck's nest floating in the canal . . . When forced to wait like that, a person will ask himself whether he was really in such a hurry after all, whether it is important to get where he was headed, and how might he change his route, should he go back or go somewhere else.

One of the oldest drawbridges in Amsterdam is Magere Brug, built in 1670. Let us imagine now that up in the sky, there among the countless divine bureaucrats, sits an angel in charge of storing the thoughts of the pedestrians who were waiting for Magere Brug to be lowered. Imagine if we were able to listen to the inner voices of all those waiting people. Imagine how the voice of a vegetable vendor who is hurrying to sell her produce at the marketplace intermingles with the voice of a prostitute who has just earned her wages, the voice of Peter the Great who turned up incognito in Amsterdam, the voice of Jan Steen on his way to purchase more paint . . . If such a thing were possible, it would be the most unique and most true-to-life history of Amsterdam.

Museum

Amsterdam, its center, is a complete whole. You can always take hold of a little detail of the dollhouse with tweezers and remove it, brush away the dust, repaint a little table on the first floor, change the miniature curtains on the second floor, you might even redo the full facade of the dollhouse, but nothing more than that. Any further undertaking would destroy the house's value, any rough handling might smash its whole structure. All you have to do is tug on the wrong thread and the entire city would unravel. That is why Amsterdam urbanists spend most of their time extracting cobble stones that have sunk too deeply into the sand, leveling the sand, and putting the cobbles back exactly where they were before.

Some inhabitants of the city behave like museum volunteers. Over time, some become exhibits in their own right, while others become the curators. Human museum exhibits date from the glorious 1960s, from the days when time still flowed; these men and women have long grey hair now, they are elderly *flower children*, the remnants of the European student Left who live on generous welfare stipends, former rock-and-rollers, aging squatters, and marijuana smokers. These exemplars show their wizened faces around town, faces on which, like some tic, there is a fossilized youthful brashness. Other museum curators gripe about the filth, the sleazy tourism destroying the city center, and the consumerism that is cheapening the golden Dutch past.

Perhaps it is precisely this museum side of Amsterdam (without the pomposity of a museum) that provides the energy that stirs the circulation in its population. Fresh immigrants who come from traumatic environments where life was unstable and unpredictable find the calm certitude of life in a museum unusually soothing. On the other hand, there are many Amsterdammers who suffer from claustrophobia, as if it were an endemic disease. For people like that, Amsterdam gets too close after only a few months. People like that emigrate to other countries temporarily, although they mask their neuroses with serious reasons. This temporary emigration is known as the Sacred Vacation, "Vakantie"—a visit to a second home in France, Portugal, Spain, or elsewhere. If they can't do that, they get on a waiting list to buy an apartment in a completely new Amsterdam which is waiting to be built, and in their mind's eye they tend the floating gardens in front of their future homes. If they can't do that either, then the Amsterdam claustrophobes hop on a train and off they go to Rotterdam, The Hague, Utrecht, or Leiden for a cup of coffee.

And if they can't do that, the claustrophobic Amsterdammers enroll in cheap classes which are usually taught by immigrants: courses in Egyptian belly dancing, Argentine tango, Bulgarian folk singing, Indian yoga, and the Serbian circle dance.

Dear Anne . . .

There is a detail I am almost certain I share with many others. The detail binds my childhood to Amsterdam. I no longer remember when, perhaps when I was in fifth or sixth grade, I read the *The Diary of Anne Frank*. The little girl who spent her days hiding in a house in Amsterdam became my hero, and for a long time she ruled my childhood imagination.

After we finished seventh grade, the whole class went on a month-long camping trip. At night, by the light of a flashlight, hiding from the others, I wrote in a diary. I'm only guessing, because I no longer remember, that at the moment I needed someone who would be mine alone, in whom I would confide my stormy feelings. I couldn't address myself to a dead notebook. I needed someone alive to write to. The most natural person would be someone who had written a diary herself, and who was close to me. Anne Frank became my imaginary interlocutor. That must have been how my childhood diary entries started: *Dear Anne, you won't believe what happened to me today . . .*

Later I was ashamed. The little notebook disappeared out of shame. I never kept a diary after that. Who knows, perhaps it was the shame, the liberty I had taken by addressing my silly childhood scribblings to an "inappropriate" addressee, that prompted me to become a writer. Anne Frank remained stored away in a box where I keep my most intimate belongings, many of which have murky, shameful associations which I have never articulated.

I used the word "inappropriate" although I'm not entirely sure I should. My knowledge of Anne Frank was sealed in the child's edition of her diary, from which the fact of her death had been expunged, or perhaps only masked. It was a little like a child's edition of *Snow White*, the full version of which, with the addition of the step-mother cannibal, I read only as an adult. I identified completely with the fate of Anne Frank, but neglected to take on board the fact of what really happened to her.

Only later, much later, did it occur to me that Anne Frank had not, in fact, been saved. Her life, like that of most of her fellow

Jewish Amsterdammers, had ended in a concentration camp. As with many other cities in Europe, Amsterdam also played a part in the dark and disgraceful history of betraying its own citizens. The lives that have been erased and the culture which has been destroyed can never be restored. That is why Europe is full of museums that are designed as places of collective shame. A "musealization" of shame is one form of expiation for sins.

I often wonder what gives the European politicians, people in positions of power, the media, and the on-duty thinkers, the confidence to pass judgment on human morals and arbitrate in things such as democracy and human rights, as they do so often in areas foreign to themselves: Eastern Europe, the Balkans, Africa, Asia . . . I wonder where Europeans get the confidence in their right to arbitrate: does this come from an awareness of the crime that Europe committed only a few decades ago, or from their having forgotten that crime?

I am still not sure whether that child's edition of the *The Diary of Anne Frank* did, indeed, mention the fact of Anne Frank's death, or if it was my child's subconscious that held Anne Frank in a sort of limbo, as if she wasn't entirely dead, but not fully alive, either.

"Who are you?" said the caterpillar
I wonder whether there is a connection between two very different skills: cycling and conversing. Have the Amsterdammers, in cultivating one, lost their ability to handle the other? Because nowhere have I met people more agile on a bicycle, and less spry in conversation.

The absolute champions in the skill of conversation are the Russians. They have honed their skills for decades in salons, at home over long winters, at their summer estates. Russians have been practicing the typical Russian conversational genre known as *razgovory po dusham* in camps, in the long lines where people waited, sometimes for hours, in shared apartments (*komunalaya kvartira*), in their underground life (*podpolye*), and in gatherings of drunken bingeing full of hubbub, smoke, love, and bitterness. The skill of conversation was as valued as fine literature, and an agile conversant earned applause and the admiration of his friends. True, as encouragement for developing their skill, the Russians had something they no longer have today: the iron curtain and an infinite amount of time. The English and Americans are the best in the skill of light conversation, which they call *small talk*. Small talk may crop up anywhere, in buses, on the front stoop, on the street, in passing, in stores. It is a gift of everyday life and is given freely. Small talk lifts the spirits. We are not alone in the world, nor are we lost. Someone's smile and warm words greet us at every corner.

Conversation with some Amsterdammers is like a visit to the dentist. Everything is in the dentist's hands; there is no way to reverse the power relations. It would be hard to imagine a patient leaping upon a dentist and wresting the drill free.

During those painful conversations, my interlocutors asked me what my name is, who my mother and father are, what their names are, if they were alive, what my parents do and where they live, if I had brothers, sisters, if I had children, where I was born, when and where I went to school, which schools I attended, what I did, where I lived, what my phone number was, when I was going on vacation, where, and when I was getting back, and when I would be going on vacation again . . . During the conversation my interlocutors didn't seem to notice the beads of sweat springing out on my face, nor did they answer the questions I put to them.

Who knows where the Amsterdammers got this conversational style. Perhaps they experience small talk like a ride on a bicycle, where the only thing the rider is interested in is pumping the pedals and mastering distances. Perhaps it is the Dutch landscapes that dictate this kind of style, and the familiarity, for inhabitants of the lowlands, of a clean, open, unobstructed view. Perhaps, who knows, this is a reflex that is subconsciously stirred in the inhabitants of a country which once was an empire, and is now "occupied" today by immigrants. Perhaps my longing to talk about myself is written all over my face, though I myself don't know it, and the sensitive Amsterdammers are simply responding to that longing.

Whatever the case, after I had several instances of light conversations like those, I started carrying a list with the answers written on it, as a precaution. As soon as a person seems inclined to "light conversation," and I sense the conversation heading in this direction, I silently hand my interlocutor the list. I watch him peruse the list while puffing at his cigar; he puts down the list, and looks at me for some time in silence; finally he takes the cigar out of his mouth, and addresses me in a languid, sleepy voice: "Who are you?"

And I answer:

"I hardly know, sir, at present, at least I know who I was when I got up this morning, but I think I must have been changed several times since then . . ."

Filled cookies

The *gevulde koekje* is an ordinary, round cookie. In bakery display cases it looks as if its chubby cheeks are a little sunburned. The little filled cookies have either a smooth or a zig-zag edge. There is one kind that has an almond pressed into the middle, which makes it look like an oversized button. All in all, the *gevulde koekje is* a plain form of pastry. There is nothing that sets it apart from all the other homely cookies. But, when a piece is broken off, inside the cookie gleams a fragrant, rich marzipan paste filling.

This hidden marzipan heart is a metaphor for the glorious past of Holland, its famous people, Spinoza, Erasmus, Rembrandt, van Gogh, all those researchers, seafarers, cartographers, builders, merchants and dreamers, the army of anonymous alchemists who made land out of water. Inside the plain cookie with its marzipan heart lies the power and continuity of Dutch history, the severe black clothing that the Dutch wore in the seventeenth century, lined with the most precious fur, the little houses along the canals that concealed great fortunes. The homely cookie that unexpectedly offers forth its rich and fragrant filling is a pastry version of the city of Amsterdam. Amsterdam, too, has a marzipan heart, while its outside edges are dingy and unremarkable. Nibbling the cookie I recall the fact that Amsterdam gave birth to New Amsterdam, one of the most beautiful cities in the world; the horizontal produced the vertical. New Amsterdam is an orgiastic fantasy of Amsterdam; it is what Amsterdam could not be. Snail-like, Amsterdam hugs a turf that is green like a fresh leaf and thin as a matzo, while dreaming of a city that would soar skyward to the clouds. Amsterdam is Europe, New Amsterdam is America.

A visitor chooses some venerable Amsterdam café with big picture windows, finds a corner with a view of the canal, with today's newspapers spread out on the table, with a warm cup of coffee, and, while gazing around at the passersby and reading snatches from the paper, nibbles a filled cookie. He begins to feel he is growing into the Amsterdam landscape. Pampered by travel, the visitor might suddenly feel that this whole landscape is, in fact, his, and that, furthermore, it always has been his, but he had never had the opportunity before to know this. The visitor feels himself sinking with ease into the landscape, as he might into an easy chair. The visitor could get the notion, furthermore, that he might linger, lounging in the easy chair; suddenly, he can't remember any reason why he should get up and go.

If this visitor to the café is a woman, it might happen that she gets a little confused and slips off her shoes, to relax her aching feet. And just when she should be getting up to leave, the woman might poke around for her shoes with her feet, and it might just happen that she can't find them.

"Excuse me, have you seen my shoes?" the woman will ask the waiter, after getting up, lifting the chair she'd been sitting on, and looking all around.

"What did they look like!?"

"Ruby red slippers . . ."

"I haven't seen them, sorry . . ." the waiter will say, after a brief inspection of the café. He'll ask, with sympathy:

"What will you do now?"

"Don't give it another thought. I was thinking I'd get rid of them anyway," the woman will reply, calmly.

"There is a shoe store right around the corner . . . So you don't have to go home barefoot . . ." the waiter suggests in a friendly fashion.

"First I'll buy a new pair of shoes, and then a home, so that I have a home to go home to," says the woman.

That, or something very much like it, was what happened to me. I speak from experience.

2001

USA NAILS

A man of sense, I am conceding,
Can pay attention to his nails;
Why should one quarrel with good breeding?
With some folk, custom's rule prevails.
—*Alexander Pushkin,* Eugene Onegin, *Chapter 1, verse 25*

So, it is true. Things aren't what they used to be. I can't pinpoint precisely when it was that the Vietnamese arrived: whether after September 11th or before. I know they weren't there two years ago. But this spring when I visited New York, I immediately noticed a change in the landscape at 76th St and 2nd Avenue, where I always stay. Second Avenue, and much of the rest of the city, was alive with NAILS signs. New York looked as if it had tumbled straight out of *The Twelve Chairs* by the Russian writing duo Ilf & Petrov. The novel opens by saying that there were so many hairdressing establishments and funeral homes in the provincial town of N. that the inhabitants seemed to be born to get a shave, a hair cut, a splash with toilet water, and then to die. The people of New York have recently become obsessed with caring for their nails. Their fingernails and toenails. New Yorkers have started *having their nails done.* And their nails are being done by—the Vietnamese.

Since I am one of those people who believes you can learn the most about local and global political trends at hairdressing salons (and barbershops!) and in taxis, as soon as I got to the city I went straight out to the nearest hairdresser. As I sat in the chair, I realized that everyone working there was Russian. Second Avenue—a single street can provide a view of how the world works, why not!—was peppered with Russian hairdressing salons. The provincial town of N. had come to New York, at least as far as hairdressing salons were concerned. My first impression was that the institution of the hairdressing salon was on the decline. No one was talking politics. As far as the Russian language is concerned, it had long since sallied forth from its New York ghetto and moved from Brighton Beach to Fifth Avenue. I found this out during a walk one morning. Uniformed doormen stepped out of the fancy buildings along Central Park speaking Russian, and stopped long, shiny limousines whose drivers also spoke Russian.

Yes, things aren't what they used to be. A scowling taxi driver with a full mustache and bushy eyebrows asked where we were going, as if he wanted to know where the world, not I, was going. The sign in his cab sent an unambiguous message: Ahmed Muhamedanov.

"Where are you from?" He asked.

"The former Yugoslavia," I told him.

"Can you believe what they're doing to us, those creeps?"

I quickly learned who was doing what to whom and who the creeps were. He praised Milošević. He damned the Hague Tribunal, that had no clue what was really going on in the world. Milošević, now there was a fine man. He was the first to take on the struggle against Islamic fundamentalism. Because they, the Muslims, damn them, were rocking the foundations of our Christian civilization.

"Aren't you a Muslim?" I asked, looking back at the sign with his name.

"Me?! God forbid!"

"Well, what are you then?"

"Jewish."

"From where?"

"Uzbekistan."

I am an impassioned rider of taxis whenever I stay in New York but I had never heard anything quite like that before. Ahmed Muhamedanov was an isolated supporter of Milošević, the man who had "anticipated" the struggle against Islamic terrorism. True I did not run into many American Serbs—except for the nice saleswomen in Saks Fifth Avenue, my favorite department store. They are usually Russian, but I was beginning to find women from Belgrade there as well.

I did keep meeting people from Bosnia who, in the meanwhile, had become Americans. I met a young Bosnian woman on Wall Street who was working as a broker.

"No big deal," she said to me.

I met other people in the States from the former Yugoslavia. Edin was a young painter, who had become an interior decorator.

"I only do apartments on Park Avenue," he said.

I met Bego, in Manchester, New Hampshire, a refugee who was held for a time in a Serbian camp for Muslims before he came to America.

"I had no idea I was about to land in the United States. I expected it to be Manchester, England," he said.

In the space of the seven years since he had arrived as a refugee, Bego found work, bought a house, married off his daughter, put his son through school, and planted a garden. He has a goldfish pond and an oriental-style gazebo in his garden. At his birthday party, where I met him, Bego danced an inspired *sirtaki* in his moonlit garden. His American neighbors think he is Greek because he looks like Anthony Quinn, and because of the *sirtaki*. Bego danced with a triumphal flourish at the end of his birthday party. He has left Bosnia behind. His people are here, in America: his family, relatives, friends.

Yes, it does seem as if nothing is the way it used to be. But what do Russians, Uzbeks, Bosnians and the Greek *sirtaki* have to do with the Vietnamese?! Nothing. Or, only as much as New Yorkers have to do with waiting in line. The lines I saw in New York reminded me, with their length, of the lines I had seen some twenty years before in

Moscow, in front of a store called *JADRAN* (meaning Adriatic) where Yugoslav products were sold, from sofas to shoes. I saw a line in front of the newly opened *Neue Galerie* on the Upper East Side. New Yorkers were waiting to taste the famed Sacher torte, leaf through American editions of Freud, Broch, and Musil, and see the paintings of Egon Schiele and Oskar Kokoschka. There were very long lines in front of MOMA for a show of Gerhard Richter's work. East Germans used to languish in lines to buy laundry detergent. New Yorkers today—precisely as if they are returning the favor—languish in even longer lines to see the paintings of painters who used to be East German.

Nothing may be the way it used to be, nevertheless I found New York to be every bit as much the city proportioned to people that I've found it before, and, thank goodness, every bit as "obscene." I am one of those people who adore New York with an unconditional love: I love the homeless people sleeping in cardboard boxes, wrapped in filthy rags, and I love Zoran's transparent blouses, which sell for several thousand dollars each and gently drape the shoulders of the more fortunate. By the way, Zoran, the fashion designer, is someone from the former Yugoslavia who has really made it. Zoran is the man who has put "our" name on the fashion map of "obscenity."

So could obscenity possibly have anything in common with fingernails and the Vietnamese?! It could indeed. In the fantasies of the poor only the rich pay money for someone else to do their nails. Because only the rich have the time, and time, as we all know, is a luxury. We are finally back to the fingernail, the smallest human unit of value. There is a saying in my language for comparing one person to another: he is worth less than the nail on her little finger. Many ancient peoples believed that the nails and hair were the most mystical parts of the body (only the nails and hair continue to grow for a time after death). They are the body parts most associated with taboos. To possess a little of the hair from someone's head, their nail clippings, and some molded wax is enough to hold that person in our thrall. Some of us remember the small-town boys in the 1960s who grew out the nails on their little fingers, that visible substitute for the invisible penis.

If New York is the center of the world—and I, as someone from the provinces of Eastern Europe, have no doubt that it is—then one could say from the vantage point of the center that nails have now become the center of the body. I was initiated into the new trend at a salon on Second Avenue. The boss, a Vietnamese man, greeted me with a courteous smile, and his colleagues settled me into a comfy leather chair. One offered to massage the weary back of my neck. Another got to work on the nails on my hands and feet. *Abra, abra*, a third asked me. *Abra, abra*, the Vietnamese woman insisted, and then explained what she meant through gestures. *Abra* means *eyebrow*. For another ten dollars I could have my eyebrows plucked. I declined. The offer sounded a touch licentious to me.

It was the end of the work day. I was the last customer. I entertained myself by watching how the Vietnamese proprietor was teaching a young Mexican woman with plump fingers how to groom nails. The Vietnamese man was gentle and patient. First he applied polish to the nails on her hand, demonstrating how to brush the surface of the nail properly. Then he stretched his own hand out to her so she could demonstrate what she had learned. They made a perfect picture. Lit by light from the street, the teacher and pupil polishing each others' nails was a scene worthy of Vermeer.

The scene was one of contact between two people from distant worlds, a Vietnamese man and a Mexican woman, on Second Avenue in New York. The two stretched their fingertips toward each other, touching like two aliens. I thought about how people burrow, vine-like, making secret passageways all over the surface of the earth. Unstoppable. Unflagging. I thought about how people migrate, pouring themselves from one place into another like sand; how they appear suddenly in one spot like mysterious messengers, masked as promoters of small and, at first glance, meaningless skills such as grooming fingernails. I, both Dutch and Balkan, the Mexican and Vietnamese women, and this Vietnamese man, all of us happened to find our selves engaged in a mysterious project at the end of a New York day, the meaning of which we could not divine.

It occurred to me that the world is righting itself—using some internal logic that apparently has nothing to do with ideology or ideological systems. The nail salon was a symbolic juncture at that moment, an affordable temple of affordable comfort for the people of New York, for the people in the neighborhood, for tourists such as I was, for fresh baked emigrants.

That nail salon was a place of symbolic global reconciliation. It occurred to me that American citizens leave dozens of pounds of their nail clippings and pounds of eyebrow hair in these new grooming salons. It occurred to me that they are leaving them in the care of the Vietnamese! If we consider those ancient beliefs, this means that the Vietnamese, should they want to, could have their customers permanently in their thrall! Because the Maori, the Australian Wirajuri, the west African Mani and Jumbes, the Tahitians, the inhabitants of the Solomon Islands, the ancient Incas, Patagonians, South African Makololos, and many other peoples carefully hide their nail clippings and hair trimmings so their enemies can't get a hold of them. In other words, Americans are cheerfully putting their heads on the chopping block. The Vietnamese, instead of working at the job of righting "historical wrongs," are courteously massaging the weary necks, hands, and feet of the people who brought them so much tragedy forty years ago, miring themselves in tragedy in the process.

Perhaps the Vietnamese, disguised as groomers of hands and feet, actually bear an important message? Are the Vietnamese calling on

all of us to show some compassion for their partner in the historical chain of trauma between the colonizer and the colonized, the
exploiter and the exploited, the power-monger and his victims? Are
the Vietnamese suggesting that the sum of their wisdom lies in massaging the power-monger's neck and trimming his nails? This is a
possible symbolic reading of the global map of the world. Just as the
whole world rushed headlong to read the symbolism of the terrorist
attack on America, I have the right to approach global symbolism
from the other end, from the vantage point of the reconciliatory, the
"hedonistic," from the nail salon.

Returning to Amsterdam, I found myself at the Osdorpplein
shopping center. The first thing I saw was a new shop with the sign:
USA NAILS. I peered in. A Vietnamese woman greeted me with the
seductively aggressive mantra: *Enkbra, enkbra . . .* I knew exactly
what this meant. Again I declined her offer to pluck my eyebrows.
Nee wenkbrauwen, alleen nagelen (Not eyebrows, but nails), I pieced
together in my equally broken Dutch. There, for those who are so
inclined, I leave the interpretation of the unusual global migration
of Vietnamese nail groomers who, bearing the sign USA NAILS, are
quietly and courteously conquering Europe. I am not complaining.
I frequent the USA NAILS salon in Amsterdam. As far as cutting
fingernails and toenails, I look to this as my guide:

> *Cut them on Monday, you cut them for health,*
> *Cut them on Tuesday, you cut them for wealth,*
> *Cut them on Wednesday, you cut them for news,*
> *Cut them on Thursday, a new pair of shoes,*
> *Cut them on Friday, you cut them for sorrow,*
> *Cut them on Saturday, you see your true love tomorrow,*
> *Cut them on Sunday, your safety seek,*
> *The devil will have you the rest of the week.*

September 2002

3.

"Writing?" asked Ukhudshansky listlessly.
　　　　　　—Ilf & Petrov, The Golden Calf

WHAT IS EUROPEAN
ABOUT EUROPEAN LITERATURE?

European Literature and the Eurovision Song Contest

The notion of the European literatures, as employed by European
Union politicians, those who manage culture, the publishers, the old-
fashioned literature departments at universities, and, often enough,
the writers themselves, is not so very different from the notion of
the Eurovision Song Contest for the top pop song of Europe. The
Eurosong is the hottest fusion of spiritual European unification; the
Eurosong is a grandiose (*European-style* grandiose) parade of European pop-music kitsch. Other features of the contest provide far more
entertainment than the music itself, such as the outfits (*This year the
performers from Cyprus were best dressed!*) and the spectacle (*The Irish
smoked the stage up so much this year, they nearly started a fire!*). The
voting is always loads of fun (*Croatia, ten points! Belgium, two points!*),
as are the TV-postcards from different countries, and the little visits
to the studios in Tallinn or Dublin. There is entertainment to be had
in the "politics" and its transparency (*What do you bet that Croatia gives
the most points to the Slovenes, and the Slovenes give all their points to the
Croats!*); the participation of new European presenters (*Wow, this year
we've got the Bosnians!*); and the absence of certain non-presenters (*No
Serbs are going to sing to me in Europe!*). As far as the music itself, it's
assumed that the Turks will come up with oriental kitsch music and
that the Swedes are always working to replicate ABBA's smash hits.
The biggest show in Europe has a didactic side (the audience learns
the names of new states: *Latvia, Estonia, Lithuania*) and a political
and ideological side (*OK, so we've brought in the Estonians, but no way
are we going to allow the Turks to join, their singing here is as far as it*

goes!), and along the way, of course, it brings in some serious money. Occasionally, there are eyebrow-raising moments, like Diva (*Viva la Diva!*), the Israeli transvestite, but a little eyebrow raising in such a mainstream context can only be refreshing.

European literary life isn't so very different from the Eurovision Song Contest. It, too, has its big names behind whom always (always!) stands the name of a state. It is, admittedly, less spectacular. But the broadcasts of the annual award ceremony for the Man Booker Prize prove that literature, too, can become a spectacle on the silver screen. The award winners bound vivaciously up onto the stage (*Canada, ten points!*), and announce their gratitude in a way that is strikingly reminiscent of the pop stars. The judges give a more eloquent statement, which is hardly surprising considering the fact that words, rather than musical notes, are the substance of literature. The commercial impact of the Booker show supports our initial comparison, no matter how unjust, malicious, or inaccurate some may think it.

Gregor G. Drubnik's part in it all

Some thirty years ago a fabricated news item appeared in an issue of the *New York Times*. It was about a Gregor G. Drubnik, a Bulgarian writer who, in 1971, was supposedly awarded the Nobel Prize for Literature. The article was crammed with discriminatory epithets, such as the *remarkably stupefying quality* of Drubnik's works, and it was supposed to be hilarious. The very idea that some Bulgarian could win the Nobel Prize for Literature made readers grin.

Had I come across this article when it was first published, I, too, would have grinned. I was studying comparative literature at the time, and I was full of myself. I read European and American writers, wrote papers on Proust and Joyce. I read the well-known and less well-known Russian writers, studied the schools of literary theory at a time when literary theory was at its peak. All in all, I was convinced that I was at one with the great world of literature. It was a time of an upsurge in publishing in the former Yugoslavia; a flurry of translation was going on, and I followed every new thing in literature I could get my hands on. When I first went to the States in the early eighties the selection of translated books for sale in bookstores struck me as modest. I couldn't tell anyone that. Nobody would have believed me, and, besides, only a few years later the situation in American bookstores—as far as translations were concerned—had changed dramatically.

By the early 1990s the situation had also changed "at home": the local bookstores were awfully empty, and it was difficult for me to convince anyone that things had been different only a few years earlier. Around that time my books set out into the world, and I followed not long thereafter. In my conviction that I was communicating skillfully with the great literary world, whatever that meant, I forgot about the possibility that perhaps that great world was not communicating with me.

When my first novel was published in England, a critic finished his review with the question: *But still, is this what we need?* Only later did I realize what the critic's sentence had meant. I hadn't noticed there was a label trailing along behind me as I traveled: *Made in the Balkans.* When someone comes from the Balkans, he or she is not expected to produce books of genuine literary merit, but to fit the stereotype that WE harbor about THEM, the Balkans, or about the places all of THEM come from. I had, therefore, completely forgotten where I was from and where I was headed, or, in other words, I had ignored the established codes of communication between the cultural center and the periphery. As far as my literary abilities were concerned, they didn't matter at all.

It turned out that Drubnik's Cold War shadow was still lurking on the sidelines, thirty years on. The number of labels that others attached to me and my books only proliferated. New labels appeared alongside *Made in the Balkans*: the collapse of Yugoslavia, the fall of communism, war, nationalism, new states, new identities . . . For foreign readers, my texts were weighed down by baggage. I looked like a traveler lugging several suitcases in each hand, while trying to maintain a certain grace. Unlike me, my West European colleagues traveled light, luggage-free: they and their texts were all their readers saw. In my case the luggage was burying me and my texts. The situation had changed drastically "at home" as well. Labels had started cropping up there, too. To understand my writing, it suddenly became necessary to know whether I was a Croat or a Serb, and who and what my mother and father were.[1]

Ten years ago I held a Yugoslav passport, with its soft, pliable, dark red cover. I was a *Yugoslav* writer. Then the war came, and the Croats,

---

1. A new, expanded edition of a lexicon of world writers has come out in Croatia. The editors resolved to include "domestic" writers in the category of world literature—Croatian writers for the most part, some fifty of them—and then a far smaller number of Serbian and Bosnian writers (since the Serbian and Bosnian literatures are "foreign," so they, too, deserve representation in a lexicon of world writers). The number of translations a writer has, and his or her reception abroad, were not relevant criteria, but rather "the significance of the literary work," and then a numerical cut-off point, or, as the Zagreb University professor of Croatian literature (who was the editor for the Croatian writers) put it, "you have to stop somewhere." As far as the "domestic" writers were concerned, the strict issuers of literary visas for entry into world literature did not allow writers to declare their nationality for themselves (which is fine, since most of them, if given the chance, would brazenly go ahead and declare themselves American writers), but instead, with a laboratory-like precision, they divided them up by blood type. They could not allow Ivo Andrić to remain a "Yugoslav writer," but they showed generosity of spirit in defining him by blood (as a Croatian writer), by residence (as a Serbian writer), and by themes (as a Bosnian writer). "The national literatures are not unions that writers can sign up for or leave," announced the stern inspector (certain that blood is not water) who gave the fifty authors, some dead, others living, visas for entry into world literature. Another editor was more explicit in her description of her own efforts, announcing that she felt as if she had been engaged in the job of "lion taming."

without so much as a by your leave, shoved a blue Croatian passport at me. The Croatian government expected a prompt transformation from its citizens, as if the passport itself was some sort of magic pill. Since this didn't go down easily in my case, they excluded me from their literary and other ranks. Croatian passport in hand, I abandoned both my newly acquired and formerly demolished homeland and set out into the world. With impassioned, Eurosong-like glee, the rest of the world identified me as a *Croatian* writer. I became a literary representative of a place that no longer wanted me. I, too, no longer wanted the place that no longer wanted me. I am no fan of unrequited love. Even today, I still, however, haven't shaken free of the labels.

Again I hold a passport with a soft, pliable, dark red cover, a Dutch passport. Will this new passport make me a *Dutch* writer? It may, but I doubt it. Now that I have a Dutch passport, will I ever be able to "reintegrate" into the ranks of Croatian writers? Possibly, but I doubt it. What is my real problem? Am I ashamed of the label of *Croatian* writer that still trails after me? No. Would I feel any better with a label like Gucci or Armani? Undoubtedly I would, but that's not the point. Then what is it that I want? And why am I, for God's sake, so edgy about labels?

Why? Because the reception of literary texts has shown that the luggage of identification bogs down a literary text. Because it has further been shown that labels actually alter the substance of a literary text and its meaning. Because the identifying label is, in fact, an abbreviated textual interpretation, and is almost always skewed. Because the label opens up room for reading something into a text that is not there. And, finally, because the identifying label discriminates against the text. To acquiesce to identification means to endorse the notion that the field of literature is nothing more than a realm of geopolitics, which may, in fact, be the reality, but why should I embrace every "reality," just because it is a "reality."

Why should the vast majority of my colleagues feel it essential to hold tight to the label?[2] Because this identification of writers by nationality, by the country each belongs to, has become part and parcel of literary and market communications. Because in this way it is much easier and quicker to travel from the periphery to the center. Because for many writers the identifying label is also the only way they communicate both locally and globally, so that they can be accepted and recognized as Bosnian writers, as Slovenian writers, as Bulgarian writers. The label is the fundamental assumption of the outdated institutions of national literatures, but also for the modern literary marketplace. Because ethnic identity is a tried and true sales formula which has propelled many writers from the periphery—for the right literary reasons or the wrong ones—into the global literary marketplace. The market always needs a Bulgarian, a Serb, a Croat, an Albanian. But only one. Two max. A surfeit is, naturally, confusing.

Europe all the way to India

The cultural bureaucracy of the European Union, the numerous cultural managers, officers, and "advocates" (bureaucrats who "advocate for cultural matters")—all of them are doing what they can to take a position on things. Globalization (another word for American cul-

---

2. The slogan BUY THINGS CROATIAN! has caught on in Croatia. The slogan was supposed to make Croatian consumers sensible, to convince them to buy domestic goods. At the same time the slogan was a gesture of defiance to the European Union (because it had postponed talks for welcoming Croatia into its ranks) and implied that *domestic* is better than *foreign* (European). In this manner, fresh cheese and cream, a specialty brought to the Zagreb marketplace by farm women from nearby villages has become a symbol, the most authentic heart of Croatdom. In 2005, eight Croatian writers (men, of course) were invited to write a book which was published in a large edition by the daily paper *Jutarnji list* and advertised with the slogan READ THINGS CROATIAN! None of the eight men who had been chosen protested about the ad copy, or about the fact that they were all men: it is better being sold as an authentic Croatian product with a lot of publicity in a large edition than—not at all.

tural imperialization) worries the culture of the EU. While American critics use the term *imperialization* without a twinge, the Europeans flinch at it. They are afraid of being accused of anti-Americanism, as the French are, for instance—they rise every so often to the challenge of protecting their cultural products, but also what has been taken from them: their lost cultural primacy. It has been shown that anti-Americanism is not culturally, or politically, or strategically, or financially, profitable: it is not only the American merchants who make money in the industry of American culture, but also the European go-betweens.

European "cultural identity"—whatever that means—is "threatened" by the pervasive industry of American mass culture; by the East Europeans who are awaiting acceptance, each toting their cultural bundle; and by emigrants of the non-European cultural circle—the most painful point, by the way, of the European cultural subconscious—whose numbers are rising ominously with every passing second. Where do all these Moroccans, Algerians, all these Chinese, Arabs, belong? Who can even keep track of how many of them there are? What categories to use? Their passport? The language they use? The sphere of cultural reference they supposedly belong to?

Proud of their ideology and their multiculturalism, the cultural bureaucracy of the EU is perpetuating, for the time being, a tried and true approach—me *Tarzan*, you *Jane*—a formula for acknowledging various cultural identities, encouraging regional and other differences, and, of course, integration, though no one knows what that actually means. So, to each his own faith, and to each her own burka. As long as someone who is Moroccan lays something *Moroccan* on the counter, whatever that means, and we lay something *European* out, whatever that means, all is right with the world. That is how cultural products are exchanged, for the most part. That is how the market works, and the dynamics of literary life proceed according to this entrenched mechanism.

Everything would, indeed, be right with the world, if there were no non-mainstream individuals, dysfunctional cogs in the mechanism, people who erode the stereotypes about culture, about who they are, and who they are supposed to be. Individuals like that outgrow their cultural promoters, managers, and the cultural bureaucracy of the EU, which wrestles with issues of European cultural identity. They outgrow their critics and interpreters, the university professors and readers. In other words, no one knows what to do with them.

What are the Dutch to do, indeed, with Moses Isegawa, an African writer who lives in Holland and writes in English? What are they to do with me? I live in Amsterdam, yet I do not write in Dutch. What are the Croats to do with me? I write in Croatian, but I have a "bad reputation" and I come home only for the Christmas holidays. What are the Serbs and Bosnians to do with me? They can read me in the language in which I write: BCS (Bosnian-Croatian-Serbian). How do the Dutch handle a Moroccan writer, who, instead of writing about the cultural differences between the Moroccans and the Dutch that anyone could understand, has embraced the task of reconstructing the Dutch language of the eighteenth century? What are the French to do with an Arab writer who has undertaken a new version of *In Search of Lost Time*, or the Germans with a Turkish writer who is writing a new *The Sorrows of Young Werther*?

Among the dysfunctions in the existing literary system, I have a favorite example. Joydeep Roy Bhattacharya was born in Calcutta. He left India when he was twenty. He earned a degree in philosophy in the United States, and lives in New York. Joydeep wrote a novel. The theme of his novel is Hungary and a circle of Hungarian intellectuals in the 1960s. The Hungarians promptly translated the book. A Hungarian intellectual grumbled to me that the novel deals with Hungary, but in an *Indian* way. "It would have been better for him to write about India," he commented.

Joydeep is a handsome, photogenic man. The English publisher published his novel with the secret hope that with his next novel Joydeep would change his mind and write something about India—something like *The God of Small Things*, but from a male perspective. My mother, to whom I showed Joydeep's book with his photograph on the back, instinctively took the side of the English publisher. "Why doesn't he write about India?" she sighed. "He's even cuter than Sandokan."

In a world in which the "identity kit" has become something like a toothbrush—an essential which you cannot do without—Joydeep has chosen the most arduous path. He tossed his "identity kit," from which he could have made a profit, into the dustbin because he preferred the right to free literary choice, free literature. Joydeep is cognizant of the consequences of his symbolic suicide. "At home" in India, I assume, they aren't too partial to him. The countries he writes about complain because they are convinced that they, alone, hold the "copyright" to their themes. His English publisher tolerates Joydeep's East European "virus" because he hopes he'll recover and the time will come when Joydeep will return thematically to "where he belongs," to India. So in answer to the question of what would be "European" in the European literatures, I say: it is Mr. Bhattacharya, an Indian man born in Calcutta, who lives in New York and writes about Europe.

The grey zone of literature

So it goes. The Croats publish "authentically Croatian" writers with the advertising slogan READ THINGS CROATIAN! (as if readers had been overly eager to read everything that was not Croatian!); Serbs, Lithuanians, Estonians, Latvians, Macedonians, Slovenians, and others have crammed themselves into the nineteenth century concept of literature by blood group; West European literary cataloguers, baffled by the massive penetration of literate migrants into the national literary fabric, are struggling to keep up the borders between "autochthonous" and "alochthonous," "national" and "émigré" literatures, the result of which sounds like a minor revision of the Croatian slogan (READ

THINGS CROATIAN, BUT MOROCCAN, TOO!) if it were reworked according to politically correct European standards). While one group of them is preoccupied with questions of literary and historical, national, ethnic, and European literary identity, a large grey zone of non-territorial literature is growing in the European (and other) literary interspaces. That zone is inhabited by "ethnically inauthentic" authors, émigrés, migrants, writers in exile, writers who belong simultaneously to two cultures, and bilingual authors who are writing "neither here nor there," writers who, in any case, are working beyond the borders of their national literatures. The literature of the grey zone is being written by writers in their native tongue while they are surrounded by the language of their host country, and by others who choose the language of the host country over their own. There are writers who undermine linguistic conventions and move freely among languages and cultures, translating meanings; there are writers who are creating a new language and new culture out of linguistic and cultural mixtures.

These "new languages," and consequently the languages of literature, are characterized by an interaction between different languages, or deviation from the standard language (for instance Black English, Spanglish, Nuyorican, and many others). The slang of Dutch teenagers, for instance, is called "smurfentaal," (the language of the Smurfs, those little blue cartoon characters), and it is a "low" Dutch shot through with Moroccan, Turkish, Antillian, English and other languages. New dialects are being born which are gradually becoming the languages of literature: Chicano-Spanish, Turko-German, Algerian-French, Russian-American. The number of combinations is uncountable. In the post-Yugoslav linguistic constellation—in which the formerly common language, Serbo-Croatian, has been abolished and officially divided into the Croatian, Serbian, and Bosnian languages—the subversive variant for language use would actually be the retro-variant: the BCS-language (an abbreviation which officials at the Hague Tribunal use for Bosnian-Croatian-Serbian).

The writers who are writing the new literatures have mostly been dislocated from their original environments. They do not feel "at home" in the countries where they live, nor do they dream of returning to the countries from which they have fled. Those new writers are building their own place, a third cultural zone, a "third geography." The new literature is still being published within imposed, unjustly narrow and often discriminatory categories—such as exile, ethnic, migrant, émigré, disapora—partly because the literary critics and interpreters have been caught short. An adequate language of interpretation has still not been found for the new literary reality. Arjun Appadurai warns[3] that "post-national formations," for instance, can not be defined with the vocabulary of the existing political language. A language which would include the overlapping interests of numerous groups, trans-local solidarities, cross-border mobilizations and post-national identities does not exist yet.

What the name will be for this new alternative literary zone is a matter of agreement. Judging by the growing number of courses at American universities, the term "transnational literature" could be the term of choice. Azade Seyhan writes: "I understand transnational literature as a genre of writing that operates outside the national canon, addresses issues facing deterritorialized cultures, and speaks for those in what I call 'paranational' communities and alliances. These are communities that exist within national borders or alongside the citizens of the host country but remain culturally or linguistically distanced from them and, in some instances, are estranged from both the home and the host country."[4] Franz Kafka, who lived in Prague but wrote in German, is a symbolic literary figure of deterritorialized literature. A well-known notion of Deleuze and Guattari about

---

3. Arjun Appadurai, *Modernity at Large: Cultural Dimensions of Globalization*, University of Minnesota Press, 1996.
4. Azade Seyhan, *Writing Outside the Nation*, Princeton University Press, 2001.

"minor literature" could be a productive theoretical formula for future articulation of transnational culture. Contemporary deterritorialized or transnational culture is a dynamic and unusually complex process. The key concepts and themes of transnational culture—archiving ethnic, linguistic, and national memory; dislocation and displacement; cultural shifts and translation and transplantation of culture; the narratives of remembrance, bilingualism, or multilingualism, exile, etc.—constantly mutate, change, multiply, and overlay their meanings in an uninterrupted process of interaction.[5]

And while European cultural thinkers—confused by the number of increasingly famous writers who belong "neither here no there"—try to articulate the exciting migrational processes in literature, falling back, for lack of better expressions, on Goethe's old term "world literature," many "ethnically pure" European writers snuggle into the dusty concept of national literature, enjoying themselves like mice in a wheel of cheese. The holes in the cheese are, however, getting bigger, there is less and less cheese, and the Babylonian cacophony of new, unintelligible, frightening concepts (*post-national units, transnational units, cross-border mobilizations, para-national units* . . .) which

---

5. The changes experience by the European culture of exile, for instance, are most explicit in films. In the remarkable film by Franco Brusati, *Bread and Chocolate* (*Pane e cioccolata*, 1973), with the legendary Nino Manfredi in the leading role, there are two worlds: the affluent world of Western Europe and the impoverished, exile, guest worker world. There is no communication between them; indeed, any attempt to bring them closer ends in tragicomedy. In the recent film *Head-On* (*Gegen die Wand*) by Turkish-German director Fatih Akin, the protagonist, a German Turk, speaks no Turkish and despises the Turks. Between Hamburg and Istanbul there is almost no difference. There are no differences between the Turks and the Germans. Since there no longer is a "homeland," there no longer is "exile" either, so in that sense it is impossible to go "home" any more. The story ends with the protagonist's absurd return to his birthplace (even though he is barely able to pronounce the name of the town). His return is not motivated by his desire to move back, but by the genre, which has been drained of all its meaning.

penetrates from without is getting louder. Who could have predicted that this invisible, alternative world which had been discriminated against would so rapidly outgrow the previously existing one. Who could have dreamed that Lolita would turn up one day in Teheran? That Raskolnikov would be bashing grannies in Shanghai? That the son of that Bulgarian, Gregor G. Drubnik, who lives on the Faroe Islands and writes in a mixture of Bulgarian, Farsi, and Ladino has become a serious candidate for the Nobel Prize!

October 2003–September 2005

LITERARY GEOPOLITICS

A writer without a people is like shit in the rain.
—*Jonas Pshibiliauskiene-Krikshchiunas*

Zeus, the father of all gods, is smiling benevolently as he watches his favorite, Europa, at work. She can't be said to have betrayed his expectations. He had none. When he left her, he gave her two gifts that any woman would love to have: a spear that never missed its mark, and expensive jewelry.

After using her admirer as the speediest possible means of transportation to more favorable and appealing climes and after having an erotic fling with the horned beast to whom she bore her sons, Europa, satisfied and sated, married a local guy, Asterion. Poor Asterion has nothing more in his CV than his marriage to Zeus's mistress and the adoption of her three fatherless sons. With her natural talent for handling herself equally well among gods, animals, and men, and with a small but tidy sum of capital left to her, to allay any subsequent moral damage, Europa continued living the so-called full life. That first journey on Zeus's back stirred in her a yen for geography, so she went on exploring new lands and continents. Some she colonized, and then granted them independence; she seduced many of them and then dismissed them. So it was that she augmented her wealth. Many were the things she invented. She placed notions such as democracy, humanism, art, literature, and philosophy under her absolute copyright. She was aggressive, too; she waged wars and honed the art of annihilation. Several decades ago she committed the most vast and terrible crime in the history of mankind, murdering some six million of her Jews, which by no means prevents her from playing the role of moral arbiter whenever the occasion arises.

Today, Europa, like a good and wise mistress, is busy uniting her lands, although she failed a recent unification test flat-out. She, who did nothing to prevent the dismemberment of Yugoslavia and the ensuing war there, now flaunts phrases such as "post-national units" and "post-national constellations." She, who never so much as blinked an eye at the disappearance of the "Yugoslavs," for example (this was an ethnically indifferent, "mixed" minority living in the former Yugoslavia that was actually larger in number than the more nationally conscious Slovenes), is now demanding rigorous respect for the rights of minorities as a key requisite for joining her ranks.

Precisely because of this, perhaps, one of the key ideological cornerstones of European unification today is—culture. Just as each little town in the former communist countries had its "Culture Center," so the large map of European integration is crisscrossed by virtual and real "culture centers." Culture can be a tourist-instructional gift packet offering a smattering of history, a touch of folklore, a line or two of verse. Culture can serve as an *identity help-kit*, as a shadowy point of self-respect and mutual regard, or as a blank surface onto which meaning may be inscribed and read. Culture may be understood as a way of life, *whether of Berbers or barbers* as Terry Eagleton notes with wit, as the progression of cultural history from Seneca to Seinfeld, as the antithesis of barbarism, as a form of manipulation and superiority, as a marketing ploy, or as a synonym for *national identity*. The word *culture* fits neatly into the vocabulary of the administrative EU newspeak. Because in that vocabulary the most frequent words are also the shadiest, such as *fluidity, mobility, fusion* . . .

In the context of the new Europa, culture should be traditional, national, and cosmopolitan—all, of course, in reasonable measure and balanced proportion. Culture should promote local color, yet remain open; culture should open borders, yet reinforce stereotypes. Tourists end their visit to Holland by purchasing a little pair of wooden clogs, a small windmill, and a tulip bulb, despite the fact that the tulip was a fabrication of the Turkish floral imagination, wooden clogs are worn by peasants in all the muddy northern European countries, and there are windmills spinning in *Don Quixote*. All this will not shake the resolve of the visitor to bring back a genuine *Dutch* souvenir. The souvenir vendors are glad to oblige. They know full well that whoever tries to make the market of stereotypes less stereotypical ends up bankrupt.

Culture, therefore, is a representation of something. And art is a representation of something. In that most pedestrian of conceptual fusions, culture is tied to the broadly understood notion of "art." As far as art is concerned, in her rich cultural history Europa came up with patronage, a fertile partnership of art and money, which gave birth to the "Golden Age" and the European cultural canon. Europa further explored the joining of art and ideology, bringing us periods when, as Walter Benjamin put it, "fascism aestheticized politics" and when "communism politicized art." Europa explored various aesthetic ages, artistic concepts, and periods; she tested long periods of elitist high culture, then a time of "mechanical reproduction" and the stripping of the aura of art from art, only to find herself in a tangle of concepts at the end, but also in a fierce, chaotic dynamic of dissolution in which a number of things mingle: democratization of art and the rule of the market domination of a mass culture—most of it American—and the consequent geopoliticization of culture, shoulder to shoulder with the remnants of traditionalistic cultural concepts and their re-politicization. Amid this morass are Europa's needs. She treats culture as her principle ideological glue, to rearticulate and reshape herself.

At first glance, there seems to be no cause for concern. A brief stroll around the Internet will demonstrate that Europa is nicely networked today, with hundreds of highways, roads and byways; funds and foundations; umbrella organizations; and NGO networks, cultural services, and virtual offices whose sole task is to enable the flow of cultural traffic. Countless cultural managers, officers, and mediators are busily facilitating the traffic of culture and cultural cooperation. These people are salaried European enthusiasts; they are nationalists, post-nationalists, and internationalists; they are cosmopolites and globalists; they are European and regional nationalists; they are spokespeople for European local color and differences, but also for European unification. In a word, they are professionals with multiple identities, people with several heads on a single body. Current and future European cultural life exists in this dynamic, in the rich network of united European cultural bureaucrats and "workers," producers of culture, artists, writers.

Though literature has long since lost its primacy, relinquishing pre-eminence to the more appealing media, its life is still being dictated by these same givens. The contemporary European writer, particularly the Eastie, is the product of a confused cultural dynamic. He, too, is one body with many heads, and he does what he can to position himself to keep up with the changes. He discreetly attempts to retain the traditional role of the "soul of his people." In West European countries this writing function has long since been de-politicized; it's not extinct so much as available on demand. In the newly joining East European countries, which have not yet succeeded in expunging their "liberating" nationalism, the writer as the "soul of the people" has his hands full. The model, therefore, has not lost its appeal. For the "soul" of one nation best communicates with the "soul" of another nation. It is much harder to communicate with a "soul" that has no borders and no permanent address, isn't it? Under the old conditions, our Lithuanian or Slovenian writer, defending the autonomy of the "literary arts," declined, in some cases, to represent his (communist) people. Today he is prepared to assume that role again. For his (post-communist) people? Because he has changed his attitude toward literature? No. Because of the rules of artistic supply and demand. Because the European literary marketplace cannot survive an inundation of fifty Lithuanian writers (just as the Lithuanian marketplace can't sustain more than two Dutch writers, for example), and so only one or two will be welcome. This select two will be the "household names" of Lithuanian literature. Hence our Eastie (and Westie) and the European oriented "souls" who crave affirmation on the European market, and the "globalistic souls" who would sell their European affirmation tomorrow for a more profitable American reception. The emergence from the paradise of the national literatures, where a writer is always treated as a "representative" and "an artist with words," implies a further nod to market democracy. Writers from Slovakia to Slovenia, who have been surrounded by short-sighted colleagues with comfortable waistlines, are now being faced with the market. In that market, they are going to be running headlong into, among others, David Beckham, who recently was given the British Book Award because the book with his name on it brought the publishing industry a pile of money. That is why our Estonian, if he is a market optimist, will have to fit regular visits to the fitness club into his literary life. The competition is fierce, unfair, and traumatic. True, the European cultural bureaucracy, which still holds literary-national identities in high regard and promotes their exchange, is keeping the brutal realities of the marketplace at bay, at least in this transitional period. These bureaucrats take their cut for that, as any agent would. And the readers push their own agenda. They would like to get a quick handle on things and read a little something *Estonian*.

What about those who have no national identity? With the cosmopolitan, intellectual proletariat, or with the spokespeople for a European identity? A European *melting pot*, which would erase state borders, and national and ethnic divisions, and would be legally regulated by handing people a European passport and making them European citizens? People like that will have to wait. The only thing they can entrust their Utopian hope to is the movement of major capital, although this may sound like a paradox. In the future, instead of nation and state, the new "identity maker" may be a powerful corporation, and in that case it could happen that the logic of money does away altogether with state borders and identities. If this should happen, Serbia will be re-named "Ikea," and its inhabitants will be Ikeans, while Slovenia will be re-named "Siemens," and its inhabitants will be the Siemensites. Imagine a leader of a small European state sending this message to his people: "If you do not behave well, I will sell you to Bill Gates."

Life itself seems to be moving quietly in that direction. The East will not be moving westward with the acceptance of ten new members, as every anxious West European chauvinist has feared, but instead the West will be moving eastward. I know nothing of the avenues of major capital, but I do know that the Croatian coast has been sold off for a song, and that the Bulgarian city of Varna is full of the averagely solvent English, Dutch, Belgians, and Germans—the ones who are snapping up what's left because they were too late to buy apartments in Dubrovnik, Prague, or Budapest. It is entirely possible that these small, numerous, and invisible migrants, these small-time owners of Croatian, Hungarian, Bulgarian, and Romanian residential property, will determine the future of Europe, even the future of European culture. Why not? If nothing else, they know that life in the freshly incorporated countries of Europe will be cheaper and more fun than life in the expensive West European urban ghettoes. Aside from that, there is that damned "identity" stuff for export: from the amusingly oversized Bulgarian kebabs to the cosmic singing of Bulgarian women.

As far as the reception of new members is concerned, I am thrilled to contemplate the French struggling to get their mouths around Lithuanian names and the Germans polishing their Latvian. I am also delighted that the Lithuanians—who are always boasting of the fact that Vilnius is the geographic center of Europe and that the mother of the pope John Paul the Second was Lithuanian—will have to tone down their enthusiasm for their own national charms as they enter the European Union. I am also pleased that as they enter the EU, the Estonians will have to delete the verbose passages that describe the cornflower—a purely Estonian blossom, flourishing on Estonian soil for a thousand years—from their tourist guides. As we know so well, national identity is a matter of time-consuming, intelligent marketing. As I said: the national symbol of Holland is the tulip, formerly a Turkish flower.

And what about literature? Will it come out of this interaction changed? It will. I assume that, in the process of their adaptation, Slovak, Lithuanian, and Latvian writers will donate the occasional book to the existing heap of tomes on people who suffered under communism. In Belgrade, as I write this, belated souvenir vendors are selling little busts of Tito (30 Euros a piece). "These are for the foreigners, they like to take something communist home with them," say the street sellers! There will be attempts to sell similar souvenirs, but they will quickly vanish. The topography that had been lost in literature will, I assume, return. In Croatian novels in the late nineteenth and early twentieth centuries, for instance (and much the same is true for the Czech, Hungarian, and other literatures), intellectual literary heroes traveled back and forth to Vienna, Prague, and Budapest, speaking in German or Hungarian, and books were printed without a footnote that would translate all the foreign-language references into Croatian. The topography will get richer. The themes of exile, passports, and visas will gradually vanish from the Eastie's thematic repertoire, as will the division in the European world of "ours" and "theirs." But from the perspective of the negligible number of Westies interested in the European East, that superior-imperial component is also on its way out. It would, of course, be interesting if European writers were to take a good look at one another and write something about this. But the enthusiasm for unification and the code of political correctness might not allow them to. And the market will give incentive to lighter, younger literary themes.

In closing, while we are on the subject of the literary *enlargement* of Europe and literary geopolitics, it is worth revisiting the words of Miroslav Krleža: "What does one solitary book mean in today's world, no matter how deserving it may be of publication? Less than a droplet of water in the Amazon River. Four hundred years ago when Erasmus published his book in two hundred copies, this was an event for the European elite from Cambridge and Paris to Florence, while today, among the hundred-odd book fairs where hundreds of thousands of new books appear, how can a single, lost, solitary book be noticed? Great masters, who turn books into lucrative merchandise, the sovereigns of the metropoli of literature and art, govern the literary marketplace, taste and aesthetic criteria, and without the thunder of their propaganda thousands and thousands of books would disappear into a totally nameless silence. I do not mean to suggest that literary successes are manufactured by the press and advertisements, any more than fuss in the press can predict the winners of a horse race, but I hold it to be indisputable that a hypothetical re-assessment of literary values today would give a different picture of the condition of the European book than the press of metropolitan centers does in its advertising. The structural value of the average or the whole of literary production would assume different proportions. Perhaps this would not essentially change today's criteria, but it certainly would multiply the gallery of loud names coming from those countries, which are cut off from the literary metropoli by the barrier of their unknown languages. At least cartographically the boundaries of good books would be broadened."[1]

Krleža's lament stands firm even today, several decades later. As far as a just distribution in literature is concerned, we will have to bide our time. Literature is in the realm of geopolitics. There are great literatures carrying the enjoyable burden of universalist values, while small literatures are expected to carry in their bundle their local, regional,

---

1. Predrag Matvejević, *Razgovori s Miroslavom Krležom*, 1969

ethnic, ideological, and other specifics. Many foreigners (people who were tied to the territory by their work or some other interest) during the recent war in the ex-Yugoslavia boasted to me that they had read books by Ivo Andrić and Miroslav Krleža. "Why?" I asked. "To better understand the Balkan frame of mind," they answered. If I were to suggest to a German that I was reading Gunther Grass to better understand the "German spirit," or if I were to tell an American that with the help of Philip Roth I was penetrating into the inner American mindset, I believe they would be disturbed and shaken. Grass and Roth are great writers, not writers of tourist-spiritual guides. The periphery and the center, however, do not receive, nor have they ever received, evenhanded treatment, and that is why the books of Krleža and Andrić will remain no more than literary guides to the Balkans for many.

Similar differences in treatment exist between literature and—women's literature. While literature gladly bears the burden of universalist values, women's literature wrestles with narrow, inborn specifics. When women write about sex, for instance, their perspective is treated as female, while when men write about sex, their perspective is perceived as universal. Although every writer is "a personality," "a self," in the practice of literary theory, literary history, and sociology, women writers are invariably "treated" in formations, in groups of two, three or four, especially if they come from small countries. Two Bulgarian women writers, three Eastern European women writers . . . Gender-oriented female literary critics are seldom much help. It turns out that a sisterly concern for the status of writing women has contributed to the promotion of women writers, but also to keeping the sisters ghettoized, with one difference—the ghetto has become more visible and loud. The long-awaited right to create one's own self-definition in terms of gender, ethnicity, and race ultimately, in most cases, becomes a nightmare and a punishment.

Affairs on the world literary map are, in fact, a bit more complex than that. They cannot be explained away by binary relations between the periphery and the center, between big and little literatures, or zones of influence and domination among the nation-, race- and gender-marked literary texts. It is enough to dwell on the gargantuan literary production of China for our optimism about the rise of value of the Lithuanian, Croatian, and Estonian shares on the European literary marketplace to deflate. Our understanding of the complexity of relations in the world "literary republic" will surely be helped more by the economic and political perspective and discourse (such as employed by Pascale Casanova in her book *The World Republic of Letters*)—notions such as "literary capital," "the economics of literature," "the verbal marketplace," "the world market of intellectual goods," "invisible wars," "immaterial wealth," and "literary policy"— than by the more traditional literary concepts.

So, fellow writers, let us rise to the challenges of capital and—physics! Because the only ones who rely today on metaphysics, as an alibi for what they do, are—criminals.

April 2004

TRANSITION:
MORPHS & SLIDERS & POLYMORPHS

I'm doing a lot better now that I'm back in denial.

—New Yorker

1.

When I tried to explain to my eight-year-old nephew the notion of times gone by, he cut me off abruptly: *Oh, I know, that is back when the world was black-and-white!*

My nephew is a child of video culture, he never lets go of his PlayStation® controller. The world before his time was, indeed, black-and-white. I am a child from a different world. My first photographs were black-and-white, my first TV was black-and-white. People could be sorted into the good and the bad, and worlds were better and worse. Color came along later, and with it the disappearance of the black-and-white world.

2.

Much has changed over the last fifteen years in post-communist countries: states, borders, surroundings, people, signs, communications, the message, the code, the recipient of the message, and its sender. The changes have been so rapid-fire that post-communist everyday life resembles a cheap science-fiction TV series.

In *Sliders*, an American science fiction series for teenagers, the protagonists glide effortlessly through time and space. The assumption is that everything else stands still. In one scene, two of the sci-fi heroes find themselves on an American university campus. Everything is here: the classroom buildings, the students, a park and—a statue in the park.

"Hey, wasn't there a statue of George Washington here before?"

"Sure. Why?"

"Because we just went by a statue of Lenin . . ."

And sure enough, the shot shows the astonished faces of the two sliders—and a statue of Lenin.

This episode can serve as an introduction to life in the countries in transition. In the hyper-dynamic process of transition, transformation, and conversion, in this fast-paced traffic, no one seems to be factoring in the traffic jams. Semantic traffic jams are more than frequent in post-communist communication. But it seems as if they no longer bother anyone.

3.

In the zones of transition it is the mental landscape, the people, who have changed the most. The accelerated dynamic of change, adaptation, positioning, denial of the past, and much more—defy the imagination. It's all *edit, delete, save, hide, show, open, close, do, undo, cut, replace, format* on a living, breathing human text. In comparison with the transformations experienced by the citizens of countries in transition, Czeslaw Milosz's famous typology of communist intellectuals (from his book *The Captive Mind*) falls a little short. Where is the post-communist intellectual in all this? Is he changing? Is his writing any better today? Is his thinking boxed in by fewer constraints? Has he shed his real and his imaginary censors? Does he cultivate the same drive to subvert the moral, political, and aesthetic canons as he did before?

Back in the black-and-white days things were simpler. The Eastern European intellectual had a choice: to embrace what was referred to as official culture, or to descend into the intellectual "underground." He could emigrate, of course, but that was not so simple. Today, whether conscious of it or not, the intellectual sends messages to three addresses, to three imaginary recipients, three hypothetical sponsors. The first addressee is his own, local community; the second is "Europe," "Western Europe," or the "European Union," whatever those mean; while the third is the global marketplace, the "world." In comparison to American writers, for example, the situation with the post-communist writer is incomparably more complex. In efforts to satisfy all three imaginary addressees, the post-communist writer has become the perfect morph, slider, polymorph.

4.

The local addressee, our intellectual's home audience, has changed radically over the last fifteen odd years. If the intellectual is to survive, he, too, must change. The transformation was not too traumatic; it was a collective event, and politically advantageous. Giving others an example, the leaders of the transition first transformed themselves, thereby freeing their followers from any feelings of anxiety. Croats, moreover, referred to their collective transformation as a *spiritual renewal*, and this helped them see their own conversion as a spiritual cleansing. The leaders of the change were fierce nationalists, even though they had been communists before, former anti-fascists became brand new fascists, atheists became passionate believers, murderers became heroes, thugs and thieves became prosperous businessmen, ignoramuses became arrogant public thinkers. Aside from being ideologically and politically desirable, the transformation proved profitable. People who had been semi-literate emigrants became government ministers, small-town school teachers designed the new school system, librarians and bad poets became ambassadors and embezzlers of state funds, criminals and killers became generals bedecked with medals, and schizoid megalomaniacs became presidents of countries. While the transformation from frog to princess takes a little while on the popular *Total Makeover* shows on television, the make-over in the transitional countries happened literally in the blink of an eye.

5.

Our Yugoslav transitional intellectual lost his common cultural space with the collapse of Yugoslavia. Even for those who never experienced that space as shared, the potential audience was noticeably smaller. If he was to hold his head above water, he had to agree to change his thinking. He had to embrace his ethnicity as his sole identity, he had to get a new passport and a new language, and he had to move from the larger, common state to a smaller one. He had to agree to a radical break with the Yugoslav cultural legacy, particularly if he was a Croat. He had to embrace historical revisionism and make his peace with the notion that he had been living in a "totalitarian communist regime," in "communist darkness," in "Tito's Yugo-Serbian dictatorship." Our intellectual was called upon to demonize the country where he had lived, to spit, in other words, on the dead. He almost envied the Russians, Hungarians, Czechs . . . who had not only had communism, but could also point to countless proofs that communism had dealt them a bad hand; proof could be had in the history of political emigration and in the history of the dissident movements, in the pile of books that have been written, and in an intelligentsia which had been relegated for years to the intellectual underground. Our Yugoslav intellectual, on the other hand, had nothing, not a shred of evidence that he had been dealt a bad hand. Hence he cultivated *false memory syndrome*, and transformed himself into a "victim of communism." Luckily, everyone around him had become *victims*, too, so no one asked him for proof. He had to master a new rhetoric. He had to swallow the host and embraced Catholicism or Orthodoxy, depending on his background. And if he didn't swallow the host, he had at least to mouth respect for the priests. Because they, the priests, were opening exhibits, blessing school bags, libraries and university buildings, new cat scan equipment, hospitals, new stretches of road. Indeed the priests not only crawled into his conjugal bed, they even started writing introductory essays for books that had nothing to do with their spiritual territory, very nearly stealing the bread from the mouths of the intellectuals.

Our intellectual had to embrace a new notion, that fascism and communism were one and the same. He had to deny the anti-fascist legacy within which he had been raised. He had to close his eyes to the dumping of books, particularly in Croatia, to the sweeping of the shelves in libraries of unsuitable titles. He had to close his eyes to the destruction of statues, even those that had been raised to his literary predecessors.

But things didn't stop there. Only a few years later the intellectual had to change his rhetoric yet again. This time with the promise of joining the European Union. Quickly he mastered the new, European code of decorum. He found a hook in language. He started with striking frequency to use the phrase **Yes, but** . . . The **Yes**, as a claim that he had a firm position on an issue, and the **but**, his cloaked form of defiance. The **Yes** was directed to a single recipient, while the **but** opened the possibility of revision and cooperation with another.

Our intellectual is currently getting accustomed to the thought that life is packed with paradoxes. The most important, however, is the fact that young states need culture. To be a writer, an intellectual, a representative of a young state is to be guaranteed an income. Our intellectual has mastered the tricks of survival. He has learned first and foremost how to take the pulse of his own herd.

6.

The second imaginary addressee of the transitional intellectual is the European Union. Not long ago, some ten member countries were accepted to the European Union, while others wait patiently in line. And look, culture is a key item on the ideological agenda of the nascent EU. It's true that culture in the European dictionary may mean any number of things, because it is so handy: it functions as negotiator, diplomatic mediator, as a *bridge among peoples*, because it *knows no borders*, because it reconciles and expands, because it honors *difference and divergence, identity and regional specifics*. With the burgeoning of the number of meanings of the word "culture," the number of *cultural workers, managers,* and *cultural lawyers* mushrooms as well. The European cultural bureaucracy reproduces itself with mind-numbing speed. Culture is like some a sort of spiritual euro, the ideological adhesive of the European countries.

Our intellectual cautiously takes the pulse of his hypothetical European addressee. And what he notices immediately is that the EU offers no guarantees of liberation from the constraints of national identity. Quite the contrary, he will be granted admission only as a clearly defined Croat, Serb, Bulgarian, or Albanian.

The clearest articulation of transition is in an installation with the unambiguous title, *Transition*, by Erzen Shkololli, an Albanian artist from Kosovo. Shkololli's triptych consists of three small personal snapshots, the size of an ID card photo. In the first picture we see a boy dressed in Albanian folk costume wearing a white cap, a photograph taken after his circumcision. In the second picture we see the boy in his Tito Pioneer uniform—around his neck, his red Pioneer kerchief, on his head his blue Pioneer cap with red star. The photograph was presumably taken just after he was accepted in the Pioneer organization. In the third picture we see the young artist with a melancholic expression. He stands before a blue background, and around his head is a halo of yellow stars.

The number of "patrons," "donors," and "commissions" of artwork has proliferated, and the intellectual notices this immediately. In the old days, during communism, it was seen as a disgrace to accept a state commission for a work of art; only the lowest of the low sold their soul to the devil. These new NGO devils seem to be good guys. If they want you to play their song for the money they've paid, then why not? They have the right. *Soc*-realism, *Euro*-art, give what you can, what matters is that the music plays on!

7.

The third imaginary address to which our intellectual sends his messages is the global marketplace, the world. He attends carefully to the pulse of the global marketplace, and though it may all be a question of luck, he will first send the message that is expected of him. By all accounts, the global marketplace is happiest dealing in "identities." That is why our intellectual will try to dispatch his message in this direction and sell something post-communist (which still implies something anti-communist), something "made in the Balkans," something "exotic." In doing so he won't shirk from fabrications, from tooling and re-tooling his "identity," precisely like any other vendor of souvenirs.

Travelers on Croatia Airlines may find a *paprenjak*, a sweet cookie made with black pepper, in their lunch pack, which the package claims is a traditional Croatian cookie. On the decorative label is a text by the Croatian writer Zvonimir Milčec, a model example of fabricating identity for the purposes of the market: "The pepper biscuit, traditionally made in Croatia, is not unlike Croatian history: its ingredients include honey, walnuts and pepper, a rather self-contradictory combination which gives the biscuit its characteristic sweet and spicy flavor. And this, indeed, is the flavor of Croatia's history. Through history, until the most recent time, foreign invaders and aggressors have reached for this land which mixes Central Europe and the Mediterranean in ideal proportions. They were after the honey, leaving us the pepper. Now when we are finally on our own, we can enjoy both qualities of this traditional biscuit (which the Croatian writer August Šenoa described in his *Goldsmith's Gold*) and share all the nuances of the rich flavor with our friends and visitors. Enjoy the flavor."

8.

It turns out that our transitional intellectual is a hyper-rational being, a mutant with precise inner mechanisms that allow him to position himself perfectly in all three cultural zones: locally, in Europe, and in the world. And yet this isn't, in fact, so. Our intellectual is an ordinary human being.

When I was recently out walking in Amsterdam I caught sight of a restaurant with an appealing name, the Lisbon. When I went across the street, I discovered to my disappointment that under the name Lisbon stood the words "Turkish specialties." Though this detail is not particularly representative of the Amsterdam gastronomical scene, it can help elucidate the mental constellation of transition.

Everyday life in the post-communist zones is rife with signals of various kinds. Nothing means what it says, nor does it mean what it used to mean; the sign no longer coincides with the meaning. The whole system of communications has been turned topsy-turvy. The system of shared references is no longer shared, the communication code has changed. The semantic nodes, a confusion of meanings, are only one of the consequences of the destruction, erasure, and negation of their own fifty years of history by the former Yugoslavs.

9.
Doctors claim that moving to a new place is one of the worst stresses a person experiences in a lifetime. Young people put up with moving more readily. It is said that moving homes may be a death blow for an older person. The people of the former Yugoslavia were supposed to move overnight. Ironically, many of them lost their home as they moved. Though they keep repeating that they are finally masters on their own land, their insistence on repeating this phrase signals that with each repetition they have to persuade themselves of it anew.

Serious damage resulted from the maniacal project of Franjo Tudman, president of Croatia, a historian by training, according to which fifty years of a shared Yugoslav past was supposed to be expunged and the continuity established for a Croatian state, tying it to the time of the four years of Nazi rule—when Croatia was, indeed, an independent state. He opened the door to reinventing the past and a positive re-evaluation of the Nazi puppet state under Pavelić's rule, while he stigmatized the recent past as "Yugoslav" and "communist."

The Croatian example apparently demonstrated that a ten-year ban on the culture of the former Yugoslavia sufficed—including the movies, books, TV, mass culture, popular culture, products, public figures—to convince ordinary people that they had only dreamed their past. The older population lives today in an imposed amnesiac limbo, while the young do not even know that there was a former Yugoslavia. The Ministry of Education saw to this by changing the school system, changing the textbooks, revising the history, and the language.

10.

All in all, the fear of being ostracized from the community, the self-positioning and conformism, the pervasive "culture of lies" and voluntary engagement with it, self-censorship, the violent rupture with the past, the discontinuity, therefore, the relativization of value, conversion of value and its ridicule—all these form the constellation in which our intellectual found himself, but even more, he fostered it, to a large degree, himself. In environments in which the recent past has been erased—in which there no longer is any stable system of common reference, reliable history or historical expertise, trustworthy media, critical debate, dialogue and polemic, experts to furnish reliable knowledge, or public figures of reliable moral credentials; in communities in which all the values have been turned inside out, and an absence of critical awareness reigns supreme—our intellectual finds himself in the schizoid position of a lack of authenticity. The messages that our intellectual sends to his addressees resemble the Lisbon, that Amsterdam restaurant offering Turkish specialities. Our intellectual is an "unreliable narrator" (as if there is nothing that obligates him any more to be reliable): he shifts as the momentary ideological demands require. His most frequent strategy is to adopt a discourse that is desirable to one of the sides, and pack into it contents that are desirable on the other side. And that is why he so readily becomes a morph, slider, polymorth.

A large part of the post-Yugoslav women's writing scene is characterized by speedy adoption of women's (pseudo)feminist discourse which slips misogynist, patriarchal content in with the packaging. The media, especially the newspapers in Croatia and Serbia (in the other countries in transition too, I guess), prefer women authors who write about sex without restraint, but at the same time they are shown in photographs ironing their husband's shirts. These women writers are well-paid newspaper columnists, and they are not disturbed by the thought that these same newspapers are controlled by the local political and financial mafia. They urge a moral cynicism as a formula for successful market behavior, and, at the same time, a "sentimentalism" (interviews crammed with private, emotional details related to general, "women's" themes, illustrated by photographs that confirm the stereotype of a "good mother, wife and lover"). Affirming by their ambivalent public behavior their pseudo-subversiveness, their fake political articulation, and their faux feminism, the transitional feminists support the status quo and mock the possibility of genuine political change. The men's literary scene uses the same strategies, but they are not engaged in manipulations related to gender identity (since their primacy is not threatened), but rather they are positioning themselves on the domestic "ideological" market.

11.

The laws of the contemporary literary marketplace "force" most intellectuals to adapt. Alina Vituhnovskaya, a contemporary Russian poet, found herself in prison, rightly or wrongly charged with drug dealing. From there she sent her parents the following message: "Phantomas says: these are times when even a great man is nothing without the media." The parents immediately notified the media, provoking a media uproar, after which Alina Vituhnovskaya was released. Her comment: "I understood the period of my incarceration as a conceptualist action, a performance. It was a perfect opportunity for me to become a hero, in fact it was a gift. I thought: why would these pitiful agents of the secret service become the authors of my life? I preferred to orchestrate a spectacle."

The interpretation of the transitional metamorphoses of our intellectual may, of course, be read differently. His efforts to satisfy his domestic addressee seem to have paid off many times over. Was the transformation he underwent at home what he needed to become a marketable "player" abroad? Was the lack of authenticity of his position precisely what made him so authentic?

Only in times ruled by firm, frozen values—political, religions, moral, aesthetic—has the writer enjoyed (and in some places still enjoys) a special status, the role of the "voice of the people" and the position of moral arbiter. Today, in the contemporary post-political, post-modern, market-oriented cultural zones—an intellectual is simply a "player." First he must fight to be heard at all. If he should step outside his local environment, he will soon discover that his voice is only one of a million other voices. Our intellectual will further discover the ironic, but liberating, fact that he is nothing more than a product of the market, that his books are products, and that, consequentially, the degree of intellectual subversion is gauged by its market impact. Finally, with relief, he will discover that the writer, the intellectual—whether transformed or untransformed, authentic or faux, conformist or non-conformist—is merely a participant in the global marketing spectacle, hence he is a performer, a circus performer, an entertainer, a vendor of "cultural" souvenirs.

In order to complete his metamorphosis, our intellectual will attempt, without a trace of moral restraint, to affirm his own polymorphism as a common value. *Most of the people living in these times, including me, can be described as spineless. That is not such a bad thing,* claims Svetislav Basara, a contemporary Serbian writer who served as ambassador to Cyprus. At the doorway to Europe, to the "world," our intellectual is greeted by welcoming words written by a man of his own ilk—Bernard Henry-Levi. Our intellectual reads the message with relief. It coincides with his own expectations—*The Intellectual: masculine noun, a social and cultural category, first observed in Paris during the time of the Dreyfus affair, became extinct in Paris in the late twentieth century.*

The public intellectual is extinct, but his craft—providing intellectual services—still flourishes. Here is the paradox: the more disgraceful the moral death of the intellectual, the more urgent the need for his services. As far as ex-Yugoslavs are concerned, those who had been card-carrying members of the party immediately rushed to support their nationalist leaders Tuđman and Milošević. Their leaders, after all, were themselves converted communists. Those same intellectuals today—if they have survived—are the most passionate supporters of post-postmodernism, the ideology of cynicism, games (*Ah, everything is just a game!*) and image (*This isn't my real identity, it is merely one of my public personas!*), the carnivalizing of ideology and politics (*Everything is a carnival, and I am part of it!*), and marketing strategies (*This is my marketing strategy, not what I think!*). Those who are pushing anti-nationalism today (*Why, after all, everyone knows that national identity is nothing more than a construct!*) were cheering as the boys went off to battle a dozen years ago—the Serbs seeing off the Serbian soldiers, and the Croats seeing off their own, Croatian troops—to slaughter each other. Today's passionate propagators of the theory of simulacrum, virtuality, and multiple identities (*I feel fine in any one of them!*) are mainly those intellectuals who use postmodern theory (Poor old Baudriallard!) as an alibi for themselves and others for the practice of moral conversion. If we proclaim that everything is a game, we cease to be responsible. We become children. And look, before us opens a world in which we are left identifying with valiant Buffy, the Vampire Slayer. Because far and wide there is no one braver.

October 2004

OPIUM

Be not angry
Not long ago, I happened to spend three days in a small European town. All because I am easily swayed: the organizers of a local literary festival won me over with their effusive invitation. A young woman from the literary festival met me at the airport and kindly dropped me off at the hotel. I settled in. I explored the town, visited the local point of interest built by the ancient Romans. The next day in the morning the young woman drove me to the local university campus. "This is a famous writer . . ." said a professor with buck teeth and a face well-streaked with capillaries, and shot me an apologetic grin. Obviously she had no clue who I was nor any notion of what to do with me. The next professor was livelier. She managed to pronounce my name (my first name, not my last), but did not let me say a word. I got through it somehow. The morning was, fortunately, over. Afternoon and evening were still to come.

Outside a chill March wind was blowing. The hotel was saving on heat. I set out to walk around town. To warm up, I went into a local bookshop. The tables were heaped with memoirs: *The Memoirs of a Geisha*, *My Life* and *My Life So Far*, and even *How to Turn Your Memories into Successful Memoirs*. A book caught my eye with its unprepossessing cover: *The Prophets*. I took the book and someone's *My Life*, also on sale, paid, and left.

At another store I bought two sweaters, one black, one beige. I found some crescent-shaped flaky pastries at a bakery. At a local movie theater I bought a ticket for *Syriana*, but the show wasn't going to begin until 8:00. The two or three local pubs I peeked into looked a bit grim. There was nowhere left. My imagination had dried up, and it was barely noon. The organizers of the literary festival were going to pick me up in the afternoon the next day to take me to the literary event, and I was heading home the morning after that. I went back to the hotel room, put on the sweaters, the black and the beige, got into bed, and pulled up the covers. I reached for the channel changer. The global tempest over the Danish Anti-Muslim cartoon—which satirized Mohammed and brought the entire Muslim world to its feet—was subsiding. Flags, mostly Danish and American, were no longer burning. I clicked off the television, which made the room even colder. My situation was bleak. I opened the book with the unprepossessing cover. The author promised he would provide instant and thorough guidance on questions of faith. *Every faith is good*, the author remarked with touching generosity.

Learn to know yourself
I don't know much about religious belief. I have been mentally stuck on Marx's slogan—that religion is the opium of the people—and there I have languished until now. I am an atheist. My grandmother did not sneak me off to church to have me baptized (the ace up the sleeve of many East Europeans of my generation). My parents were atheists. My grandfather on my mother's side was eager to join the communists when it meant taking a risk. As soon as the communists came into power, Grandpa lost his taste for them. Grandpa hated priests with a passion. His hatred for priests, apparently, had nothing to do with his communism. But it clearly did have an effect on my mother. She, too, hates priests.

Unlike my grandfather and mother, I am flexible, which isn't hard for us non-believers. I am open to faith-related experiences. I am capable, for instance, of staring for hours at those people who hawk cleaning fluids in the marketplace, making stains vanish like magic. The sleight of hand tricksters—those shifty guys on the street who switch a ball around under a matchbox, now you see it now you don't—have a hypnotic effect on me. Magicians who turn silk handkerchiefs into doves thrill me. But despite all that I have never taken a serious interest in the fellow who turned water to wine. From a global perspective I belong to a less than significant part of the human population. I barely count. Some demographers of religion claim that only 8% of the world's population is like me. We, the flexible and not-so-flexible atheists, agnostics and skeptics share that percentage with pre-Christian and tribal believers, palm-readers, futurists, horoscope fans, and those who believe in UFOs. Everyone else, ninty-two percent of humankind, is part of one of the major religions, or so claim those who monitor the global "religion-casts." Ninety-two percent is no trivial percentage. Even if we take the numbers with a grain of salt, they still are hardly trivial. Some scientists claim that the incredible receptivity of the human mind to this "opium" relies on a religion gene.

Seek knowledge from the cradle to the grave
I read the whole book quickly. The recent prophet scandal had piqued my curiosity for religious matters. I had been wondering why it was that such a huge number of people felt compelled to defend the honor of someone who has been dead for centuries, whose honor—if you consider the fact that it has been sustained for hundreds of years, has inspired millions of the faithful and will last for eternity—should by all counts be in good shape! Had the defenders of his honor brought the same ferocity to protesting the millions of African and Asian children who are dying of hunger, AIDS, and violence, I would have understood. But a cartoon! Oops. Sorry! Here I bit my tongue. Weren't there people in my country who tore down, torched, and killed in the name of defending the honor of the dead? Didn't my countrymen disinter the dead, cart around the bones of their ancestors, and swear oaths on them? And wasn't I proclaimed a "witch" because I raised questions like that publicly? Might it be better for me, therefore, to stop talking and start learning something?

Who are the prophets? Prophets are people who believe that they speak in the name of the Lord. Prophets are a "mouthpiece of God," people who in the ancient times served as some sort of divine microphone. All God's creatures are potential microphones for God, I guess, but if God were to use everyone as a microphone, things would end up like that children's game of "telephone." That is why God chooses only the best microphones. None of the squinting, tapping, *one, two, three, do you hear me*, trying to make a connection to those of no faith. God wastes no time chatting. Once uttered, God's word is law.

In bygone days there were plenty of people prepared to be "God's mouthpiece." Only a few, and only men, were recognized out of the initially impressive number of self-proclaimed prophets and prophetesses. Not all the prophets are equally great. The most important are the "fathers," those who set in motion the creation of the biggest monotheistic systems: Judaism, Christianity, Islam. Within the various religions the prophets enjoyed different standing: one status, already mentioned, is that of microphone, the second is the status of PR (public relations), and the third is that of a demi-god. The greatest of the prophets brought together all three of these things. Religious systems are complicated; God's bureaucracy is the oldest and most rigid in the world.

The prophets, therefore, were people of flesh and blood. Each had a CV. The sudden appearance of God to them—in the form of a burning bush, a voice in a cave, a code of laws carved in stone, an inner voice—was not like winning the lottery. Because at first no one, except their wives and children, believed them. That is why, for them to earn the admiration of the simple people, they fell back on tricks: they would knock a stick against a stone and water would gush from it, they'd part the seas, turn water to wine, walk on water, raise the occasional person from the dead, draw rain from the clouds. People stoned them, hammered them to crosses, humiliated, tormented, persecuted them, chased them into exile, proclaimed them insane, but they kept on their path, and in the end they won their moral victory.

Aside from the spiritual part, there was also a practical dimension to the prophets: they fought for monotheism, morals, and a messianic belief, they were the first to call for a civil society, they were social reformers, lawmakers. Or, translated into the language of today: they were activists without NGOs, without financial backing, offices, computers, phones, or bills. Some of them were institutionalized within the faith, while others became powerful religious institutions.

The great prophets—Jesus, Moses, Abraham, Muhammad—were each a human being with a life story. We have heard of them because they brought along with them not only followers, but also biographers. The biographers noted down every detail of their lives. God has no biography. God's prophets do.

The most appealing part of the story about the prophets is the fact that they were genuine, ordinary people, though, indeed, with special talents. The books of their lives could, therefore, be the books of our lives. And hence, we have biography!

Say what is true, though it may be bitter and displeasing to people
The title of the well-known rock opera *Jesus Christ Superstar*, by Tim Rice and Andrew Lloyd Webber, puts forward a simple notion: in those ancient days, the prophets were the first mega-stars, the first *celebs*.

When *TIME* magazine invited its readers to vote for the most influential personality of the century, Elvis Presley (with the most votes) found himself in the company of Yitzhak Rabin, Pope John Paul II, Adolph Hitler (what can we say, Hitler, too!), Mother Theresa, Madonna, Princess Diana, and Mohandas Gandhi. What did these people have in common? Nothing, except the fact that they were famous.

One can easily imagine the crew who followed the prophets. Perhaps there were among them philanthropists, statesmen, God's servants, singers, actors, fans, and sympathizers, people like Bono, Bill Clinton, Luciano Pavarotti, Kofi Annan, Bob Geldof, Pope John Paul II, and Angelina Jolie. Perhaps they were people who traveled worldwide, giving others a warm word and hope for a better world.

Prophets were the celebs of their day. That's why the celeb is a sort of prophet of our day. Unlike the heavens of old, our global media sky twinkles with thousands of stars and starlets. Theology has, apparently, solved its problems. *Celebrytology* has yet to do the same. One of the main problems of *celebrytology* might be a paradox of a demographic sort: celebs multiply like amoebas, and tend to live forever. And something else: the chance that ordinary people will become celebs is growing with astonishing, god-like speed. Not even ordinary people, it seems, can make their peace with the thought that they are in this world only to reproduce and dissolve like salmon on a river bottom.

At the Topkapi museum in Istanbul I saw an unusual relic: a hair from Muhammad's beard. There are many hairs in a beard; I assume that hairs with the "authentic" stamp exist elsewhere as well. There are other remains of the prophet there as well: a tooth, slippers, hair, clothing, and swords. Among the souvenirs for sale at the museum, I really liked the key clasp with a Mecca-compass showing only one direction: Mecca.

When I was in Memphis once, I visited Graceland, Elvis Presley's museum. They have as many souvenirs as they have relics there, so a fan of the King can buy sandals, a bag, a button, a key clasp, a scarf, a cigarette lighter, glasses, an umbrella, a jacket, boxer shorts, a hat, a copy of one of Elvis's stage outfits, a souvenir for pets, chess, a wall clock, a lamp in the shape of a guitar, wallpaper, jewelry, a toy, a pillow, and socks, everything in Elvis's style. Some of Elvis's fans believe that Elvis is still alive, others are sure he will rise up again one day from the dead, and a third group—convinced that he is going to live forever—celebrates his birthday every year, while a fourth group is calling for his beatification.

In Berlin I saw an unusual item on display at the historical museum: the hide of a boar from which a portrait shone, done in a hologram-like image, of Erich Honecker. The patient hand of an artist had squeezed and trained the hair on the boar's hide until a portrait of the East German communist leader, with his glasses perched on his nose, emerged.

In 1981 (a year after Tito died!) in Međugorje, a Croatian village far off the beaten track, six village children confessed to a parish priest that the Virgin Mary had come to them. The Virgin Mary promised the children that she would gradually confide secrets to them—ten in total—and all of these secrets would be crucial for mankind. The Madonna has been communicating on a daily basis with the chosen six ever since. The children are adults now, but the Madonna still sends them text messages. The pilgrimage to Međugorje has meanwhile become one of the most famous in the world, and several hundreds of thousands of pilgrims traverse it every year. The incredible success of the Međugorje story has heightened religious sensibility among Croats. A year or two ago a foggy splotch appeared on a window in a village in Međimurje. The owner of the house claimed that it wasn't a splotch at all but the Virgin Mary. Pilgrims have been lining up ever since in front of her house. Some of them arrive on bus tours.

I never went to the Lenin Mausoleum, the tomb of the most famous, and youngest, mummy of our times. I didn't feel like waiting in the endless lines. But I grew up in a place that spent about thirty years adoring Tito. As school children we used to go on our own "pilgrimage" to Kumrovec, to visit the home where Tito was born. We were particularly taken with the wooden cradle where baby Tito had slept. We were raised with the Tito legend. The most popular story was the one about how Tito, when he was a boy, once stole the head of a pig, cooked it up, and fed it to his hungry siblings. The Yugoslavs dreamed up the slogan *After Tito—Tito*, and celebrated his birthday for several years after he died.

A friend of mine, an actress, was on a popular American science fiction television series for several years. This catapulted her into the world of celebs. She often appears at conventions. Conventions are a modern twist on the more traditional religious gatherings. Conventions are like a traveling Mecca or Lourdes that go to where the believers are. Stars, like my friend, come down for a moment from the media sky and allow their devotees, collectors, believers, curiosity seekers, and sympathizers to see them close up. While they are there, the stars answer their fans' questions, sell photographs with (healing) autographs in gold, silver, or pencil. Their fans recite whole dialogues by heart, and strut around dressed up as characters from the various science fiction series. This religious gathering promotes polytheism. Among the many stars (saints), the fans (the faithful) choose their favorites. Souvenir versions of relics are brought home from the pilgrimage (t-shirts, photographs, dolls, buttons, autographs) by the fans and added to their household reliquaries.

And by the way, as far as souvenir relics are concerned, I myself am not immune. I admit to owning a Native-American dream catcher; a small Russian travel icon; a keychain with St. Christopher, apparently the patron saint of travelers; Peruvian worry dolls that are meant to spirit away troubles; a needlepoint portrait purchased at a Zagreb flea market of Tito wearing his marshal uniform; *vibuti*, a holy dust, which someone brought me from a trip to Sai Baba; a chunk of the Berlin wall; and a little foot made of wax that someone brought me a long time ago—when I was flat out, immobilized by a bad back—from a religious fair that is held once a year in Marija Bistrica. Amulets in the shape of body parts are believed to have the power to heal.

What is it that these apparently unrelated, randomly selected examples have in common? The religion gene. The whole world was awash in tears when the day dawned, a year ago—"popeless." Millions rushed off to the Holy See to pay their last respects to the Holy Father. The entire world wept when Princess Diana was killed several years ago: there were Russians, Chinese, and many others who lit candles for Princess Diana, though nothing bound them to her. Some three hundred million people wept when Stalin died. Yugoslavs sobbed when *the greatest son of the Yugoslav nations and nationalities,* Tito, died. There were even some Serbs who shed tears when Milošević died recently. They would have cried more if the times had been more sympathetic. As it was, Milošević left this world quietly, like a Tamaguchi.

All these people, including Hitler from *TIME*'s list of the famous, are the massive icons of our time: light, dark, entertaining, or trivial.

Modern celebrity culture perpetuates the rituals of religious culture. Perhaps celebrity culture is a substitute for religion, perhaps its supplement. In other words, opium laced with cocaine. If it is no more than a supplement, which is the more likely, then—thanks to the media that blast us night and day—we live in a time that is more obsessed with religion and religiousness than ever.

The ink of the scholar is holier than the blood of a martyr
Hagiographies are the biographies of holy people. Unlike a biography, a hagiography is an instructive cult text, which uses the life of a saint to conjure the ideal of the holy life. Although hagiography includes supernatural events and phenomena related to the lives of saints,

historiography treats the hagiography as an authentic testimony of the customs and way of life of certain communities. The instructive passages and the simple language of the genre make hagiography the precursor of popular literature.

Today's biography and autobiography are modern hagiographies. There is also a third genre—the memoir. Celebs have won the right to all three. And memoirs needn't be written after a lifetime of experience. Celebs write them whenever they feel like it: as teenagers, like Britney Spears, or in parallel to their lives, like Wayne Rooney, the twenty-year-old soccer player who recently signed a contract for his autobiography, which he will be writing and publishing in installments for the next twelve years.

How do the people, the ordinary people, manage at a time when stars, gods, and idols are popping up on all sides like popcorn, and the media keep massaging our religion gene? Many Muslims wear a beard to be closer to their spiritual leader; many Buddhists shave their heads to be nearer to theirs. Yet it never occurs to any of them that by doing that they, themselves, might become Buddha or Muhammad.

Cindy Jackson, on the other hand, an ordinary girl, took her own transformation more literally. She suffered through a series of operations (made the sacrifice, took risks with her health) to get closer to her goddess—Barbie. Today Cindy Jackson, a surrogate woman, is more famous and authentic than her idol. Having gone through many years of self-torment, Cindy Jackson fully qualifies as Saint Barbie.

There are many Japanese who are crazy about karaoke, a technical gimmick they invented some thirty years ago. The voice of the singer is removed from a popular song, while the background music remains, and an anonymous performer jumps in to take the lead.

There are a lot of people, for the same reason, who are wild about the *Big Brother* show. Here, too, anonymous people take control of media that were in the recent past intended only for the stars.

Famous people write their autobiographies; biographies are books that someone else writes about famous people. A memoir is equally accessible to all, both to the famous and to the ordinary. The market demonstrates that ordinary people have mastered a genre that was intended, until recently, only for the select few. Memoirs are a kind of literary karaoke, a form suffused with the personal. Just how personal is it?

Be aware of suspicion because suspicion is a great falsehood

What does it take for a memoir to be successful?

"Unsuccessful" memoirs (such as *Speak, Memory* by Vladimir Nabokov) rarely call on the reader to identify with the author's story: the author's story is either too "exclusive" or it is narrated in an "exclusive" style. Unlike the unsuccessful ones, the successful type of memoir (often called a **personal memoir**) aims for a high level of identification between the reader and the author's story.

A successful memoir must, therefore, follow a religious model. Confession is what makes it work. The memoir is a confessional genre. A successful memoir must hold to certain conventions, just as the hagiography did before it. A successful memoir must display motifs from the religious repertoire: suffering, sin, forgiveness, and enlightenment. The most popular memoirs on the market are about personal misfortune, overcoming illness (memoirs about the statistically more frequent illnesses, are, of course, the most popular), dependence (bulimia, anorexia, alcoholism, drug addiction), all kinds of humiliation (sexual abuse, bullying, mobbing), and the hardships of life (the death of our nearest and dearest). Every successful memoir must be a story about weakness and overcoming weakness; about sin, overcoming sin, and forgiveness; about the errors of our ways, coming to terms with those errors, and self-forgiveness; about hardship and overcoming hardship. Every successful memoir is a story about achieving wisdom, serenity, harmony, and spiritual purification.

Aware that he is daring to compete with the saints, the author of a memoir builds an apology into his narrative. The apology expresses the hope that the author's story will be of value to others. The author's intention is not, therefore, to show off, to earn money, or to become famous (or, if the author is famous already, then even more famous), but to help other people. This apology is expected from the author: the memoir is, indeed, a highly egocentric narrative form. The content of a memoir (a story of passing through temptation, suffering, and humiliation) camouflages the authoritarian voice. The voice of the prophet is authoritarian too, but prophets need no excuse; they do not pretend to authorship, they are simply God's microphone, the transmitters of God's authority. The authors of memoirs have no such alibi, they have no intention of relinquishing their "copyright," hence they employ the rhetoric of modesty.

Literary critics and reviewers contribute to the success of the memoir genre. They are likely to say that every memoir is *wonderful* or *beautifully written*. Critics know that there is nothing frivolous about a personal confession. After all, how could one say to the author of a confession—in which s/he is describing a struggle against some nasty disease or other personal misfortune—that the confession isn't *beautifully written*? This is the purview of religion.

Following the logic of cultural context, genre, and the media, every celeb assumes the role of prophet, just as every author of a successful memoir does. And this is precisely what we, the readers, expect of them. So it is that the star and her fan, the prophet and his follower, authors of memoirs and their readers, find themselves in a perfect spiritual bond.

Furthermore many celebs tend to be have a multi-functional relationship with the market. The stars are our idols (Oprah Winfrey), our prophets, entertainers. They are spokespeople for our political views (Bono), or our religious (Richard Gere), ecological (Pamela Anderson), or other convictions. Stars own the television programs we watch and the magazines we read (Oprah Winfrey); the stars are the subject and/or author of the books we read. Stars write the books our children read (Madonna, Travolta). Stars design the clothes we wear (Jennifer Lopez, P. Diddy), the food we eat (Paul Newman); stars are our guides through the endless realm of consumerism (David Beckham, Cindy Crawford, Britney Spears, Uma Thurman, Brad Pitt). In a word, stars satisfy our every need; they are our total "shopping mall." But are they not, in their own way, also prophets? Total (and totalitarian) designers of our everyday lives?

How is it that the "personal memoir" has become one of the most popular genres of our age? Because of a new cultural context. It used to be considered impolite for someone to make the details of his or her private life public. There is broad cultural acceptance today of "baring one's heart," of "peeling the onion," of **coming out**. Today, people confess to their weaknesses and misfortunes publicly. The currency of these weaknesses and misfortunes is quickly exhausted: sexual abuse was in fashion for a time, then addictions (drugs, alcohol, eating disorders), and now depression is in. While most people around the world are barely surviving (starvation, wars, illness, poverty), and can do nothing but bite their tongues, a powerful minority is howling publicly about their misfortunes. The media (Oprah Winfrey, Larry King, and many others) merely confirm the unquestionable truth that we are all human, and that, therefore, each of us in this "vale of tears" has a "cross to bear": while some die of hunger, others are at risk of dying of overeating. While some die of thirst, others are at risk of dying of alcoholism. While some die in local wars, others are being killed by drugs, or in car accidents. The assumption is that some poor woman in Uganda and her children, dying at this very moment of hunger and AIDS, will be doing so with a lighter heart. And what if she, too, could **come out** . . . However, there is no need of it. Our world is just: our saints are there to suffer in our stead.

He who knows his own self knows God

Wynonna Judd, a popular American country singer, wrote a memoir called *Coming Home to Myself.* Her book is a *memoir of survival, strength, hope and forgiveness, filled with an exultant and empowering message certain to resonate with those who have dreamed of finding them- selves, and who only needed the courage and inspiration to begin their own journey.* Wynonna writes *simple and straight from the heart* (masters of purple prose would say her work is inscribed with lifeblood taken straight from her veins), her book is a *life lesson* (just as literature was referred to in socialist textbooks, as the "teacher of life"). Wynonna Judd by no means holds the copyright to writing straight from the heart. The problem is that the genre of memoir is registered as a literary genre, yet all its elements—intention, author, language, sub- stance, interpretation, and reception—are edging over into the realm of religion.

I assume that it must be a difficult and agonizingly bureaucratic job in the church to authenticate a prophet and that prophet's message. Some cite three simple rules for authentication. The prophetic mes- sages are qualified as authentic if they are a) **simple** and **coherent;** b) **truthful** (one false message among thousands of truthful ones is enough to disqualify a prophet); and c) in line with the accumulated wisdom of humanity and the teachings of the church, in other words, **compilatory.**

James Frey, a man with literary ambitions, wrote a book called *A Million Little Pieces.* At first he did not set out to make the book into a memoir, but (apparently at the urging of his editor) that is what it became. A memoir about a bad boy, who overcomes his dependence on drugs to become pure as the driven snow. With his *sincerity* and *authenticity* he captured the hearts of millions of readers. James Frey became a prophet whose teachings were greedily embraced. Frey's healing message was relatively succinct, clear, truthful, and non-original: *Hold on!* Later, of course, it turned out that Frey had fabricated most of what he'd written in the memoir. The "prophet" had failed the exam test of truthfulness, but in the happy interval he managed to sell more than three million copies.

Do prophetic messages differ in essence from those that the writers of memoirs, whether celebs or ordinary people, send us? In fact they do not. In all three cases it is desirable that the authorial persona be in the role of "victim" for us to identify with him or her (because each one of us, every day and in every way, is a victim). The repertoire of messages that we are prepared to hear is perfectly proportionate to the repertoire of messages our idols send us (like the messages in fortune cookies). All these messages are here to convey to us something about love, sympathy, self-sacrifice, self-respect, respect of others, achieving harmony and the fullness of life, about avoiding envy, hatred, and so forth. (In this most basic sense, even my socialist schoolbooks were impossible to distinguish from religious books!) As simple, coherent, truthful, and compilatory, the messages sent to us by our celebs and prophets are both beautiful and quotable. In this category, Vladimir Nabokov loses, while Paulo Coelho takes home all the prizes.

Whosoever plants a tree and tends to it diligently, looks after it until it matures and bears fruit, is rewarded
Paulo Coelho, whose books are devoured by millions of readers worldwide, qualifies with equal success as a saint, a prophet, a writer, a missionary, a benefactor, a statesman without a state, and a global guru. Coelho is a unique example of a writer who satisfies the whole gamut of criteria: he is respected on all continents, as are all the greatest prophets, and in all the religious zones; he is a spiritual leader to the famous and the anonymous, the rich and the poor, the young and the old.

Coelho's biography is rich with particulars, which qualify it both as the biography of a prophet and of a star. Coelho was a rebel as a boy; he was confined to a psychiatric clinic three times by his parents because he had said he wanted to be—a writer. Young Coelho fled from the clinic and persisted with his offbeat hippie lifestyle, writing lyrics for pop music and comic books (earning hand over fist all the while). After his hippie phase, finally obeying his parents, he began to live the life of a changed man (interestingly, in this phase he was also financially successful). He went to Europe on vacation and visited the Dachau concentration camp, and while he was there the apparition of someone he had never seen before came to him in a powerful vision. Two months later, Coelho met the man from his vision in an Amsterdam café. The man, whose identity Coelho has never divulged, advised him to dedicate himself to Catholicism and to go on a pilgrimage to Santiago (de Compostelo). Coelho did as the stranger told him, left his job, and described his pilgrimage in the book *The Diary of a Magus* (or *The Pilgrimage*). This book was a huge financial success.

Today, Coelho, a famous man, sends his followers brief daily messages over the Internet, and every year at Christmas he writes a Christmas story and sends it around the world. *Being a writer*—says Coelho—*is sharing your love through books.*

There are many attractions to be found on the Coelho website: Coelho's interviews, audio programs (where you can hear the voice of Jeremy Irons reading Coelho's texts), photographs (showing Coelho as he is greeted everywhere by fervent throngs, and both secular and religious leaders, such as Pope John Paul II). At Coelho's Internet stationery shop the visitor may purchase souvenirs, notebooks, diaries with Coelho's messages (*Start each day of the year with words from Paulo Coelho!*), Coelho's anthologies (*Read words of universal wisdom collected by Paulo Coelho!*), CDs, and Internet games (*Pilgrim*). And the visitor will be able to find information on the site about the

Paulo Coelho Institute, which is dedicated to the poor children of Brazil; detailed reports on Coelho's pilgrimages; reports on Coelho's participation at world conferences held in places like Davos, or on conferences about Coelho himself (in Athens, where 4,000 people gathered, while thousands more waited outside because there wasn't room in the hall); and information about Coelho's translations and the number of copies sold. Not wanting to give the wrong impression—that it is all just about money and promoting the author—there is a meditation corner where the visitor to the site can meditate while gazing at religious relics (of all the faiths!) selected by Coelho.

In our modern religion-and-celebrity culture, Paulo Coelho, "a warrior of the light," is a phenomenon without parallel. His books,—**compilatory, simple, clear**—are literary *vibuti* powder, a holy mixture, a tutti-frutti made of all the religions. Paulo Coelho is a modern prophet, a great magus, and a spiritual acupuncturist who faultlessly finds the acupuncture points in millions of people, regardless of the nature of their beliefs.

Literary reflection is not Coelho's strong point, but, in fact, he doesn't need it to be. Mega-popular writers (as celebs, or prophets) are mega-popular precisely because they offer their readers the illusion that literature (fame or God) can happen to absolutely anyone. (*Tell your story: Tell everyone it is possible, and others shall feel the courage to climb their own mountains,* writes Coelho.) That is why Coelho likes heart-related metaphors (he writes from the heart), "religious" landscapes (mountains and deserts), or metaphors from folk almanacs. *Whether in literature or love, the creative process must follow the cycle of nature,* says Coelho.

That other, fictitious gardener, the unforgettable Mr. Chance (from the film *Being There,* which is based on a novel and screenplay by Jerzy Kosinski), might add: *All is well—and all will be well—in the garden.*

Do not monopolize

According to Catholicism, an indulgence is forgiveness for a sin. The sinner was able to earn that forgiveness with repentance, prayer, and good works. In practice, however, forgiveness from sin was often purchased, for cash (apparently the church of St. Peter's in Rome was built with revenue from the sale of indulgences).

At a symbolic level, memoirs are also a kind of purchase of indulgences. The memoir writer goes through a form of repentance by pen. This indulgence, too, may be purchased for cash. There are a whole series of agencies in the vast market that offer to facilitate the writing of personal memoirs. The Association of Personal Historians, with their certified instructors, offer clients reliable services. The instructors interview the customer, jot down his recollections, leaf through the documentation (family photographs, letters, diaries, and similar items), and for a mere $10,000 to $25,000 they hand the client his very own personal memoir. The agency that hires personal historians advertises its services with the slogans: *Create your personal history. Share family stories with your loved ones. Everyone has a story to tell. Only you can tell your own. Add your experience to the archive of our lives.*

There are people who would like to write their own memoir, but don't know how. For potential memoirists like these there are licensed coaches and therapists marketing their services, there are trainers and creative writing instructors who specialize in memoirs. These instructors help beginners to "unlock their buried memories," and through the "healing experience" to write their memoir. The instructors will furthermore instruct the students to find stirring quotes (*The voyage of discovery lies not in finding new landscapes but in having new eyes*, Marcel Proust; or: *There are two ways of spreading light—to be the candle or the mirror that reflects it*, Edith Wharton). And most important of all, the coaches need to convince the student that his/her life is worth describing. Every life is, after all, "special and unique." A ninety-year-old student who had gone through creative writing therapy and written her memoir announced: "I've had a wonderful life. I just wish I'd known it sooner."

Isn't that what all of us want to hear? The admission that our life is special and unique? And since this is so, and if it is possible, why, indeed, should we depart this world without leaving a written testimony that says what was special and unique about us.

An hour's contemplation is better than a year's worship
I was recently in Zorgvliet, the Amsterdam cemetery. It was as if I'd turned up on a Polynesian island (Although the comparison is suspect. I have never been to Polynesia!). The association with Polynesia was amplified by the sandy soil, and the many tombs that resembled primitive, tribal art. If the person had been a barber, the shears he used might be there; if he was partial to drink, maybe there'd be a glass and bottle. I saw some Chinese take-out on one grave, fresh chicken wings and rice in a plastic container.

On a bench by the grave of a child sat a crowded, damp family of some thirty plush teddy bears. I was surprised to see that many graves had no headstone. Pressed into the sand around them were sea shells, pebbles, plastic toys, painted eggs (for Easter), plastic Christmas trees decorated with candles, and little gifts. There are reliquaries—in glass boxes the size of a household aquarium—in place of a headstone, displaying little objects that belonged to the person: a comb, a toothbrush, a letter, a favorite book, a CD.

These arrangements belong, I assume, to the burial subculture of a new tradition. They are brief biographies of the dead written by the amateur hand of their nearest and dearest. At Zorgvliet there is a syncretism of religion and culture. The relics live here in happy communion: a cross and a dream catcher hang on a bush, an embroidered velvet slipper brought from a trip to an Arab country, a little Buddhist oil lamp, a plastic airline food tray, a Chinese wooden rattle . . .

There was a black marble sculpture of a gorilla, full size, on one grave. The portrait of the deceased shone on the headstone, engraved in marble. The deceased, they say, was a famous Amsterdam criminal.

Sit together and eat in company

Chopped onion should be sautéed for quite a while. Good health is what matters most. It is tough to get rid of wine stains. Liars are the worst people. Lettuce is good for you. Old age is a terrible tragedy. Beans are best in salad. Cleanliness is next to godliness. Stand up straight when you walk. Always throw out the first water when you cook kale.

I took note of this authoritarian voice of hers. I am sure she has been saying truisms like these her whole life; it's just that, amid the sea of other sentiments, I hadn't spotted them. But now, everything has gotten smaller. Her heart has shrunk. Her veins have shrunk. Her footsteps are smaller. Her repertoire of words has narrowed. Life has narrowed.

She has reduced her movements to a daily visit to the nearby open market. She takes this little walk by relying on a shopping cart on wheels. (*I always buy meat at this butcher's. As far as lettuce is concerned, I only buy the most tender heads*). She uttered her truisms with special weight. Truisms give her the feeling that everything is fine, that the world is precisely where it should be, that she has things under control, that she has power, because, here she is, deciding, here she is, buying something, here she is, knowing which kind of lettuce is best. Her mind still works, her legs still go, she can walk, though only with the help of a walker, but walk she does, and she is a human being like any other, and she still has her business to see to.

She wields her truisms as if with an invisible stamp of approval, which she smacks everywhere, eager to leave her mark. The desire grows stronger with her growing awareness of death. (*When I die, this porcelain coffee service will be yours. When we bought it, it was the most expensive service around. It cost us a whole month's wages!*) She has intended the service for me. In her opinion it was the most valuable thing in the house. She had something different in mind for my brother and his family. She explained this to me not long ago on the phone . . .

"You know, I have decided to have them over for dinner even more often from now on. The children love everything I cook for them. They say to me: Grandma, you are the best cook in the world! It tires me, but the way I see it, I'll cook for them even if I have to do it on my hands and knees. That way they will have something to remember me by . . ."

"There will be plenty of things for them to remember you by . . ." I said cautiously.

She didn't answer. Instead she asked me . . .

"You sound a bit congested. Do you have cold? Do have some tea with lemon. Tea with lemon is the best way to fight a cold."

I hung up the phone and sighed with relief. All was right with the world. My eighty-year-old mother was doing fine. Her message—what she'd said about the tea with lemon—foamed, buzzed, and shimmered into the air like the lively colors of a divine sparkler.

Who are the learned? Those who practice what they know
Back in my hotel room—forgotten by God and central heating—I suddenly felt a terrible loneliness. It seemed as if the whole world was part of God's light show, except me. I have never had a "vision" the way Paulo Coelho did; I've never experienced an "epiphany" the way Haruki Murakami did (his hit him during a baseball game). The divine light has never signaled to me that there is a special reason for my existence.

I shivered with an inner chill. I wished I could warm my spirit on something. There was nothing there. I picked up the crumbs of the sweet crescent pastries that had scattered around on the bedspread with a moistened finger and spread them on my tongue like the host. And then I flicked on the television . . .

A scene shone forth on the screen. Some guy was jamming five cent pieces up his nose. He was a serious looking middle-aged man with an unhappy look on his face. The scene was fraught with tension. The five cent pieces were about to fall out. One did. The man grabbed the coin and worked it back into his nose patiently. The man's expression as he looked into the camera was one of glee. The victory was absolute; he had inserted fifteen coins into his nose, and had just set a world record!

God created man in his image, they say. The man on the screen was God's creature. What inner drive moves a man to push against his limitations? God's creature on the screen was trying to get closer to his Maker and delight him with what he did best. Was God, perhaps, entertaining himself in a similar fashion? Perhaps he never had anything more than that in mind in the first place? Perhaps therein lies the whole mystery . . .

On the open page of the book I'd been reading I noticed the hadit: *God has not created anything better than reason or anything more perfect and beautiful than reason.* Isn't it a paradox, I mused, that in a world that is richly steeping in a religious marinade, it is only religion that is calling for **reason**?

At that moment I was startled by a sudden, loud sound. The old pipes of the hotel's central heating system had come alive and were gurgling, to announce the imminent arrival of warm water.

2006

4.

"No, this isn't Rio de Janeiro!" he said at length.
—*Ilf & Petrov,* The Golden Calf

THE STENDHAL SYNDROME

I am stuck, up in one of the bell towers of the *Temple Expiatori de la Sagrada Familia*. It is close in here. I need air. I recognize these symptoms, I know what it is: a panic attack. Breathe! Puhhhh! Puhhhh! I have to breathe; it will pass. A mangy pigeon struts by at eye level, separated from me by iron bars. The pigeon is aggressive. Obviously, it would gladly scratch my eyes out. These damned tourists, it thinks. Damned pigeons, I think. Maybe one day it will take the offensive. Maybe one day this species of city-dwelling bird will mutate and crowd out the people. "Scat, murderer!" I hiss. The pigeon flaps its wings in response and sweeps dust up my nose.

Thinking about the famous Gaudi spiral staircase that I need to descend makes my head spin. What possessed me to go up them in the first place? How many steps are there left to go? Will I ever get down or will I be stuck in the bell tower—looking through the narrow little window at a scrap of sky—forever? Ah, Gaudi! I waited in line from early morning yesterday for the famous *Casa Mila*, "*La Pedrera*," to open. Gaudi's roof, with those astonishing chimneys (*espantabruixes*), as if it anticipated the future invasion of camera-clicking tourists: no one can escape being caught in someone's picture. I watched the tourists explaining eagerly to their fellow travelers what anyone could have seen for themselves; they made curvy gestures with their hands, mimicking Gaudi's concrete curves. They tried to capture with pantomime what was staring them in the face: Gaudi's balconies resembled, or so they say, a heap of seaweed tossed out on a beach by the sea.

I am sorry I didn't get to see the glass dome of the *Palau da la Musica Catalana* in Barcelona, but so it goes: my visits to cities over the last ten years can be reduced to the things *I haven't* seen. I had been longing to see the Sistine Chapel for years. Once it was closed for renovations, another time it was a Monday. On a day off, the third time, I pushed my nose up against the closed door yet again.

It was on my fourth visit to Rome that I was lucky enough to show up when the Vatican Museum was open, and with it, the Sistine Chapel. I finally found it after a half-hour of racing through the labyrinthine museum. I stopped at the doorway to the little hall. People were packed in like sardines, their heads tilted back towards Michelangelo's ceiling. My eyes were caught by twins, babies in a stroller; they, too, had thrown their little heads back so that they could see the ceiling. I tried to turn and retreat, but couldn't, as the people were pressing in behind me. I made my way further in, and without even looking at the ceiling, I began to maneuver diagonally through the mob toward the other exit, which disturbed the people with their heads thrown back. I felt the sweat drip down my back. The panic rose in me like the head of foam on a mug of beer. I felt I'd die if I didn't get out of there that instant. I was only semi-conscious by the time I reached the main entrance. On my way out I grabbed a cheap *Capella Sistina* video, paid for it, didn't wait for the change, and flew out like a shot. I never even watched the video, of course. Since then I've gotten rid of my VCR. Now I have a DVD player.

Lately, I never manage to see anything. There is some comfort in the fact that I saw the Louvre, Hermitage, and Metropolitan a long time ago, in those less than democratic times when plane tickets were expensive. Because since then the cities, and with them the museums, have been occupied by consumers of cheap air fares: people resigned to every physical and mental humiliation; tourists with nerves of steel and astonishing physical endurance; human specimens outfitted for combat, armed with backpacks, cameras and bottled water; people waiting patiently in long lines, latter-day pilgrims who are paying penance for who knows what sins; hunters on the lookout for tourist relics and collectors amassing cheap souvenirs; people who have taken the metaphor of the world as a global village literally. Those of us who are less resilient in mind and body have no other choice than to retreat to a tavern in Madrid—poking at our not so fresh tapas with a fork and staring at a cheap reproduction of Picasso's *Guernica* on the wall—wondering anxiously where all this is headed. We losers have no other option than to sip our espresso, as watery as chamomile tea, in some Amsterdam café, ogle a bad copy of Rembrandt's *Night Watch* on the shelf over the bar, and muse on the state of affairs.

It has always been them and me. They used to spend their weekends shopping in malls while I visited museums; they sweated buckets, ransacking Ikeas for furniture for their lairs, and I, with no concern for the cost, hopped off to London for the latest exhibitions. What happened!? The last ten years or so they have caught on to the fact that there are cheap flights and now they are flooding my (my!) places. World museums today are not expanding, of course, for me, but for them! They are building new ones like the one in Bilbao, so that they (not I!) will have a reason to go hopping off somewhere over the weekend. The cosy little bookstores where I use to spend a big part of my life have expanded into vast book supermarkets, all because of them. They have emancipated themselves, and they are shoving me aside. They are taking my space, nervously flapping their wings, sweeping dust up my nose. They have elbowed their way into my places—they are coming to the cities, walking around the old excavations, taking photographs of holy places, visiting cultural monuments, sitting in concert halls, walking around galleries, bookstores and museums. They have left me holding a cheap mug with Picasso's signature or a Malevich reproduction, a balloon in the shape of a woman performing the Munch "Scream," or a chunk of plaster with bits of ceramic tile stuck to it which is supposed to remind you of Gaudi, and also serve as an ashtray.

However, they no longer bother me. I, too, have been emancipated. I have changed my lifestyle. It doesn't even occur to me to travel.

Now I live on the Internet. And after all, if our lives are already virtual, why should our travel, including our visits to museums, have to be real?! I can find everything I want on museum websites. The Met and MOMA are my favourite Internet destinations. I explore the halls, stop and admire artwork, zoom in, zoom out, meanwhile listening to the music I want, and, best of all, there are no crowds, no people, no reason to panic. And as I leave, I can stop off at the MOMA museum souvenir shop and buy an Isamu Noguchi lamp, or a Muji shelf made of recycled paper. I can check and see what the Guggenheim is offering and buy a nice scarf with Kandinsky motifs. And as far as the Vatican Museum is concerned, now I can peruse the Michelangelo frescoes on the ceiling of the Sistine Chapel at my leisure. No dizziness, no heart pounding . . . And when I leave the museum, I can buy myself a cap, just for fun, that says *Veni, vidi, vici* (we're in Rome, after all, are we not!). The Tate, the Pompidou, the Uffizi, the Prado, the Hermitage, the British Museum—I have them all at my fingertips, and they are mine, all mine.

Yesterday, however, while I was strolling a bit around the Louvre, something happened . . . Was it a moment of weakness? Perhaps I felt a touch of dizziness. Was I zooming too quickly? Was I zeroing in too abruptly on the details of the Mona Lisa? Who knows? Suddenly, as I pulled back from the painting, I saw heads of museum goers along the lower edge of the computer screen. The heads were looking at the Mona Lisa. For a moment it felt nice, running my eyes over the visitors' heads, and then zooming in and out on Mona Lisa. But then one of the heads in the crowd turned and froze, astonished. At first I watched the anonymous visitor with curiosity as he peered, baffled, in my direction, and then a hand tugged at someone else's sleeve, one shoulder bumped another, the heads of the museum goers —the first, second, third, fourth, fifth!—swiveled around with the speed of falling dominos. Some of them stood as if hypnotized, others gesticulated, yet others pointed, and some, craning their necks, stood on their tiptoes the better to peer at me, precisely as if the edge of my computer screen was a windowsill. I felt like King Kong. Panic stung me like a whip and stole my breath, my heart pounded out an alarm signal, and the first visitor began flapping his arms nervously, as if they were wings and he was stirring the dust up around him. Then he tilted his head oddly, and his little black eye bore menacingly into mine . . .

Gasping for breath, I yanked the computer cables out of the wall and the screen went black. I sank down in front of the computer screen and panted, expelling air in short breaths. Puhhh! Puhhh! Puhhh! Breathing rhythmically, I felt the panic slowly ebb. The fear diminished, thinned, and then evaporated. My heart was beating in a regular rhythm; the inhaling and exhaling slowed. Getting up from the desk, I noticed a tiny, grey feather and a layer of dust on the black computer screen. Puhhh! I blew the feather away, and then went to get a dust rag to wipe away the dust.

LEAVING IT TO LOLITA

Tito and the Partisans laid the groundwork for a new Yugoslavia on November 29, 1943 at a clandestine meeting in Jajce, in Bosnia, right in the middle of the most grueling part of World War II. Thanks to their boldness (at that point they had no idea how the war was going to play out), their courage, and the overall outcome of World War II, the people of Yugoslavia got a new state. For years Yugoslavs celebrated November 29th as Yugoslavia's birthday. Until it collapsed. Now each of the five (soon to be six, and perhaps, indeed, seven) little states that hatched out of the ex-Yugoslavia celebrates its own birthday.

A few years ago several of us thought we'd get together at an Amsterdam bar to celebrate the birthday of the no longer existing state. Whether as a joke, or out of nostalgia, or out of a need to get together and sniff at each other (the stuff emigration is made of!), Yugo-emigrants began drifting into the bar at the agreed time: Croats, Bosnians, Serbs, Slovenes, Albanians, all of whom had turned up in Amsterdam as a result of the war.

There were two Bosnians sitting at one end of the counter. One of them made a pretence of grumbling angrily.

"Screw you, Tito, you creep!"

"Why?"

"Who ever heard of starting a country in November?"

"What's wrong with November?"

"Well, if it were May, right now we would be sizzling up something tasty on the grill."

The bartender—who was probably seeing a gathering of these proportions for the first time in his bar-tending career—asked:

"So what are you people celebrating, anyway?"

"A birthday."

"Whose?"

"The birthday of ex-Yugoslavia."

"Tito's dictatorship?"

"Yes, that's the one, the ex . . ."

"Wait a minute, does that mean that all of you are pro-dictatorship?" The bartender squinted, suspicious.

"No, we are pro-democracy," the Bosnian replied calmly.

"Then why are you celebrating the day a dictator came to power?"

"Because democracy came hand in hand with dictatorship."

"You must be crazy," muttered the bartender.

"We sure are," replied the Bosnian calmly.

How can a person start claiming something different—once sweeping generalizations have gained credence, aided by the media and widely held beliefs? How can a person explain to a bartender that things were not as he imagines? Especially when we can no longer tell whether things were different from how the bartender thinks they were. Haven't we—for the sake of life as it moves ever onward—touched up our personal histories, bringing them closer to those sweeping generalizations?

Once when I was trying to explain to a western European friend what was happening during the war in Yugoslavia, she interrupted impatiently:

"A thing like that could never happen here!" she said, using the phrase "thing like that" so that she wouldn't sully her mouth with the word war.

"And why not?"

"Because we have democracy!" she said with conviction. Instead of her pitying me, I found myself pitying her. With such a holier-than-thou attitude she could equally have been saying, "Because we have communism." It wouldn't have changed the substance of the matter.

In communist dictatorships ordinary people were not as ideologized as my bartender presumably thinks they were. Most of them, like anywhere else in the world, thought of nothing but how to get by. But dictatorships were, if nothing else, a free school for political smarts: even the most illiterate cleaning lady had politics at her fingertips. People did all sorts of things to make ends meet. They lied, cheated (homo duplex, homo sovieticus), and brown-nosed; they performed their mini political slaloms with remarkable agility. They'd balance on the high wire above the abyss. They were flexible. Yes, they were compromisers, corruptible, scum, you name it; there is just one thing that cannot be said about them: that they were politically unaware. They snatched at political nuance in the blink of an eye. They knew the whole system of signals; they knew how to publish newspapers "between the lines," and how to read between the lines with canny insight. They kept their fingers crossed behind their backs; they sported a simpering grin. They learned how to be perfect hypocrites. True, the Yugoslavs were less politically agile than the Czechs, Hungarians and Poles, simply because people fared better in "Tito's dictatorship." They got lazy, and lost their muscle tone; perhaps that is why they failed to see the signs of their own impending doom.

Back to our bartender. How can I explain to him that in post-communist democracy, in our new "democritatorships," I have to fight for the rights I had enjoyed freely in the communist dictatorship? The right to gender equality. The right to reproductive choice. The right not to attend religious instruction classes if I chose not to. The right not to wear a cross around my neck. The right not to declare my nationality. The right not to hate my neighbour. The right to say out loud that though I may not have been living in the glow of democratic fireworks, life was not so gloomy either. (After all, electrification was a big communist priority, wasn't it?) How can I now reclaim the rights I had under communism without sustaining big losses? Losing my job; losing my public voice. Losing friends who claimed they had been blind but now they see: a plumber who refused to work for "Serbs, Gypsies, and Yugo-nostalgians;" an editor who became chief of police; a publisher who chose to live off the fifth edition of *Mein Kampf*...

Two Russian Lolitas, Lena Katina and Yulia Volkova, set the Eurovision Song Contest on fire in 2003 with their sexy on-screen smooching. There were many viewers who were delighted, as if this had been a glimpse of a new, sexually-uninhibited Russia (sure, during communism there hadn't been bananas, hence there must have been no lesbians).

The pair recently cropped up on YouTube with a musical number called "Yugoslavia." Lena Katina hums a sad little ditty, and meanwhile images follow one after another. A black-haired Volkova—who has taken it upon herself to personify Yugoslavia—appears. Her cute face fills the screen. It never occurs to her or anyone else that she is concealing all the dark, greasy heads of Yugo-murderers and criminals with her shoulder straps. And why should this occur to her? Why should she or anyone else make a connection between things that are entirely separate from one another?

The verses grieve for the demise of Big Brother and invoke the Soviet Army, that army from long ago 1949—when there was genuine danger that the Soviets might occupy Yugoslavia, to save it, just as they had "saved" the other countries of the Eastern bloc. I cannot imagine, nor do I care, how it happened that the long-dead Big Brother—having traversed light years—insinuated his way into the song. What does worry me is the ignorance behind Katina's and Volkova's pretty faces. They play with the war as if it is chewing gum. I am even more saddened by the media reach of these mish-mash messages—and the popularity the video spots enjoy among many of the younger ex-Yugoslavs and young Russians (there are even several versions of it, including a cartoon). They, and their pop idols, have no clue about who's who in the whole story.

My bartender would jump right in to defend them and pull the customary card out of his sleeve: those tasty television shots—which jump from the screen like a devil from a jack-in-the-box each time they're needed—of a group of embittered old people waving tattered red flags on Red Square.

"Are you going to tell me the alternative is better?" the bartender asks in an orthodox tone I know so well. Ah, I don't want to say anything. I agree, they're old commies, ugly cabbages that sprouted in some field near Chernobyl . . .

But there is a thing that seems more dangerous to me than old people who grew up under dictatorships. So many young people, the sated children of democracy—in the East as in the West—are emptied of all ideology but the ideology of success. Comfortably snuggling into democracy, like mice nibbling leisurely at the cheese, they are harmoniously working at some future great hole. Perhaps I am worrying about the hole because the future of the world rests on the young (these last words emanate from the grave of communism). Because from there, from that empty hole, an obedient army may one day emerge, an army that will place itself in the service of a future manipulator. And just an ordinary manipulator will suffice. There will be no need for a dictator.

LET PUTIN KISS A WET SLIPPERY FISH

I cannot recall when I last saw a more pornographic image. The picture is a close-up of Putin holding a fish and kissing it. It was taken during the president's visit to a fish farm in the village of Ikryanoe, near Astrakhan, on the Caspian Sea. He is kissing a sturgeon, the fish that produces the finest caviar. The eye of the fish, visible just below Putin's nostrils, is, it seems, warmer and more tender than Putin's own. Several moments after the photograph was taken he put the sturgeon back into the water, to the applause of the assembled locals and employees.

Putin, like the great masters of self-image management, is here killing several semantic birds with one stone. The sturgeon is a long fish with a pointy head. With the gesture of an experienced porn star, fixing the observer with his chill gaze, Putin is sending an indirect kiss to the gay population: the long, slippery sturgeon in his hands could be a penis, and Putin is kissing the organ at its sensitive tip.

But there is another, strictly heterosexual, interpretation. In the slang of many Slavic languages the word "fish" means woman, or, rather, the female sexual organ. This metaphoric sequence starts from the male assumption that the female sexual organ "smells like a fish." Putin fearlessly embraces the smelly fish (though his sensible woollen gloves suggest the fish-kisser prefers safe sex).

The president is also sending the kiss to the subconscious mind of the Russian people, who know their fairy-tales. The main hero of "By the Pike's Wish" is stupid, ugly, lazy Emelya, a fisherman who amasses wealth, a kingdom, and a beautiful princess because he releases a pike he had caught. The pike is his powerful helper. All Emelya has to say is, "By the pike's wish, at my command . . ." and things are instantaneously resolved in his favor. Putin, therefore, is suggesting to his people that they should stay where they are and place their trust in a higher order, because they can be pulled out of deep shit only by the will of God—or fish. Putin himself, like Emelya, is a lucky fellow, and the fish's favourite. One way or the other, the kingdom is his.

Many and varied holy fathers have had their picture taken wearing purple berets, tiaras, turbans, and fezzes—more penis symbols—clearly signaling an ancient potent fraternity (God, after all, is male). So why, then, wouldn't Putin send a similar love message to his most ardent macho fans, the many Russian neo-Nazi gangs? If hundreds of tons of paper and millions of dollars were spent some eight years back when the Clinton-Lewinsky national lottery spun, and if all of America was caught up in measuring the diameter of the stain from Clinton's sperm on Monica's dress, then why shouldn't Putin publicly kiss a slippery, wet fish? If Mikhail Gorbachov can advertise Pizza Hut and Louis Vuitton (photographed by Annie Liebowitz, no less), why shouldn't Putin have a snap taken with an impressive Caspian sturgeon?

But I am not interested in Putin, or the fish, but in hunger, the hunger for the limelight. What has provoked this massive yearning? Some twenty years ago, expectations called for the opposite behavior. It was once considered vulgar and a sign of bad upbringing to speak of yourself, to tell the public about your private life, to cosy up to people you don't know, and to show undue interest in the private lives of others. How did it happen that what used to be vulgar has become an essential part of daily life?

When I first went to Moscow many years ago, my Russian friends held to an unwritten rule: the less you said about yourself, the thinner the police files would be. Why is everyone now rushing to fill their files? Why do we treat the former bogeyman of the totalitarian system, Big Brother, like a household pet? Isn't there anyone left in this world who suffers from healthy paranoia?

Foreigners who live in Holland often complain that the Dutch hardly ever invite them over. They say this is due to their Protestant culture of privacy, one of their most fundamental values. This may be so, but all you could care to know about the Dutch is right there on their front doors. All a foreigner has to do is stroll through a suburban neighborhood, and he will see an array of photographs on the front doors: displays of their vacations, genre scenes with the kids, children's drawings, verses penned by the poetically inspired, announcements about newborns or a death in the family . . .

The media induce the hunger in millions of ordinary mortals. It is all-consuming and on the rise. The gullible millions do not have the kind of access to the main headlines that Paris Hilton and Putin have, but they have found their own media to propel them out of anonymity: mobile phones, blogs, websites, Internet forums, television programs in which they perform as the "gladiators" of our time. Then there's the street as the medium: in Amsterdam everyone knows about the guy who from time to time streaks through the city, buck naked, on roller skates. Outsiders on the outskirts strip the mufflers from their motor scooters and roar around the quiet neighborhoods all night just to let it be known they exist.

The paradox is: the more we eat, the hungrier we are. The more opportunities we have to inscribe our name on the map of the world, the greater the fear of disappearing. The more traces we leave behind us, the faster these traces are erased. The more books we publish, the quicker they are forgotten; the more movies we watch, the less able we are to remember what they were called.

An American university recently started buying up the archives of famous writers who write in English. Some young writers have sold their archives to the university in advance. Whence the panicked fear of disappearing, when not only are we living longer, but our possibilities of leaving proof of our existence are incomparably greater?

All our ancestors left behind were a few photographs, usually family pictures. We record absolutely everything today: our inception, life in the womb, emergence from the womb, games, growth, every minute, every month, every year, the operations, excursions, sexual acts, pulling of teeth, concerts—absolutely everything. Even when we don't do all the recording ourselves, there are many services at work recording our biographies: somewhere our every purchase of an airplane ticket is on file, our dinners, the shoes we bought, the times we went to the doctor . . . And when we record and re-record everything, when we write everything down, when our archives are full even before we are born, there is a great risk that we all, along with earth itself, will pop like a vast, bulging plastic bag. After each of us will remain a heap of photographs, cell phones, video recordings, movies, digital recordings, bills . . . Perhaps, protruding from that rubbish heap, will be a photograph of a stranger with a chill gaze kissing a fish. But until that global blast happens, let us satisfy our hunger, let us seek the limelight, let nothing stop us in this, for we only live inasmuch as others know of us.

On the same day the picture of Putin kissing the fish appeared in the press, *The Lancet* published alarming findings from a research project conducted by the World Health Organization. It turns out, apparently, that one third of mankind suffers from some form of mental illness. And of that horrifying number, two thirds will have no treatment. What possible connection could there be between Putin and the world's mental health? The answer lies in the lack of equilibrium. While thirty percent of mankind is truly maddened by starvation, poverty, war, and disease, the rest of us are rapidly losing the plot.

A LITTLE STORY ABOUT
REMEMBERING AND FORGETTING

A ten-year-old friend of mine recently spent his Easter holidays with me in Amsterdam. I took him to the Anne Frank Museum. He had never heard of Anne Frank. I tried to recall whether I had known who Anne Frank was when I was his age. And then my childhood diary came to mind. I had written to an imaginary friend in that diary, and my imaginary friend's name was—Anne Frank.

Last year I was very fortunate: I spent two months teaching students of comparative literature at a German university. Several spoke a number of languages fluently; they were young and already remarkably worldly, a little international group. Some of them were also socially privileged diplobrats.

I was free to speak on whatever I liked. At one point I realized that out of a natural desire to help the students follow me I was turning my lectures into a list of footnotes. My students knew who Lacan, Derrida, and Žižek were, but the number of books they had read was astonishingly small. I would mention a name, such as Ceszław Miłosz, but my students did not know of Ceszław Miłosz. I would give them a word such as *samizdat*, but my students did not know what a *samizdat* was. This is all entirely understandable, I thought, and I did what I could to explain: in some former communist countries manuscripts were distributed clandestinely, in copies typed up on a typewriter, I said. Then I realized that it was more than I could do to explain what carbon paper was and what copies were, simply because I was not able to explain—the typewriter! Typewriters now dwell in the limbo of oblivion: they haven't yet surfaced in museums, yet they can no longer be found in stores. Of course they can still be seen in movies . . .

The East European culture that had been created under communism dwells in a similar limbo of oblivion. This was an intriguing culture and the shared ideological landscape gave it a certain consistency—the landscape of communism. It was a fact that the finest part of that culture was born of its defiance of communism, split into the "official" and the "underground" sides. Aspects of that cultural landscape are a part of many of us. Among us there are many who remember the brilliant Polish, Czech, and Hungarian movies; the stirring theater; the culture of *samizdat*; art exhibits and plays held in people's living rooms; critically oriented thinkers, intellectuals, and dissidents; and great experimental books whose subversive approach was built on the tradition of the avant-garde movements of Eastern Europe. All of this has, regrettably, gone by the board, because all of it has been stymied by the same merciless stigma of "communist" culture. There are not many today in the younger generation who know who Bulgakov was, though his and other books have been translated, the movies have had their audiences, and artists such as Ilya Kabakov have been enshrined in Russian coffee table picture books.

But is the stigma of communism at fault (if "fault" is the right word) for the lack of interest? Of course not. Most of the reason for the cultural oblivion can be ascribed to the global marketplace. Global culture means the global marketplace first and foremost. The global marketplace, like any market, is guided by a simple law: survival of the fittest. Add to that the built-in reflex each of us carries, the fear of being left out. The market feeds on precisely that consumer reflex and survives therefrom. In other words, if all the kids on the block wear Nike sneakers, I, too, must wear Nike sneakers, because I do not wish to shunted aside, right? Or, if I am a rebel, the market will find a way to commodify my rebellion, and I'll wear my anti-

Nike sneakers. The young global consumer therefore devours Michel Houellebecq and considers Houellebecq the most subversive writer in the world, completely forgetting the fact that his subversive voice is being marketed in airport bookstores, in millions of copies. We live in the age of the information revolution and the global marketplace (so our consumer will wear a t-shirt with Malevich's signature on it, despite the fact that he or she will not be entirely sure who this Malevich fellow is).

Most of the guilt for cultural oblivion can be laid at the doorstep of those at work on cultural history. The hysteria around that past still goes on, the past is the favorite chewing gum of intellectuals, historians, writers, member of the Academy, the media, and politicians. In Croatia, for instance, the word "Yugoslavia" is nearly forbidden. Fifteen years ago many libraries were purged of "communist," "Serbian," and "Cyrillic," books, but also other books that were considered inappropriate.

My ten-year-old friend, for instance, may not find the verses of Ivan Goran Kovačić, a fine poet, in his curriculum. Kovačić joined the Partisans and was killed in the Second World War. Vladimir Nazor penned a famous onomatopoetic line of verse which every Croat knows by heart—*I cvrči cvrči cvrčak na čvoru crne smrče* (meaning: a chirping, chirping cricket on the knot of a black spruce)—which teachers of the Croatian language often foist on foreign students who are studying Croatian. (Try it! *Tsvrchi, tsvrchi tscvrchak na chvoru tsrne smrche*). As they struggle with this tongue twister, foreign students have no idea that during the anti-Yugoslav and anti-communist hysteria of the early 1990s there were attempts to expunge the name of Vladimir Nazor. An elderly poet at the time, Nazor had joined Tito's Partisans, like Ivan Goran Kovačić, and wrote a poem celebrating Tito. Neither of these poets is alive today. They are being rehabilitated by members of the Croatian Gay movement who recently claimed that the two men had been homosexuals, and lovers. The anti-communists (needless to say, everyone, today, is an anti-communist) are secretly hoping that this rehabilitation with a twist will succeed, because if it does, it will distract from the fact that the purists had tried to expunge all mention of these writers. In other words, the historical intervention of the gay community will serve to suppress the (no longer acceptable) suppression of everything communist, and make public the (now acceptable) homosexual bent of the two poets. This is only one small example of the schizophrenia of transitional, post-communist culture.

So why hasn't my ten-year-old acquaintance heard of Anne Frank?

During a recent stay in Zagreb I watched my mother's favorite morning TV show. A brief historical piece gave the story of a little girl, Lea Deutsch, an actress, "Zagreb's little sweetheart," the "Croatian Shirley Temple." The pleasant voice of the speaker accompanied a sequence of photographs appearing on the screen: *And then one day Lea Deutsch was put on a train headed for Auschwitz, but she never made it because she breathed her last while still on board the train. It was only last year, after so very long, that a Zagreb street was named after her . . .* Why was that little girl put on the train? Who put her on that train? And does the fact that a street was given her name, after so very long, imply that the communists would not allow a street to be given her name? Does this mean that the street was given her name thanks to the new democratic government?

Lea Deutsch was a child actress much, indeed, like Shirley Temple, and she was Jewish. After Himmler visited Zagreb and Ante Pavelić in 1943, the Nazi government of the Independent State of Croatia put Lea Deutsch and her family on the train for Auschwitz, in order to ingratiate themselves with Himmler. And the street was given her name only now because the new government—which has at the very best only half-heartedly distanced itself from the fascism of the Independent State—decided to whitewash its image a little and make it more politically correct.

Back to my ten-year-old friend. The story doesn't end here. Why did I take him to the Anne Frank Museum in Amsterdam? Because the museum and the story of Anne Frank are accessible to kids his age. Sure, there is always a long line of tourists at the museum, most of them adults, but then the museum is right in the center of town. Most visitors take away the story about the valiant Dutch family who hid the Franks. There is another museum in Amsterdam, the Dutch Resistance Museum. It is a little further out of the center, and there are no lines of tourists waiting to get in. Though its name would suggest otherwise, the visitor can learn about how the Dutch were eager to denounce their own fellow citizens, the Dutch Jews. In fact, they were more eager to turn Jews in than other Europeans were, and furthermore, they received a small remuneration for every Jew they reported to the authorities.

In their redesign of their own past, the Croats are not so different from the Dutch, just as the Dutch are not so different in their redesign of their past from many other people. In other words, we are all human. All of us—the states, state institutions, the media, and the politicians, historians, schools, teachers, parents, and the watchful family friends who have assigned themselves the task of setting things right—work on arranging and rearranging history, each of us in our own way, each for our own reasons, each in our own realm. And so it was that I took my friend to the Anne Frank Museum. Perhaps I'll take him to the Dutch Resistance Museum the next time he comes to visit.

ALL FOREIGNERS BEEP

I was in Stockholm recently. Stockholm is a rare European city—every Euro-idealist's dream of the "real Europe." The city is amazingly clean, elegant, and beautiful. The design is lovely and thoughtful, there is almost nothing to rub the sophisticated observer the wrong way. It all functions, it all slides, it all works, everything is, sure, a bit slow, but always modern, built to human proportions. The people are generally courteous, and they do not kiss you too many times. They are frank, while never slipping into impassioned monologues, and they show no arrogance. All in all, I would like to live in Stockholm —had I the choice—more than in any of the other, more celebrated, European cities.

Perhaps this surprising fondness for Stockholm springs from a detail. In the three days I spent in this city, my presence set off the city's alarm systems without fail. The alarm systems of the stores, that is. Every single time I went into a store the alarm would go off. And every time I left the same thing, *beeeeep*.

"You probably purchased something at another store and they forgot to remove the magnet," said the courteous saleswoman.

"But I haven't bought anything . . ."

"Then maybe you have an iPod?"

"No, I haven't got an iPod!"

"A cell phone, perhaps?"

"Right here . . ."

I left the cell phone with the saleswomen for a moment and stepped out the door.

"There it goes beeping again," said the saleswoman.

"What should I do?" I asked, anxious.

"Relax," said the saleswoman kindly. "All the foreigners are beeping."

I suddenly felt a rush of relief. After so many years of living abroad, the Stockholm alarm systems had an almost epiphanic effect, like the declaration of a long sought truth. Of course, I am a foreigner! Why was I suddenly so surprised by this? Hadn't I left my home country to become a foreigner? I have been living abroad for more than ten years now, and these last ten years I have been supporting the policies of integration in each country where I have spent time. As I have changed countries, I have adopted each one with my whole heart, adapting with the speed of lightning, believing that integration is the only way. But it was only recently, while I was visiting Stockholm, that the nice Stockholm saleswoman lifted the burden from my shoulders. Why integration? I am a foreigner! I beep because I am a foreigner, I am a foreigner because I beep.

Home, for me, is where I am allowed to be a foreigner. The famous Italian Italo Calvino said something along those lines. So let me be a foreigner. It is a costly choice on my part. You have your hairdresser, your massage therapist, your butcher, your childhood friends, your cousins, your family and family get-togethers, your streets, your spots, your hang-outs, your waiters and your dentists, all of them are yours because you are at home, while I am away. I am the one who has no hairdresser of her own. I go through life with awful haircuts. You are left bearing the consequences of your at-homeness. Recently, while we are on the subject, a Russian guy bashed his hairdresser with a hammer because he disliked the haircut she'd given him. His very own, Russian hairdresser. Because a person can only allow himself to bring a hammer along to the salon when he's at home.

Allow me, therefore, to remain in ignorance of how the country in which I live is organized, who the minister of foreign affairs is and who the minister of the interior is, and don't make me feel guilty in the process. I knew all those things far too well back home, which is why I chose to be a foreigner. Don't roll your eyes if I do not know who all the local media stars are, and who that guy is who stares at me from the TV screen every time I press the button on my remote. I knew all that far too well at home, and the knowledge did me no good at all. Perhaps it is partly because of this that I chose to become a foreigner. Don't snarl at me because there are many things I do not know. I am the one who pays the bill. Don't despise me because I haven't read the work of the local literary genius, the loss is all mine. But have no fear, when push comes to shove I'll know, and I'll know what to do. When important things arise I won't fail, you can be sure. It was thanks to that reflex that I became a foreigner in the first place. My small private statistics show that if you stumble and fall, I will be the one to offer you a hand sooner than "yours," your own local people, will. Because when I needed help, it was "foreigners" who lent me a hand. Most of the "locals" were quicker to hurt than to help. Don't grumble, and don't urge me to integrate: remember, with my integration your risks grow larger.

The Italian government recently passed a law which authorizes the police to deport anyone, even a citizen of the European Union, who threatens public safety. I have a feeling that other countries within the European Union are going to introduce similar laws soon: there are too many foreigners threatening public safety. The Italians passed their law because of Romulus Nicolae Mailat, a Romanian man of Romani nationality who had robbed an unfortunate Italian woman and beaten her to death. Half a million Romanians poured into Italy after Romania became a member of the EU. Incidents of torching Romani settlements are nothing new; they date back to before Romulus Nicolae Mailat brought Italians to their feet. Italy is a country in which Russian waiters in Italian restaurants serve Chinese guests, as a Russian fellow who was visiting Italy for the first time recently observed. Public rage, however, was directed at the Romanians, who comprise no more than an eighth of all the emigrants living in Italy, and most of them are probably Roma. So everything is the fault of Romulus the Gypsy. He is the straw who broke the camel's back. As many as 5,000 requests for the express deportation of citizens of the European Union who held Romanian citizenship were filed the instant the law was passed. The Italians apparently are not concerned about the Italians who rob and rape unfortunate Italian women: they cannot deport Italians.

Who knows, perhaps the Stockholm detectors and the awkward words of the Swedish saleswoman are an introduction to a new age for united Europe.

After all, in the age that is facing us there will be more "foreigners," and hence more "locals." Perhaps the foreigners will be forced to wear magnetic gloves so that detectors can beep and alert locals to their presence. Or maybe it won't be magnetic gloves they'll wear, but subcutaneous chips in the shape of tiny yellow stars. Ah, who knows what we have in store! For the time being all of us, locals and foreigners alike, can enjoy an old-fashioned remedy: a lone poetic voice. Ivan Slamnig, a Croatian poet, inspired by a line of verse by Emily Dickinson (*I am a nobody, Who are you?*) wrote about all of this fifty years ago . . .

> *I am a foreigner! Good evening.*
> *Are you foreign, too?*
> *That makes two of us. Don't tell, because*
> *they'll chain us up, me and you.*
>
> *It's grim being a local*
> *and, boorish, like a frog,*
> *croaking all God's long night*
> *amid the steaming bog!*

What can I say to that? Foreigners of all countries unite? No, no, foreigners of all countries do not unite! Unless you want to become—locals. And you, locals, be kind to foreigners, because without them you wouldn't know that you are—locals.

Warmest regards, *beeeep*!

THE UNDERCLASS

A friend of mine, a ten-year-old, is in fourth grade. He is a child of his times. He is forever hunched over his video games. Recently he proudly showed me an interesting computer "teaching aid," an enhancement for the fourth-grade curriculum. The "teaching aid" was approved and recommended as a "genuine Croatian product" by the Croatian Ministry of Education and Sport. All in all, the entire thing is beautifully designed.

A cartoon boy appears on the screen (a boy, not a girl!). He is entering a school building . . . Each classroom door has a sign: Mathematics, English, Croatian . . .

"Which classroom should we go into?" my little friend wants to know.

"How about Geography . . ."

"Good choice! That's my favorite!"

I quickly see why. A relief map of Croatia appears on the screen and above it a little spaceship. My friend skillfully maneuvers the spaceship over the Croatian mountains, cities and valleys, it races along the Adriatic Coast, circles above the Adriatic islands . . .

"Do you know where Dubrovnik is?" asks my friend.

"No. Show me!"

He stops the space ship and immediately a cloud shows up, sporting a brief description of the history of Dubrovnik.

"There, that's Dubrovnik . . ."

The next thing to appear on the screen are photographs of the head and deputy head of Dubrovnik county and the city's mayor. Above their heads more little clouds pop up, with bios touting their accomplishments and party affiliation (hardly necessary since most of them belong to the party in power). I notice that their bios, though brief, are longer than the history of the city of Dubrovnik.

I pick up the computer mouse and now I am guiding the spaceship. Split, Rijeka, Zadar, Osijek . . . Everywhere I see the names and faces of the people at the zenith of the Croatian political elite.

"Hey, give me the mouse, this is my game," says the ten-year-old.

My friend is entranced by the game, but I am seething. I bite my tongue. It is not my job to confuse the child, to tell him that the mayor, county head, or deputy head is in fact a crook, a black marketeer, a member of the local sleaze. The ten-year-old already knows the names of all the politicians by heart because they are forever on television, in the newspapers, at sessions of parliament. Politicians are the media stars of societies in transition. In the press, my ten-year-old friend sees photographs of the villas, apartments, and factories these politicians own, their medical diagnoses and operations, their wives and children, and he can even read how the daughter or son of some politician has just graduated from Harvard University. He can hear every day how they go on about morale, patriotism, injustice, how they attack each other, how they brownnose. They're all the same. The computer game with snapshots of these politicos perched here and there on the relief map of Croatia is something utterly natural for my ten-year-old pal. And while I grumble to myself about how all this is an appalling crime, how crooks have wormed their way into everything, how they are now elbowing their way into the school curriculum, how they have fashioned themselves into historical monuments, my friend is overjoyed. He knows the name and face of every half-literate thug who overnight became a defender of the homeland, a general thick with medals, the owner of a factory, which he purchased for the price of a slightly better pair of shoes, a flourishing entrepreneur, a mayor, and an esteemed member of parliament.

Transition priests, like the crooks, are also busy raising monuments to themselves. Croatian Catholic churches are popping up like popcorn on all sides, in every backwater, in every neighborhood. The poured concrete apartment buildings put up by communists in New Zagreb neighborhoods, the buildings that guaranteed cheap housing for thousands of people, have finally found their complement: an immense concrete church. These towering concrete churches often have glass towers with an elevator gliding up and down. The transparent elevator towers—the fashion statement of new ecclesiastical architecture—should suggest to even the most unimaginative passerby a celestial connection, or, in communist lingo: the promise of a bright future. Some New Zagreb neighborhoods even have two churches. In smaller towns the church is all they've got. While Croatian hospitals have too few hospital beds, while people are dying before their time because they haven't enough funding even for the most ordinary bandages, let alone for fancy diagnostic equipment—the church is building consolation pyramids. This is the truth, as simple as it gets, even though it may sound like rhetoric targeting the church. The priests, exactly like the politicians, are everywhere: in the parliament, political forums, on television, in the media, in the schools. The front door to every hospital, and the door to every hospital room, is hung with a crucifix. My ten-year-old pal attends catechism classes. Catechism is, of course, his free choice. He has as many classes of catechism as he has of English language every week. Saturday mornings—when there is no school—he goes to church again.

"Aren't you off to soccer?" I ask.

"We have so much fun at church, everyone is there, we play games," he answers. The real answer is: *everyone is there.* For the moment, luckily, he still isn't watching the televised debates and hasn't begun proclaiming that abortion should be banned because the official spiritual leaders of the majority of Croats have said it should.

The church does some good as well. The church is the chief organizer of public kitchens, or so they say. People line up outside waiting for hot soup. Soup is the cheapest investment with the biggest bang for your buck: for two carrots, a bouillon cube, and a little hot water you get a big ideological return: religious loyalty. The church does not, of course, set aside funds for MRI equipment. They find it costs less to hang a wooden crucifix over the hospital door. Nor does it occur to them to use these sacks of cement—the ones that were left over when they finished building the church—to build a nursery school. Their responsibilities, after all, are in the spiritual realm.

Is the "landscape" I am surrounded with in the Netherlands any different? I am not sure how to answer that question, but I know that I recently visited one of the largest European markets, a bazaar (that is what it is called: *De Bazaar*) in Beverwijk, a little town about a half hour by car outside of Amsterdam. The Bazaar has been there for about twenty five years. Everything started with an underground flea market. Today it looks like a fairgrounds, neatly arranged, with roomy parking lots, and halls where literally everything is sold: computers, television sets, furniture, food, clothing . . . The most attractive section is the part that sells Middle Eastern food. The Turks, the largest émigré population in Holland, call the bazaar Little Istanbul.

The prices are low, and the already cheap Dutch chain Hema (reminiscent of the communist NaMa, the people's store) offers five items of any kind of clothing for only fifteen euros. Though the Chinese seem to have the monopoly on computer games and the Moroccans and the Turks on food, all of them buy and sell everything. The Bazaar is open every Saturday. Families go there with their kids and spend the whole day shopping, eating at the ramshackle stalls; the children play in children's play groups and fun parks. Music hums on all sides. The hundreds of different ethnic groups that live in Holland stream through the fairgrounds. And while there is a fierce debate going on in Dutch political life about integration (which seems to have become a question of life or death for the government), about loyalty to the Dutch state, identities, ethnic rights, cultural and religious differences, about ethnic tensions, about build-ing yet another mosque (this time a gigantic one in Amsterdam to ease tensions), about all the things which are meant to ease tensions but may just as easily exacerbate them to the point of war, here, at the Bazaar, there is a different law at work. While I watched people, lit by the pale March sun, nibble at fries and mayo and drift from stand to stand looking for something or other, and walk loaded down with plastic bags, it hit me that an old-fashioned concept which has been erased from every way of thinking, including the political, is the notion of class. All these people are of the same class. All of them—the white-skinned Dutch, the swarthy Moroccans, the black-skinned Surinamese, and the yellow Chinese—wear the same clothes here, each item costing no more than ten euros. They all have the same taste. They all buy the same cheap sofas, the same plastic toys for their kids, the same TV sets; they wear the same watches. They are all of them "trash," stripped of any awareness of their own position. Clever politicians and the even cleverer clergy have slipped them a toy to play with: the right to religious, national, ethnic identity. Turks feel it matters that they are Turks, the Moroccans feel the same way about being Moroccans, the Dutch about being Dutch, the Croats about being Croats, the Serbs about being Serbs . . . And all of them chew and stretch that identity of theirs like chewing gum, without seeing that what they have been given is a cheesy substitute, ignorant of the fact that they can chew it because they all belong to the same class, the *underclass*.

"So who is the mayor of Osijek?" he wants to know.

With pain I manage to spit out the name of the local crook—the mayor.

"You have aced geography!" announces the ten-year-old.

I aced my intro to the underclass, I think to myself.

A REQUIEM FOR THE
YUGOSLAV GUEST WORKER

I saw an installation at a show in New York by a Mexican artist whose name I have, unfortunately, forgotten. But I have not forgotten her show, though some twenty years have since passed. It was a powerful confrontation that stole the breath, gave that infallible pain of instant recognition. A brutal heap of things, American things, was exhibited in a glass case, the things a poor Mexican family had acquired in the course of their lives as laborers. It was a consumer profile of an anonymous Mexican family. The smoke was still rising from the "smoking ruins" before my eyes, from the dream of an anonymous Mexican for a better life. Before me, moving in its simplicity, was the realization of that dream on display: plastic, synthetic, flimsy trash tossed in a heap. It was a "Guernica" of a different kind, a different time.

The history of our lives is bound to things and stirs feelings that seem to be stronger than photographs, picture albums, video-recordings, memoirs, autobiographies, or biographies. Discarded things stand as mute proof of our absence, the ephemeral nature of our lives, the life energy invested . . . When we are gone it seems as if only the things remain. For the nameless, things take the place of monuments, before which one genuinely sheds a tear.

Yugoslav guest workers were people who, in the 1970s—along with the Turks, Italians and Greeks—set out to work as laborers in Europe. The men who came before them, before the Second World War, were called *pečalbars* or "sorrowful toilers," but the guest workers (probably called that because they most often went off to Germany as *gastarbeiters*)—were nicknamed *gastosi, gastići*.

I knew no guest workers, nor was there anyone who had ever lived abroad in my immediate community. I am using the term "abroad" here the way we thought of it at the time: Germany, France, England, or America. That was why I envied my friend Lidija who had a grandmother in America and wore the first genuine American jeans that any of us had seen. In the early sixties—before the Yugoslavs had passports and before they had started their famous pilgrimages to Trieste—jeans were a treasure. Nothing can compare to this today, not Prada shoes, nor Louis Vuitton bags, the bags Mikhail Gorbachov is advertising as I write this piece. And that is probably why Gorbachov looks like a nickel-and-diming Balkan smuggler who is hawking Vuitton knock-offs to me.

The first item of clothing I had from abroad was an American organdy dress (I have no idea why the dress was called or thought of as American!), which my mother bought for me at our small-town open market. In those days rare items—that had come in aid packages for post-war Yugoslavia, or in the packages of relatives who were living abroad—sometimes surfaced in the stalls, among the heads of cabbage and the onions. The amazing organdy dress fluttered off the counter like a rare butterfly. Perhaps my mother bought it because it was the first thing of beauty she had seen for years. That was back in the days of post-war poverty, and not only were there few "things of beauty," there was very little available at all.

Someone I knew had a father who was a "guest worker." The guest worker was from a village up in the hills near Šibenik. He got married, had a couple of kids, and moved to Zagreb, and right after that he went off to Germany. In Germany he toiled at the worst possible jobs for thirty long years. He squirreled away every Deutsch mark. In his village, on his land, he began building a house. Meanwhile, the children grew up and started families of their own. His wife left him. He kept his nose to the grindstone and spent every vacation in his village, working on the house. The house mushroomed into a three-story monster, with thick walls and little windows that looked more like rifle holes than windows. The guest worker did not rest until he had fully outfitted the house with appliances, furniture . . . And then he came back from Germany, withdrew to his village, though not to the new house he had built, but to the little shack from which he had set out into the great wide world. No one lived at the house. He was saving the house. The guest worker kept the keys to the house under his pillow and waited for the day when everyone—his wife, children, and grandchildren—would come back. If he hasn't died, he is waiting still.

Yes, the guest workers knew how to toil. Most of them knew little else. They were barely literate. They left their backwater villages and went to Germany, Sweden, France, Holland. Many of them never learned the language of the countries where they worked for years. There was never time. They spent every free moment "going back down" (from north to south!), bringing presents for everyone, arranging with masons and tile layers to lay a bathroom, a new floor, install a window, or put on a roof . . . Most of them did not invest their money "wisely," because they had no idea how. That is why they built houses in their villages, bought television sets, refrigerators, cars and—built lavish family tombs. See who has the fanciest gravestone! Most of them were guided by one thought alone, to come back one day and leave their bones in their homeland. What did they leave behind? Nothing. A culture of money spent in vain on tombs, houses (many of which were destroyed during the recent wars!), and cars, because that was all they could warm their aching egos on. They were menial laborers in foreign countries where they never belonged. They were menial laborers in the former Yugoslavia, and they were the first to come out in support of the nationalist demagogues in Croatia, Serbia, Bosnia . . . Democracy was not their problem; they had huddled with their village tribe, their village church, their village graveyard, their whole life long. Sure, there are songs that remain, the occasional joke, but these are all vanishing now. There is no record of their lives. There was the occasional movie, but it was other cultures that made the best movies about them, like Franco Brussati's fine film, *Bread and Chocolate*. They had children who despised them. Their children despised them because the parents never mastered German or Swedish properly; their kids were ashamed of them. The next generation hurried to become proper Germans or Swedes as quickly as possible.

Today in European cities I run into young Poles, Bulgarians, Romanians . . . They are not guest workers. They are enveloped in the catchy verbal packaging of EU-newspeak. They are the generation putting the slogans about the mobility and flexibility of the work force to the test, so they are a sort of gymnast of the working front. And they often live in trailers, like the guest workers of yore did, and the work force managers drive them off in vans to the fields of tulips, strawberries, asparagus, and who knows where else. Off they go, making their living. Is there any difference between them and the guest workers?

The guest workers brought consumer wonders with them. They brought us a first glimpse of wallpaper that covered the wall in a gorgeous photograph of the sea and the setting sun, of plastic lamps in the shape of a palm tree, of detergents that cleaned every stain, of splendid mixers, children's toys, technical goods, the first chewing gum, the first pineapple . . . Returning guest workers assembled a marvelous array of little delights. The mobile, flexible workers of today don't bring much, and do little to delight anyone. After all, anything they might bring is readily available in all the local shopping malls. They cannot impress anyone with new cars, because there are cars everywhere already. They cannot show off or justify their long absences with presents; they cannot bring the first blue jeans. They cannot quench the consumer thirst for novelty. All they can bring is money. Aseptic money stripped of legends about how it was earned, fairy tales about a better world in which everything functions, a legend about countries where everything is better than it is at home.

The old guest workers are dying now. One of them recently passed away in Amsterdam after spending more than thirty years in Holland. He refused to go home, to Split. He died in his little Amsterdam apartment. The doctor who visited him told me that during his last months the guest worker had completely forgotten all his Dutch. He died when the very last Dutch word he had known was gone. Before he died he cleaned his apartment from top to bottom, the doctor told me, because he left nothing behind except his body and a clean, nearly empty apartment.

A MONUMENT TO THE POLISH PLUMBER

Cultures in transition change their relationship to the past by adjusting their mindset, but even more so—by literally changing things. Such is the case in transitional Croatia, for example, where some three thousand monuments have been literally destroyed or only literally damaged, or so they say. These monuments were put up in memory of the anti-Fascist struggle of Yugoslavs during the Second World War. Today old monuments are being replaced with new ones, which are going up in memory of the anti-Yugoslav struggle of the Croatian people for their independence. In the recent war many old religious structures were destroyed, and others have been built since the war: new mosques, new Catholic and Orthodox churches. All of them follow the lead given by the maniacal Serb who lobbed shells at Dubrovnik, shouting: "Who cares! We will build a better and an older Dubrovnik!" No one remembers these words any more, and meanwhile Dubrovnik has been bought up by the very rich. There is every likelihood that Dubrovnik will be soon reborn better and— older. But that is another story.

I live in the Netherlands, in a country with the some of the littlest public monuments. They are easy to miss, some are barely ten inches tall. I am particularly fond of the fact that the Dutch put up statues to their favorite literary characters, not just to their writers. There is a new monument on Rembrandt Square in Amsterdam to Rembrandt's *Night Watch*. It is a tourist attraction, allowing tourists a proper vantage point from which to photograph the figures so they don't have to feel like Gulliver among the Lilliputians. The figures in Rembrandt's painting are given in life-size versions. But even in a country as small and densely populated as the Netherlands there are some instances when they overdo it. A magnificent mosque is under construction which, judging by the drawings displayed at the construction site, will outdo many buildings in its size.

I've often wondered why people don't raise monuments to the potato (though the Dutch did think to give each newly naturalized citizen a porcelain Delft-blue potato at the swearing-in ceremony!) but no, people—subjects as we are at heart—prefer monuments to politicians. Yet the potato nourishes us, while politicians hurt us. The stubborn human exemplar continues raising monuments to its heroes, who will turn out, ultimately, to be crooks. What can you do, the human soul is subservient, always prepared to serve, waiter-like, even when there is no tip.

The Croats—who apparently wearied of tearing down one set of statues to put up new ones furnished with new political messages— recently raised a monument to Bruce Lee. The statue was put up in 2005 in the Zrinjevac city park in Mostar. Bruce Lee symbolizes the principles of the fight for justice stripped of complex ethnic connotations. The statue was damaged by unknown vandals the second day it was up. After all why should the Chinese—who threaten to infiltrate the fragile Croatian national fabric with their cheap stores and restaurants—get their own statue?!

Having heard of the Croatian initiative, the residents of the Serbian village of Žitište, not far from Zrenjanin, decided to put up a Rocky Balboa statue. The newspaper *Politika* reported that members of the Association of Žitište Residents sent a letter to the authorities in Philadelphia, where Stallone's movies are situated and where there is already a statue to Balboa.

After the news about Mostar and Žitište, the townspeople of the Serbian city of Čačak chimed in. According to *Kurir*, a local tabloid, a number of Čačak inhabitants set in motion an initiative to commemorate Samantha Fox, a pop icon of the 1980s. The townspeople of Čačak planned to invite her to an event during Pop Days, at the same time unveiling the statue put up in her honor. "She deserved it, the woman, damn it! If they can go around putting up statues to Bruce Lee in Mostar and Rocky in Žitište, why can't we honor the authentic sex symbol of the 1980s in Čačak?" asked one of the initiators of the idea. If they should follow through on this idea, the people of Čačak plan to design the statue to Samantha based on what she looked like before she removed the silicon implants from her silicon breasts. "Why would we skimp on those God-given curves! If need be, we'll order twice the marble, just to be sure that everything is done as best as it can be, true to her figure in the 1980s when she was at her peak!" announced this anonymous man from Čačak for the *Kurir*.

I have had Poles on my mind recently, which is easy because wherever I turn, I run into them. I was recently in Cambridge, England, and in the lobby of the hotel where I was staying I happened upon a young Polish woman. It turned out she was a law student from Białystok, that she had come to England with her boyfriend, and that her boyfriend was a plumber; she occasionally worked at the hotel, cleaning, at six pounds an hour.

Polish is a language you are always hearing in the London tube. The young Poles seem to be the most loquacious users of mobile phones. Last year I happened to be in Bath. The children of the less affluent "new Russians" are studying there at the university—the School of Management, of course—while the poorer kids from Poland mostly work as—waiters.

Here in Holland there are stories going around that the Polish plumbers have taken over the Dutch plumbing market, keeping the local plumbers out of work. I have also heard stories that capable local people are raking in profits by charging the Poles three times as much rent. These are only stories, after all, because I haven't met a single Polish plumber myself. The phantom Polish plumber follows me wherever I travel in Europe. In Germany, they regularly ask me if I am Polish, which I immediately take to mean: am I the wife of a Polish plumber. All in all, the Polish plumber is the new European threat. He is the boogeyman who wends his way around Europe in overalls, with a wrench, terrifying the local working class. Because clearly there can be no life for hard-working local people while the Polish plumbers fly threateningly, Batman-like, overhead.

Inspired by the inventiveness of my former countrymen, the Croats and Serbs, I propose that a statue be raised to the Polish plumber in many European cities. Why? Because the Polish plumber is the first victim of European unification, and, particularly, of European expansion. Since everyone speaks of the Polish plumber with such fear and loathing—outstripping even the legendary hatred of the Roma—the statue should consist only of a pedestal. And on that pedestal should be the words: *Statue to the Unknown Polish Plumber.*

And while I'm on the subject, I need a plumber. If you know of one, please write me. I don't want just any plumber, I want a Polish plumber, so that I finally come face to face with the new European phantom. I know how to work with repairmen. You need to meet their every need. First a beer, nice and frosty, and then the rest . . .

MARLENE

The movie *Adam & Paul*, by the Irish director Amy Rowan, depicts a day in the lives of two Dublin good-for-nothings, alcoholics, druggies. Young people on the bottom, as if they had dropped from some Beckett play, wandering through today's Euro-Dublin in search of money, drugs, and booze. On a bench in a park where the two of them go to sit, they find a chubby dark-haired man with a small mustache. A gold tooth gleams every so often from his mouth, he has a gold chain around his neck and is wearing a peasant's cap.

"So you are a Romanian?" asks one of the bums. The guy on the bench first gets angry, and then erupts in a long and bitter tirade against the fucking Irish who think that every fucking foreigner in Ireland is a fucking Romanian.

"Well, then, what are you?"

"I am Bulgarian!" the proud Bulgarian snarls, and continues with his tirade about how Bulgaria is a marvelous country, but the Irish know nothing about it, and how Sofia is beautiful ("Is she your mother?" asked one of the Irish innocently), and how it always rains in Ireland, but the sun shines in Bulgaria . . .

"Then what are you doing here?" asks the bum.

"And you, what are you doing here?" fires back the Bulgarian.

Ireland has more Poles than Romanians and Bulgarians. During a recent stay in Ireland I heard Polish being spoken as soon as I arrived at the Dublin airport, where the employees of the airport, Poles, left the terminal building to smoke expensive cigarettes. Yes, the Poles have "occupied" Ireland. Even the Irish *Evening Herald* decided to start putting out a regular addition, *The Polish Herald*, for the two hundred thousand Poles who are currently living in Ireland. There are Lithuanians here, and Czechs, all of them have flooded the promised land of Ireland, just as the Irish during the five centuries of their émigré history inundated North America. Though they are living well now, even the carefree Irish are not standing still. Word has it that those with money are buying apartments and houses in Dubai, while those with less money are buying apartments and houses in— Bulgaria and Romania!

It seems as if the EU formula for economic fluidity and work force mobility is functioning, or at least it is that way as long everyone does what they are supposed to. In other words, as long as the young Lithuanian woman works as a waitress, and the Pole as a plumber, things are fine. Just as it is fine if every swarthy fellow with a little mustache and gold tooth is identified as a Romanian. As soon as it turns out that the fellow is in fact a Bulgarian, things get confusing. And when it turns out the fellow is actually a "Traveler"—an Irish nomad—things become as tense as the relations between the Croats and the Serbs.

Recently several thousand Poles apparently applied for jobs in the RUC, the Royal Ulster Constabulary, in Northern Ireland. The Irish Republicans immediately published a protest note, in which they welcome all migrants, regardless of race or faith, but were extremely concerned about the Poles who, as mercenaries of the RUC, would be getting entangled in a quarrel that was not theirs. The Poles, the statement reads, might find a better way to integrate into Irish society than "collaborating with the occupying forces." It was all the more complicated because the Poles are Catholics. I do not know how it turned out, and whether or not the northern Irish "mercenaries" will be bolstered by thousands of Poles, but that situation certainly stirs the EU imagination—kindred problems may arise in the future.

The notion of better ways for integrating émigrés in a society is a murky one. I do not know how it goes in Ireland, but I do know that in the Netherlands, physicians who received their training at East European universities cannot find work. Their medical schools and residencies do not count for much in Holland. If they decide to continue to work as doctors, they must go back to school. A Dutch reporter wrote a book about how he tried to find a job for his wife, a highly qualified doctor with a Russian diploma. Is Dutch medical training so superior to East European training? I assume it is not. Is it essentially different? No. Dutch doctors, aided by inflexible laws, are simply protecting their turf. I know a fellow from Belgrade with two residencies who finally found a job as—a nurse.

As to Marlene, she knew nothing of any of this. She knew nothing about Poles applying to the Northern Ireland police force, nor about the Russian doctor with no job who was married to a Dutch journalist. Marlene arrived in Amsterdam through a new age, tutti-frutti Belgian Buddhist center (how she got there I have no idea), where she got to know a fellow from Negotin. The boy had two brothers who were living in Amsterdam. Hardworking, capable fellows, they got here before the Poles, who are also hardworking, capable fellows. Marlene got to know all three brothers. She also knew their mother, who would visit the sons from time to time and stay for a month. The sons were good lads. Before going to sleep they'd read a page from the Bible, which their mother appreciated. One of the boys from Negotin spent all day painting apartments, and on Saturday and Sunday he'd dance the salsa. He even took a salsa class. He enrolled in a school for shiatsu massage. Marlene's Negotin fellow repaired bicycles. The third brother, who did nothing but smoke hashish all day, recently returned to his mother in Negotin. So Marlene learned Serbian instead of Dutch. Though I never met the young man, I have to say that he couldn't be worth even as much as her little finger. Because Marlene was tall and slender as a birch tree, with a transparent, milk-white complexion, and light blue eyes, a true northern beauty. Only her hands are large, red, and chapped, as if someone attached them to Marlene's fragile arms by some terrible mistake. Marlene works as a maid in a cheap Amsterdam hotel on the sly. Working as a maid in a cheap hotel means spending half the day with your nose buried in shit. And the boss is a nasty woman, to all of them—to Marlene, a Bulgarian woman, a Croatian woman, and a Serbian woman—she treats them all like slaves. Sometimes Marlene cleans houses as well, and in her spare time she makes cute little bags that can be worn like necklaces. Marlene looks after her family, her grandfather (she has a special fondness for her grandfather), and for her new found family. She identifies with the stories of Negotin, though she has never been to Negotin. When one of the brothers gets sick, she cooks healing chicken soup for them. Marlene also looks after her own little "Dutch" family: a turtle, a rabbit, and a cat who live with her in her tiny Amsterdam apartment. The rabbit and cat can hardly wait for her to come home, and they are happiest when she lets them sleep with her. Marlene is not entirely without dreams of her own. You can see by the gleam in her eyes that she is no ordinary young woman. Something is cooking in Marlene, though for now she has no idea where to take herself, to the left or the right . . .

One day Marlene told me . . .
  "I've decided to go upwards . . ."
  "Upwards? What do you mean, upwards, Marlene?"
  She had met some people by chance who ran a puppet street theater, and the actors needed someone to stand on stilts, and Marlene, thinking of her grandfather—who had delighted her by walking around on stilts—said, "I will!" And what do you know, she stood on stilts. At first she wobbled dangerously, of course, but now she struts around with the ease of a fish in the sea. Marlene wears a giraffe costume. Her head is in the clouds, and somewhere way down below are the nasty hotel manager jostling with her friends from Negotin; her rabbit, cat, and turtle; her family in Poland; her

mother; her grandfather . . . She uses the money she makes up on the stilts to buy everyone a little something: she gets a terrarium for the turtle, a carrot for the rabbit, a ball for the cat, a scarf for her boyfriend from Negotin, a little basket woven of matches for me . . . It isn't the money that matters, it is how Marlene feels. Up there, with her head in the clouds, with her eyes two and a half meters, maybe more, above the ground, Marlene feels like someone who has finally reached the height she deserves. Some Dutch people feel that Marlene's integration into Dutch society has been a success. The only thing they hold against her as a giraffe is that she hasn't yet learned to speak—Dutch.

GO, BUREKANA, GO!

The dynamic movement of the work force from one side of the Europe Union to the other defies the imagination. Our assumption is that the average EU resident lives where he happens to find himself and is unlikely to travel unless pressed to do so. Why should they take the trouble to take cheap flights (where the crew treats the passengers like livestock, manifesting that special sort of sadism that the poor vent on those poorer than them), when the world will come to them anyway. While one set of people stands in place, others are on the move, and the process is visible. Only the mobility of the Europe Union mafia remains invisible. Here and there I learn from the papers that some Serbian-Russian mafioso has murdered some Croatian-Albanian mafioso in a European-Japanese restaurant.

That is why the mobility of the East European sexual work force is visible, or rather the tip of the iceberg—which is afloat in deep, dark, illegal waters—is visible. I was recently in Oslo. Oslo is a small city, and the fact that there are Bulgarian prostitutes pounding the pavement around the newly opened Nobel Peace Center needn't be seen as especially symbolic. They are everywhere, around Hotel Opera right by the train station in the middle of downtown Oslo. Just as the Nobel Peace Center is. I wonder, why Oslo? As if the EU pimps had taken some sort of secret decision on the division of European territory, in such a way that the Bulgarian women of the south belonged to Oslo in the north. And while the Bulgarian women trudge through the gray, rainy streets of Oslo waiting for customers, Western European pedophiles—camouflaged as customers at cheap Bulgarian wellness centers—have been pouring into Bulgaria. They go after Bulgarians boys and girls there, yet the Bulgarian parliament is seriously considering shaking off the backward prejudices of communism and passing liberal laws on the legalization of prostitution. Meanwhile, following the Swedish example, the Norwegians have adopted a law to penalize those who use sexual services. Norwegian clients will have to count, in the future, if nothing else, on an additional financial risk.

People who are constantly killing one another—the Russians, Ukrainians, Albanians, Serbs, Turks, and who knows who else—deal in fresh female flesh. They go off to Estonia, Moldavia, Ukraine, Lithuania, Latvia, Russia, Romania, and lure girls by promise them jobs as au pairs and maids in Europe. The girls end up as sexual slaves in Hamburg, in Tel Aviv, in Albanian bordellos, in the grim Serbian enclaves, in Bosnia, in Southern Serbia, in the Arab countries, everywhere.

Trafficking is one of the most flourishing businesses in Eastern Europe; according to the most recent reports of the British Helsinki Human Rights Group, it brings the tycoons of the sex industry billions of dollars a year. A woman may be sold, resold and exploited until she dies or goes mad, or, as often happens, decides to take her own life. Suicide is better than Turkey, where women in the Turkish city of Trabzon are sold at the open market as slaves. From Bosnia to Israel the price for each women depends on the "quality of her flesh." Women are obliged to return the money spent for their transport and passport, which, of course, the pimp holds for them. Their owners starve them, beat them, and put them through "gang bangs," a test of sorts. The examination committee, five to seven of them, rape a woman collectively to prepare her for her future job. The woman works seven days a week, and she has ten to thirty customers a day, making a huge profit for her boss. In return she is given a little food and the occasional cigarette.

Arabs, who swathe their wives from head to foot, have nothing against a wild fling with East European flesh. Jews in Israel, whose faith does not allow the waste of human semen, disperse their semen into the flesh of cheaply purchased Russian women. Apparently they find Russian women the most exciting. The flashy Bollywood films (that Europeans have been crazy about recently) veil the dark Indian reality of thousands and thousands of bordellos, where women have children while they are living in the bordellos, and their children, too, become prostitutes; in turn, their children have children who become prostitutes. Rich Russian bosses, or so I've heard, have their own kind of entertainment; at their baths they use naked girls as ashtray holders. The Russian men tap their cigars into ashtrays that are balanced on the kneeling girls' backs.

Global trafficking—which has its well-traveled paths and perfect organization, where women are sexual slaves who bring in profits that far outstrip drug trafficking at a much lower risk—is one of the most horrifying realities of the contemporary world. According to official statistics about one million women fall victim to trafficking every year.

Every year a million new women are beaten, raped, stripped of their rights, turned into sexual slaves, and subjected to the most terrible humiliations. Every year men get rich on the new million women, selling their flesh to other men. The women earn nothing in the process. Their bosses treat them worse than dogs.

In this vast, appalling global tragedy there is the occasional grain of bitter joy, just as in the heartthrob American movie fairy tale, *Pretty Woman*.

They immediately dubbed him Giano Piraneze because he turned up in Rijeka with a Great Pyrenees dog from the Pyrenees. Piraneze was a small man, barely five feet tall; his whole family was like that, what can you do, his parents were barely five feet tall. Though a small man, Piraneze was nicely built, with black, shiny, curly hair, green eyes, long black eyelashes, teeth like pearls, well-muscled arms, shapely, small hands, and round fingers with perfectly groomed finger nails; in short: a man doll. He enrolled in dentistry in Rijeka, as many Italians had done; they say it is easier to earn a degree in dentistry in Croatia than it is in Italy. In Rijeka he made a whole horde of friends in an instant, and camouflaged his lack of inches with money. He paid for lunches and dinners, nights on the town and parties, and he gave expensive gifts. Burekana arrived shortly after he did. Burekana was a big, strong Albanian woman, three times bigger and broader than Piraneze. When the local fellows nicknamed the Albanian woman Burekana they had in mind her broad round bottom, which reminded them of the round aluminum pie plates the local Albanians used to bake *burek* cheese pies. Burekana had turned up in Italy as a prostitute, brought there by the Albanian mafia, and no one knew how she ended up with Piraneze, or how she got away from the mafia. She was a calm, quiet, slow girl, and she never left Piraneze's side. She was more like a bodyguard, or a Great Pyrenees mountain dog, than a girlfriend. Actually she was his body guard. She would carry him home when he got drunk, and he got drunk every day . . . And then one day they disappeared. That is, Piraneze disappeared, and Burekana went back to Italy. No one knew exactly what had happened. Rumors made the rounds, some had seen Piraneze in Barcelona, others in Madrid, yet others in Paris . . . Piraneze had, in fact, succumbed to alcoholism, which was hardly surprising considering the diminutive size of his body and the amount of alcohol he consumed. All in all, Piraneze burned out like a match. Big, calm, quiet, Burekana lived on with his parents. She looked after the little old broken-hearted couple with dedication. She looked after the Great Pyrenees dog, too, the only good memento Piraneze had left behind. His parents have no one else in the world but Burekana, so when they die they will leave her everything they own. People say they have so much money that

Burekana will be able to feed half of her Albanian countrymen for two decades with it.

And so the story ends. Go, Burekana, go!

5.

No matter how hard the frequently replaced directors tried to rid the Hercules of its hotel atmosphere, they were unable to do so. However much the office managers painted over the old signs, they peeped out from everywhere. One moment the words "Private Dining Rooms" would pop up in the sales section, then suddenly a stenciled sign "Duty Chambermaid" would be noticed on the frosted-glass door of the typistry, or gold forefingers with the word "Ladies" in French would be discovered on the wall. The hotel was making itself felt.

—*Ilf & Petrov,* The Golden Calf

THE ALIBI OF CULTURAL DIFFERENCES, OR:
HOW I GOT THE PICTURE

1.

Did you say macho-culture? You know the type: tight jeans, short jacket, usually leather (Why do the "swarthy" guys all favor leather?). Hands thrust into his pockets, he stands, rocks on his heels, mashes spit through his lower front teeth and hawks it, bullet-like, into the air. He is marking the space around himself, in a canine-like fashion. He doesn't look at you, he shoots nervous sideways glances, the same way that he spits. His gaze is dark, oiled, you can't settle on where his pupils are. Here comes another. And another. They move in packs, like village curs. Now all three, with their hands shoved into the pockets of their short, leather jackets, shoot their saliva into the wind.

2.

You see their fathers in other places, most often at the main railway stations (Why are they so fond of railway stations?), or out front, by the taxi stand (Of course, *they* most often work as taxi drivers!). One hand thrust in the pocket of a short windbreaker, the other holding a cigarette. They bounce. Bouncing, they pack down the pavement, as if the city government has paid them to. They exhale smoke into the air, suck out the oxygen. They scowl, instead of smiling they stretch their face in a grimace. When they stand or walk, their hips and bellies are angled forward. When they sit, they spread their legs and plant their behind down on the seat, as if they plan to stay sitting that way for good. What do they talk about? Mostly nothing. They rant about you. They are always railing about how cold and calculating you are. Which means, of course, that, by contrast, they are warmhearted and uncalculating. Unlike you, they have soul. You have the money and the easy life. They've got zilch. They sneer. Screw a country that is neutral, they rail. They have never been neutral. They put their lives on the line for "the cause," when they were called to and when they weren't. You, they loathe: you gave the world the wristwatch, chocolate and—cheese pocked with holes. They have only what they were born with: a sense of honor and dignity. They cannot be on your side, because you, they claim, have no feelings. They, on the other hand, have never been stingy with feelings; they have suffered too much to be stingy. They feel the pain, everything rubs them wrong. "Their lads" are at the Hague Tribunal, as if they're criminals. Always victims, they've been trampled for centuries: the Turks, Hungarians, Italians, Germans, fascists, communists, and now—this Carla del Ponte rears her head! This is how it is, happiness gives them a wide berth. Instead of calling you "the Swiss," the right way, they use their own version of the singular: a Swiss. To their minds you are—a Swiss. Instead of calling the country Switzerland, they call it Switza. *I'm heading back to Switza, I'm fresh home from Switza* . . . They have good words for you only when they are back where they come from. *No place like Switza.* They say *to their own, back there,* just as if they get the credit for making the country what it is. There's no one works harder than a *Kraut,* there's no place like *Swedeland,* no people finer than the *Dutchers.*

3.

You look at them with alarm and you wonder what they are doing here. Why do they always loiter in the same places, why don't they mingle with the crowd, why don't they disappear from your circle of vision? They stand here as if they have just landed from Mars. Why don't they go somewhere else? Each time you walk by them you automatically touch your wallet, to check if it is still there. They glance your way, indifferent, as if you are a wad of spit. You are blocking their view. And what gives them the right to grouse about you when they are living off your taxes, at your expense!? So why don't they assimilate already, why don't they get the language right so it doesn't grate the ear? Why don't they settle down already? Because of men like that you've had to replace the windshield on your car five times, because of men like that you are forced to bring the car radio into the house every evening, because of men like that you have changed the locks on the door, because of that sort you finally installed a state of the art alarm system. Yes, because of men like that you are living in your own country, as if you were in a prison, because of men like that you can't take walks any more without being afraid a bullet might come zinging out of nowhere and hit you in the head. Has it gone so far that you'll have to move out of your own country!? Where would you go!? There are people in your face like *that* in Berlin, Vienna, Frankfurt, Amsterdam, London, Paris . . . So, where can you go? To the Island of Faroe? A friend has told you—there is a Bulgarian guy living there. In the meanwhile a whole crew of them has probably settled along with him. The Bulgarians have occupied the Island of Faroe. Things have come to this.

4.

During a recent stay in Zagreb, I needed a seamstress. As these things generally go, my dentist's wife recommended one. The dentist was one of the reasons I was visiting Zagreb—as all people know who come here from Western Europe—as dental tourists. The seamstress was a young woman from one of the Croatian Zagorje villages. She travels to Zagreb every day and lives in an attic room with no heat, or even a chair for a visitor to sit on. She doesn't even have the most basic mirror. But what she does have is strong opinions. She complained to me: "A person cannot make a living with all these Chinese around. They have an easier time of getting a permit to open a small business than we Croats do. Overnight these new Chinese stores open up right in front of your nose! And they can't even speak Croatian!"

By the way, there are only a dozen Chinese people living in Croatia right now. Maybe not even a dozen.

5.

So everyone has a pet peeve. The peeves go by different names (Chinese, Albanian, Moroccan, Serb, Croat, Russian), but in essence they are one and the same. The Bulgarians stopped complaining about the Russians ages ago. Now they grouse about the Belgians, Dutch, and Germans who buy summer homes in the mountains, villages, and along the Black Sea shore for a pittance—in anticipation of Bulgaria entering the European Union, when they'll clean up on their investment. The Hungarians, by the same token, seethe at the Croats, Serbs, and Bosnians, who found the time during the recent war to snap up apartments in Budapest and make a ten-fold profit. The Croats, who got rid of the loathsome Serbs, are now badmouthing the Hungarians, Russians, and Czechs who, they say, are buying up half the Adriatic Coast. They have nothing against the German and Austrian buyers. The Croats feel more European with them around. The Germans are crazy about old wooden houses in Sweden, and as the result of their mania they spend their summers in what used to be Swedish villages, surrounded by—other Germans. The Dutch are fleeing Holland to escape the Moroccans and are seeking a haven in Portugal. There they end up in Dutch ghettoes. The Turks are everywhere in Europe, there's nothing more to be done about that, but in the meanwhile Istanbul has been populated by Russians. Rumor has it that there are already some hundred thousand of them. Apparently there is an even larger number of newly arrived Chinese in Budapest. Budapest is definitely the Chinese epicenter. Odessa, they say, is filling with both Greeks and Turks in some weird way. The Spanish complain about the Colombians: they will corner you in broad daylight and force you to clear out your savings at a cash machine. Speaking of the Colombians, they might do well to look to the Romanians who come in busloads to Spain and work diligently as, well, "construction workers." And speaking of Romania, the Moldavians are the movers and shakers at the moment in Spain, or rather one Moldavian, a serial killer, who has found he has nothing better to do than decapitate the Spanish. And so it is that everyone is pushing and shoving to get somewhere and they are all railing about one another. They migrate in search of real estate, comfort in retirement, a risk-free adventure, a risky change; they are on the move to eke a living. Europe has, evidently, embraced its multiculturalism, but the feeling of joy seems to be lacking. And what do you know, culture has suddenly become a European word of major significance. Culture is a catch-all and nothing, a field for manipulation. Culture is an excuse and an alibi. *It's a question of their culture . . . This is something inherent to our culture . . . Ah, they are so different than we are, these differences are irreconcilable . . .*

6.

As you scowl at the Serbs, Croats, and Bosnians who make your lives a misery, you think: it's probably the machismo of *their* culture that is to be blamed. What should we do with them? What should I do with the Moroccan guy who hawks spit into the wind at the entrance to my apartment building in Amsterdam? Nothing. Nothing?! Yes, nothing. As long as we are trying to find justification in *culture* and *cultural differences*, in *otherness*, in the *divergence* between *their* macho-culture (which permits all of this) and *mine* (which understands none of it), I will be coming up with an alibi not only for *their* spitting, but also for *my* irritation with them. Politically correct respect for different cultures and cultural differences is often a mask for chauvinism. And that is why, if the sole argument we use is *culture* and *cultural differences*, we will very quickly be shooting ourselves in the foot.

7.

Did you say macho-culture? As a former Yugoslav woman I was given the right to vote, and the right to equality between the sexes, in 1943, six years before my birth, during the Second World War, with an uncertain document that promised not only victory against the fascists but also a future for Yugoslavia. I was enfranchised 27 years before the women of Switzerland first voted. I believe my rights were ensured by the anti-fascist women, Partisan women, and communist women who participated on an equal footing with men in the Second World War. They organized literacy classes for the local population during the war, worked in Partisan hospitals as doctors and nurses, or fought as combatants. After the war they were a part of the public and political life of post-war Yugoslavia, but later, sadly, they were absorbed into a male-dominated world and disappeared from sight. It does seem that there were more women in the political and public life of Yugoslavia than there were in many West European countries. I went to a co-ed elementary school, a school for boys and girls. There were no other kinds of schools. My childhood women heroes were Marie Curie, Minou Drouet, and Valentina Tereshkova. I enrolled at the University, with no way of knowing that American women had been allowed to attend prestigious Yale University for the first time only one year earlier. My tuition was free. I got a job, and had an edge over the women of Switzerland, who at that time were receiving a salary 25% to 30% less than that of their male counterparts. I had an edge over Italian women, French women, Dutch women. In the 1970s, my colleagues with feminist leanings—when they were inspired by American feminism but did not have the courage to draw on domestic sources—launched a media attack and found themselves between a rock and a hard place. They couldn't fight for the legalization of abortion because abortion was legal. Nor could they protest discrimination in schooling and employment, because the system guaranteed equality. So they resorted to a preoccupation with a woman's identity, sexuality, sexism, and sexist representation of the female genre in the media, the woman's body, and its language. One of the hot topics was the limited selection of women's tampons on the shelves of (communist) Yugoslav shops.

With the break-up of Yugoslavia, with the war and the *coming of democracy to power*, the participation of women in the local post-

Yugoslav parliament dropped to 1.5%, only to rise again a year or two later. Today all post-Yugoslav women, from Slovenia to Macedonia, have available a vast and varied array of tampons and sanitary napkins in the stores, and any number of crucifixes dangling around their necks, both Catholic and Orthodox. In Croatia, the numbers of women wearing fur coats has skyrocketed, and in Bosnia—it's the burka. "Repressive" Yugoslav communism tolerated none of that, or at least not in these proportions. Today many more women attend church services regularly and watch "democratic" television programs in which the ever present religious clergymen—Catholic, Orthodox and Muslim—are heatedly calling for a ban on abortion, while other public thinkers are propounding the legalization of prostitution. Trafficking, the local mafia, prostitution, pornography, embezzlement, felonies, tycoonization, financial double-dealing, the quiet erosion of the rights of workers and labor unions, cutbacks in welfare and health coverage, a corrupt judiciary and widespread graft, catechism in public schools—which, though it is not, admittedly, a required subject, has proven to be more pervasive than math or English—all these things have been a part of the new democratic commonplace. Mass culture has imposed its icons. They are no longer Marie Curie or Valentina Tereshkova (today no one knows who they were), but Britney Spears and her countless local clones. As far as a feminist culture is concerned, it has two faces: the less spectacular, invisible version (NGO activism) and the more visible version, with its spectacular presence in mass culture, such as in the TV series *Sex and the City* or in the enthusiasm of Eve Ensler's followers (author of *The Vagina Monologues*), who have discovered her liberating formula: *I am my vagina*. A young Romanian woman who teaches French at a prestigious university in the United States said to me: "Elena Ceauşescu was my childhood idol. Not because she was a communist but because she was a scholar. It goes without saying that Elena the scholar was a communist fabrication, but I prefer to have grown up in the belief that I would be a scholar some day than a self-aware vagina."

8.

As I watch the young Moroccan man, who smashes the windshield on a car in front of my building in Amsterdam in broad daylight and steals a purse that was on the back seat (while you in Zurich complain about Serbs, Croats, or Bosnians who, I assume, are doing the same thing), I know that there is no point in calling the police because they will be deaf to my appeal. A protest rises in me. I think about how this world is constructed. I catch myself with only one wish: to go up and slap the kid in the face. As far as macho-culture is concerned, my only comfort is a photograph I possess and a little story about *how I got the picture* . . .

A few years ago I was invited to an important two-day meeting of European ministers of culture. Among the participants were all the ministers of culture of the European Union countries, the organizers, and a handful of intellectuals who were invited to contribute their thoughts on the problems facing European culture and culture in Europe to the ministers. I was one of the intellectuals. A big envelope arrived several months later in the mail. In it was a large-format photograph, which the organizers of the meeting had sent me as a souvenir of the important event. All the participants of the meeting were in the picture, standing on the steps of the luxury hotel where we had stayed. I suddenly spotted something I had failed to notice at the time. There were only three women in the group of some forty participants. These were the ministress of culture of Sweden, the ministress of culture of Luxembourg, and me. There you have my little story of how *I got the picture*!

9.

There he is again; he is back. He tucks his hands into his pockets, rocks back and forth, mashes the saliva through his front lower teeth, and hawks it out into the wind like a bullet. And you wonder what that Serb, Croat, Bosnian, Albanian, Turk, Moroccan (who knows where they are from, it doesn't matter, aren't *all of them* the same?) machismo and some meeting on European culture have in common?

At first glance, not a thing. But perhaps the ordinary photograph and doing the "math" are precisely the point at which one can start every conversation on cultures, cultural differences, differences, about one another, about the otherness, in Europe. Perhaps this conversation should start with the system of this world of ours, with those who rule, with the churches and states, with the armies and police; with those who rear us, with the schools, textbooks and curricula; with those who are "shaping" our conscious and subconscious world, with television and the media, with the market and market ideology. Only then will we be able, perhaps, to come up with an answer to the question of why that "swarthy" man, yours and mine, is standing there spitting into the wind. An answer to why he irritates us so much. An answer to why we notice some things only later, when they find their way to us as a souvenir, like the large-format photograph for example, which arrived at my address.

Local Footnote

The most influential and probably the bestselling Croatian weekly, *Globus*, ran a reader's selection in its New Year's issue of the ten most deserving Croatian men and women in 2004. Among the ten *magnificent Croatian women* was S., a local pop singer, known for her butterfly-shaped, silicon smile, her Arcadian commercials for cheese and milk, her declarations that she is a Croatian woman who is a *nun in spirit*, the Catholic crosses that sway between her generous breasts, and the fact that she gives concerts in support of a different party at every election. S. recently made a home porn video with herself in the leading role, a video souvenir, a *little memento of a lovely moment in her life* because of which S. was proclaimed not only *beautiful* but also a *very courageous woman*. M. N., the top editor of Croatian state television, known as a passionate supporter of the nationalist party in government, a former passionate follower of Tuđman's regime, declared her *magnificent* because of her (nationalistic) *unwillingness to compromise*. Among the ten *most magnificent* was a TV star of the soap opera *Villa Maria*. It should also be said that the among the *most magnificent* Croatian men was the winner of Croatian *Big Brother*, who is the proprietor of a tattoo shop.

Why bring up the New Year's issue of a local weekly? Merely because of the example of the way the media shape social concepts, among them notions of gender? Indeed, because of that, but there is another reason. That same paper, *Globus*, published one of the most disgraceful and ferocious media harangues—about five women who, in 1992, had written against the frenzy of nationalism before most people had started thinking about nationalism. *Globus* announced that these women were *Croatian witches*, thereby declaring open season for a media hunt on "enemies of the state." I remember the event because I, myself, was one of the publicly discredited five women. As a result of the nationalist media harangue, one of the *witches* moved to Paris, where she is working as a university professor, another is living in Amsterdam as a freelance writer, the third divides her time between Stockholm and Istria, and the fourth lives in Zagreb as a feminist NGO activist. *Globus*'s media "court martial" has been forgotten today. The main author of the *Globus* harangue against the five *witches* is one of the most powerful names in the Croatian media. He recently ran for president of Croatia for the second time, with significant success.

What about the fifth *witch*? Didn't I say there were five? As the story goes, the fifth was offered, as if she were a football player, an enviable sum of money to transfer from a smaller paper to *Globus*—the very same *Globus* that had made her and the four other women a public target. Today she is the leading *Globus* columnist. Her transfer is an unusually powerful message that one woman is sending to other women. And men. As they get the message—everybody gets the picture!

December 2004

THE SOUVENIRS OF COMMUNISM

1.

A year or so after the Wall came down, I paid a brief visit to Moscow. The first thing I noticed was that the taxi cab drivers in Moscow, always masters of small talk, were repeating themselves.

"Where are you from?" a driver would ask.

"From Yugoslavia."

"Has communism bit the dust there?"

"It's still holding on . . ."

"Well, here it is dead and gone!" the driver would boast.

While the drivers of taxis tried to convince me that communism had bitten the dust, in the Hotel Belgrad cafeteria I waited patiently in a long "communist" line for my first morning coffee. Some guy spoke up behind me, hoarsely . . .

"Devushka, let me buy you an eklerchich . . ."

"A what?" I asked.

"A mini-ekler for you, a mini-cognac for me . . ."

The man waiting in line had kindly offered to buy me a Soviet version of the eclair, a sad little pastry, a product of the communist conveyer belt. The display case, of course, had nothing else to offer. Touched by the sight of the squished little pastry behind the glass, nostalgic in advance for the vanishing of the landscapes of everyday communist life long before they actually disappeared, and softened by the use of the Russian diminutive, I agreed to share the table with the stranger. I sipped at my weak coffee. The man nursed his 250 grams.

"Devushka, who are you, anyway?" asked the fellow.

"Me? A . . . writer."

"Will you look at that? I have run into all kinds of babes in my life, whores and drunks, but I've never met a woman writer!"

"And you, who are you?"

"Me!? I am an lush," the fellow said courteously.

The alcoholic told me how he had sworn many years ago that he would live until he'd seen communism dead.

"Only then will I be able to go peacefully to my grave . . ."

"Well? Isn't it dead, now?" I said rudely.

"I'll be sticking around another year or so . . . Just to make sure . . ." said the self-ordained forensics expert.

2.

The threat of communism no longer hovers over Europe. No one, however, can say precisely when it was that communism gave up the ghost: some claim one thing, others something else. Some claim they personally dealt it its final blows (it is usually former party members who say that), while others say that it collapsed in on itself. The third group, the skeptics, still have their doubts and are seeking the dead heart of communism, so that they can pierce it, just in case, with a hawthorn stake.

It took awhile for the communist corpse to be moved from the formaldehyde basin to the academic autopsy hall. Today universities are embarking on anticipational (and, we hope, emancipational) post-communist studies, post-socialist studies, and the study of comparative communism—all in places that experienced nothing of communism. An American Slavic department advertises its intellectual services on the web with the cheery communist-sounding slogan: *Uchites' post-komunizmu!* (Learn the Ways of Post-Communism!). As far as anthropological, sociological, historical, and political research into the subject is concerned, it's not as if there hadn't been any before. Indeed, to the contrary. But as the subject itself—a massive ideological system with its supporters and its opponents—was read for years either from the position of the supporters or the opponents, even those who researched communism couldn't be, nor were they, held to a scientifically scrupulous standard. In that sense, in terms of research, even the Bushmen fared better.

As far as the citizens of former communist countries go, they have failed. While communism was alive and well, its inhabitants were a witty people. As soon as communism breathed its last, and bananas, previously a rare commodity, appeared in the shops, humor suddenly became the rare commodity. Today in Moscow, Bucharest, and Prague they can buy Prada shoes, but the jokes—gone.

As long as Lenin was lounging, dead, in the mausoleum, everyday Soviet life bristled with jokes at his expense.[1] When communism drew its icons, including Lenin, with it into the tomb, the tiresome, belabored debates began: what to do with the mausoleum? Should Lenin be left there or buried elsewhere? There was no one who dared propose that a Kentucky Fried Chicken be opened inside the Lenin mausoleum once it had finally become a possibility.

3.

The culture of the Russian Avant-garde which marked the twentieth century—Bulgakov, Babel, Pilnyak, Olesha, Zoshchenko, Platonov, and many, many more—wrote exciting, powerful, dark, and witty literary texts about the fantastic everyday life of communism. The novel *The Golden Calf* by Ilf & Petrov is one of the most comic and politically subversive novels written under communism. Smooth operator

---

1. I remember an amusing alternative project from the communist period designed to avoid those kilometre-long lines at the entrance to Lenin's tomb on Red Square. The idea was to re-make the mausoleum as a cuckoo clock. Lenin would pop out of the tomb every hour on the hour so that interested visitors could see him without the wait.

Ostap Bender—whose sole goal in life was to become a millionaire and move to Rio de Janeiro—is one of the great classic heroes, standing shoulder to shoulder with Cervantes' *Don Quixote* or Hašek's *Švejk*. The novel appeared in 1927, shortly before the Kharkov conference and the imposition of socialist realism, and nothing finer has been written in that genre to this day. Hungary, Czechoslovakia, and Poland all spawned top political thinkers, writers, and film and theatre directors, and created great artistically interesting and subversive culture during the time of communist rule.

Russian soc-art—a neo-avant-garde artistic movement which subverted the culture of the Socialist regime with an unusual anticipatory nostalgia—penetrated to the heart of Soviet communist everyday life and interpreted its language and symbols, ending its "commemorative" work before the death of communism. Artists such as Ilya Kabakov, Komar & Melamid, and many others moved to the West only when their artistic "mission" was done. The cult figure of Russian *samizdat*, Yuz Aleshkovsky, who made the Soviet reading public laugh with his absurdist literary texts, emigrated, and, though his books have been translated, he has not been a success in the West. Western readers did not have the feel for communist everyday life, the author's humor was not understood, the linguistic subversion left readers cold, and the absurd and grotesque aspects of the totalitarian world remained opaque to them.

That is why those writers who came after the demise of communism—the people selling damaged goods and seconds, the "translators" (those, who "translated" the complex everyday life of communism into a simpler language within the grasp of the Western reader), the writers of confessions of personal suffering during communism, the producers of cheap communist "souvenirs," all those who told of everyday communist life second-hand—enjoyed success on the Western European and American markets. The market was flooded after the Wall came down, when the Cold War was over, with works that repeated the repertoire of Cold War themes and its narrative strategies. The authors of these works revisited Eastern European toilets that had no toilet paper; rude waiters; humiliating lines; bad dental hygiene; repression of sexual, gender, religious, and ethnic identity; people who ate dog food instead of steak; unsightly architecture; ridiculous communist statues; the fat, drunk, and incompatible people; and the supermarkets in which there was nothing on the shelves but tea and cheap canned fish. The literature of the post-communist showdown with communism was just as clichéd in its ideological strategies and artistic achievements as the literature of Stalinism had been. And for that very reason, all the more penetrating. The authors of these works managed to find the pressure points in the imagination of the Western reader. It turned out that the pressure points are not the inconceivable absurdities of communism, but simple, understandable things: poor dental hygiene and empty shops.

The second switch that flicked on Western fantasies and found pressure points was the opening of the borders and the moment when the European Easties poured into the West. There were nightmarish "urban myths" about the Russian and Ukrainian mafias; about Russians who sent their children to schools in Switzerland and bought diamonds like popcorn; about a "tsunami" of Russians flooding the Côte d'Azure; Russians who bought luxurious villas in the finest places in Europe and the United States; Eastern Europeans strolling around New York, Berlin, London; about the "new Russians," a post-communist mafia; about the former communist Gotham City, Moscow, which no longer swims in tears but in cash. These stories have set in motion a complex morass of feelings: from open anti-communism to a hidden chauvinism, from an insulted Western ego to the collapse of a Western self-confidence that has been sustained for years by the notion that Westerners deserve to live far better than the commies beyond the Wall. The instantaneous post-communist mastery of the rules of capitalism—and the Russians have shown genuine talent— was the greatest blow for the typical Western European citizen.

Perhaps this is the reason for the absence of sympathy for the post-communist Romanian panhandlers playing the "Gypsy" accordion in European cities, for the Bulgarians who scrub European toilets, and for the former Moldavian and Ukrainian teachers, who are now working as prostitutes on the streets of West European cities.

4.

Soon after its demise, communism moved onto the stands of cheap souvenir vendors: they were the first to sniff out the profitability of nostalgia for the material relics of a culture which had vanished. After the fall of the Berlin wall, petty merchants in Berlin dealt in Soviet rabbit-fur hats, hats with ear-flaps called *ushankas*, old communist medals, military uniforms and chips of the Berlin Wall. A park of communist statuary was opened in Budapest, which looked as if it had been designed according to plans drawn up by some anti-communist from the McCarthy era. A visitor to the park has the impression that the museum was opened only to eradicate in every tourist the idea that there was anything to communism besides unsightly monumental statues. The only souvenir one can buy at the museum is an expensive empty can, in which crouches the spirit of communism. And the only living detail I saw when I visited the museum was a Hungarian radio from the 1950s, situated in the booth where the ticket seller sat, which was playing the Internationale, the communist hymn, in Hungarian.[2]

Out of all this—from the post-communist damaged goods and instant literature (which only reinforced the stereotypes about communism that had been set for years), and the souvenir trash—came

---

2. Before I visited the Museum of communist Sculpture I visited a large exhibit of the anti-communist dissident movement, mostly Hungarian, Czechoslovak, and Polish, in Budapest. It was as if things were being brought into balance despite the good intentions of the authors of both the museum and the exhibition. The exhibition was every bit as boring and unimaginative as the museum of soc-realist sculpture.

nothing but boredom. If by some chance America had been a communist country, American mass media souvenirs would have flooded the global market. The American comic book character Superman is your typical "communist," positive hero: a replica of Prometheus, a communist icon, a superman who does good and brings people the light. There are striking similarities between the two opposing systems: an obsession with the sky and flight, a powerful scientific imagination, a focus on the future, the desire to control the world, and maniacal, mega-repair projects. It turns out that communism fell into the hands of a part of the world that did not have a healthy market imagination, in a word: to people who didn't deserve it.

All that seems that way at the first, silly and frivolous glance. Each former communist country—Russia, Poland, the Czech Republic, Romania, Bulgaria, Hungary—relates to its recent past in its own way, using a variety of strategies: from oral history and archiving the statements of ordinary people about life during the communist era, to political, sociological, historical, and anthropological research; from Ostalgia (a post-Wall German word meaning a nostalgia for the everyday life of communism) and its many faces; musealization, archiving and collecting communist material culture; artistic—literary, visual, cinematic—research into the relations to communism; historical revision, the politics and ethics of remembering and forgetting; and even the small industry of souvenirs.

5.

What gives with the Yugoslavs and their communism?

The state of Yugoslavia was born not of a revolution, as a communist project, but during World War II, as an anti-fascist project. During World War II, the Partisans, with Tito at their head, unsure of the real outcome of the war, laid the foundations for the future Yugoslavia in 1943. When they emerged from the war as victors, Tito and the Partisans constituted the new communist state of Yugoslavia. With the Cominform resolution of 1948 the Yugoslav communists were accused of "diverging from the path of Marxism and Leninism" and an "anti-Soviet political orientation," and—after only three years—Yugoslavia was definitively thrust from the communist fraternity.

In Emir Kusturica's movie *When Father Was Away on Business*, there is a detail that foreign viewers often miss the significance of, and which will remain a riddle for many kids who have grown up in the new post-Yugoslav states, and have been raised on the new, revised history textbooks. The father, who is leafing through a newspaper while traveling on a train, happens upon a caricature of Stalin; he comments to his mistress, who is traveling with him, on the lack of taste and the insulting tone of the caricature. After that (because she denounces him to the secret police) he is taken away on "business." During that brief period, Yugoslavia was a country on a McCarthy-like hunt for (Stalinist-leaning) communist witches, using Stalinist re-education methods.

In this detail lies the paradox of Yugoslav communism. The Yugoslavs had many things that tied them to the people of other communist countries: the communist iconography, the aesthetics of totalitarian kitsch, parades, the Pioneer membership for children, massive celebrations (of Tito's birthday), and massive monuments. They had some things that the people of other communist countries could only dream of: open borders, a passport that allowed them to travel, self-management, American movies, a much better living standard, and a more liberal media. The Yugoslavs had "dissident personalities"—such as Milovan Djilas, for instance—yet they never developed the culture of defiance to communism, nor did Yugoslavs have a significant intellectual underground the way the Russians, Czechs, Poles, and Hungarians did.

The issue that was painful for Yugoslavia clearly wasn't communism but nationalism. Communism and its downfall served the Yugoslavs as a convenient interpretation, palatable to foreign interpreters and politicians, therefore as a "legal" alibi for war. The collapse of Yugoslavia (though it is difficult to pinpoint which came first, the chicken or the egg) was a prime moment for picking up where World War II had left off, this time with a different outcome. In that sense, the Ustashas and the Chetniks were the victors, where before they had been the losers. And the Partisans, fifty years later, finally lost the war.

From 1990 to 2000 in Croatia, three thousand anti-fascist monuments were ransacked. The monument in Jasenovac—dedicated to one of the most infamous Ustasha camps, where thousands Jews, Serbs, Romas, and Croats were killed during the Nazi-run Independent State of Croatia—was neglected and devastated. The names of streets, schools, and institutions—everything that had been called something even remotely anti-fascist—were changed. Following instructions from the Croatian Ministry for Education and Culture, librarians cleared the library shelves of all anti-fascist, communist, Serbian, and other books. Some books were even burned. The photograph of Biserka Legradić, the woman who dropped her drawers and urinated on a Partisan grave, was published in all the papers. The woman had decided to celebrate the final victory over anti-fascism in her own way. On December 27, 2004, Tito's statue in Kumrovec—a famous piece by the sculptor Augustinčić, which shows Tito in his Partisan uniform—was blown up. The blast blew off the statue's head. Two days later, the head of a Partisan fighter, a fragment from a sculpture which had been knocked down several years earlier, was stolen from the club of Partisan veterans in Dubrovnik. At the same time in Zadar, a parade of latter-day Ustasha sympathisers marched through town dressed in fascist uniforms, bearing photographs of Ante Pavelić and Ante Gotovina, a commander of the recent homeland war who was indicted by the Hague tribunal for war crimes. At the same time, a mass was held in Zagreb for Ustasha leader Ante Pavelić, and one in Zadar was held for Jura Francetić, head of the infamous Ustasha Black League.

At roughly the same time, the Serbian Assembly took a decision to allot the Partisans and the Chetniks equal treatment. Following this decision some Chetniks who are still alive were granted the right to a veteran's pension.

The real war for re-tailoring history, with the help of Slobodan Milošević on the Serbian side, was the one orchestrated by Tito's former general and Partisan, Franjo Tuđman. In order to provide Croatian statehood with the legitimacy of historical continuity, Tuđman skipped over the fifty years of "Yugoslavdom" and grafted the new Croatia directly to the Independent State of Croatia, the fascist state of the 1940s. As he went to work to realize his program of re-tailoring history, there were no better helpers than the "Ustashas" on the Croatian side, and the "Chetniks" among the Serbs, who conveniently furnished him with the alibi he needed. Once he'd released the "Ustashas" from the bottle, some of whom had survived World War II, others who were newly minted, Tuđman had to release their ideology with them: clericofascism, anti-semitism, the ideology and practice of ethnic cleansing, and then—because of his own schizophrenic dual personality and his latter-day conversion from communist to nationalist—he had to add anti-communism to the mix, since this was all going on within the larger context of the general enthusiasm over the fall of communism in the other Eastern European countries.

As far as communist mementos in Croatia are concerned, there aren't any. The only ones I noticed during my visit in December of 2004 were echoes. The word "Tito"—which used to be written in large letters on the faces of bare hilltops so that it could be seen from airplanes flying overhead—had been replaced by the name "Tuđman." On the lawn by the National Library—from where you have the best views of Zagreb—the name "Tuđman" was "engraved" on the dried grass in large letters. The Tito relay baton—birthday greetings for Tito's birthday that were passed hand to hand in phallic containers through all of Yugoslavia to Belgrade and into Tito's hands—was replaced by a less spectacular sacred flame, which the faithful passed hand to hand from the cathedral in Vienna to the Zagreb cathedral for Christmas in 2004. I also visited Mirogoj, the Zagreb cemetery. At the entrance to the cemetery, on land that the Croatian Catholic church had ceded, there is an astonishing black marble monumental tomb for Tuđman. It far outstrips Tito's grave at the "House of Flowers" in its monumentality. On the stone over the tomb, carved in gold, are the the words "Franjo Tuđman, first Croatian president."

The death of communist souvenirs, particularly in Croatia, suggests that perhaps there never was communism in Croatia. No one uses the word "communism" in the Croatian media any more. They call it "totalitarianism." Fascism is still called "fascism," and is often paired with "totalitarianism," suggesting to the uninformed observer that fascism was distinct from totalitarianism. "Fascist souvenirs" in the Croatian ideological marketplace suggest that there was fascism in Croatia, but also that there was anti-fascism, the proponents of which were, unfortunately, the Partisans, Tito, and the communists. With the freeing of the Croatian state from "Yugo-communist repression," the Croatian ideological marketplace became a free-for-all in the struggle for supremacy. Croatia, like other post-Commmunist states which emerged from the once shared Yugoslavia, had a serious problem with its ideological alloy. The catastrophic fall of communist shares on the world market of political ideologies forced Croatia into total denial of its communist past. The communist past was erased in a flash, communist statues were smashed, and new history textbooks—that described the time of "totalitarian darkness" and the subsequent period of light, which was secured by the "heroes" of the homeland war against Serbian aggression—were printed. On the other hand, the signals from Brussels were coming across that if Croatia was to enter into negotiations for joining the EU some day, it must shake off its warm and fuzzy feelings about its fascist past.[3] At this moment, Croatian politicians are faced with a thorny dilemma. The dilemma lies in this ideological alloy, a fusion that can no longer be teased apart. The Croatian communists were anti-fascists and the Croatian anti-fascists were communists. And, worse yet, they were—Yugoslavs.

6.

With the death of communism came the collapse of the "social imagination," which was celebrated as "the entry into the mature, post-ideological age." There is no one who is seriously considering possible alternatives to capitalism. We live in a "post-historical," "conflict-free" time, or a "time of apathy." "It is effectively as if, since the horizon of social imagination no longer allows us to entertain the idea of an eventual demise of capitalism—since, as we might put it, everybody silently accepts that *capitalism is here to stay*—critical energy has found a substitute outlet in fighting for cultural differences which leave the basic homogeneity of the capitalist world-system intact. The price paid for this depoliticization of economy is that the domain of politics itself is in a way depoliticized. Political struggle proper is transformed into the cultural struggle for the recognition of marginal identities and the tolerance of differences."[4]

After the first thrill when the Wall came down, I assume that many of the people living in the former communist countries felt a tinge of disappointment. The post-Soviets felt it, especially the Russians. Their stigma was worst: they had implanted communism. Stalin had

---

3. The same problem of the official attitude toward the past, fascist and communist, exists in all the post-communist countries. The communist past and its symbols have been deleted. The only country left that continues to use the symbol of the hammer and sickle, the symbols of workers and peasants—is Hitler's native land, Austria, which has had a hammer and sickle as part of its coat of arms for several hundred years.
4. Slavoj Žižek, *An Introduction to the 150th Anniversary edition of the Communist Manifesto*. Zagreb: Arkzin 1998.

been their monster; they were the ones who tormented the Poles, Hungarians, and Czechs for many years, and also their own Uzbeks, Lithuanians, Estonians . . . They went through the real nightmare of the Stalinist camps; through World War II where they left some twenty-seven million dead on the battlefields, which no one ever takes into account—in many West European textbooks the Russian role in anti-fascism isn't even mentioned; through a post-war everyday life that was only barely liveable; through a post-Stalinism that meant some relief, but also a vast emigration; and through the traumatic collapse of the Soviet Union, which brought with it new victims. And at the end of this nightmare tunnel they were greeted by the prize that was supposed to compensate them for all their anguish: a spacious supermarket in which they could purchase cans of Thai tuna, German yogurt, Dutch herring, and American bubble gum. They were greeted by the knowledge that they could buy all these things, yet had no money. They were greeted by a host of paradoxes that they will not be able to tell anyone about, because there is no one left who cares to listen. Besides, they figured out that a stigma, once ascertained, functions as if it were a rumor. It is far easier to set a rumor in motion than it is to prove that the rumor is wrong. The truth, later ascertained, rarely holds anyone's interest.

I assume that this same tinge of disappointment was felt by those who had had nothing to do with communism, yet the communist world was the measure by which they gauged the levels of their own happiness. With communism vanished the screen onto which they could project their darkest fantasies. The sadist suddenly lost his favorite victim.

The death of communism has also brought disappointment for those who suddenly felt they had woken up in a world from which Utopia had been banished. The most popular English sitcom of all times, *Only Fools and Horses*, ends with an unexpected twist. The Trotters, Del Boy, Rodney, and Granddad, comic anti-heroes, representatives

of the social dregs of English society, who had been amusing viewers for years with their unsuccessful money-making capers, actually
become millionaires at the end.[5] And this is not due to their hard
work—which would have suggested the ideology of capitalism—but
to pure chance. The wealth delights them at first, but cheery, ener-
getic Del Boy quickly sinks into apathy. He creeps out of his new
villa one night and goes off to his old place. There is the anticipated
encounter in the small, poor apartment. Moved by nostalgia for their
former life, Rodney and Granddad had also come back. All three of
them admit that their life lost its flavor when they thought about how
exciting it had been before, back when they were longing to become
millionaires. Del Boy perks up and suggests the only way out:

"Hey, let's become billionaires!"

And that is what all of us are left with in the end: an eternity of the
implacable logic of capital.

January 2005

———
5. Ostap Bender becomes a millionaire much as the Trotters did on television,
except that this happened several decades earlier, and in a much more entertaining environment.
   "'So now I'm a millionaire!' Ostap exclaimed in pleasant surprise. 'An
idiot's dream come true!'
   Ostap suddenly felt depressed. He was struck by his humdrum surroundings; he felt it wrong that the world hadn't changed that second, and that
nothing, absolutely nothing, had taken place. (. . .) He felt bored, like Roald
Amundsen, who, when passing over the Pole in his airship *Norge* after a lifetime of endeavor, said to his companions without any enthusiasm, 'Well here
we are!' Underneath was broken ice, crevices, cold, and emptiness. The secret
was discovered, the goal achieved, and there was nothing left to do except
change professions."

A POSTCARD FROM MY VACATION

1.

I required the services of a doctor once while I was visiting the United States. The doctor's eyes lit up when she heard I was from Europe.

"From Europe? I know Europe well! Where did you live?"

"In the former Yugoslavia . . ."

"You don't say," she sighed.

The physician and her husband, it turns out, were American Jews with roots in Eastern Europe, and spent their summer vacations traipsing along the byways of the Holocaust. While "normal people" went to Spain or Greece, they went "camping" at Auschwitz, Treblinka, Buchenwald . . .

"Sometimes I think we're nuts! I live with this man who is obsessed with remembering the pain of his predecessors; my children were conceived in thoughts of the Holocaust! Every summer I go on a pilgrimage to Holocaust sites . . . Whatever possessed me to marry such a kook!" she said, although the expression in her eyes was that of a happily married woman.

2.

It is auspicious that the tribe of Croats broke through once, long ago, to the sea and have remained there. Thanks to this, the Croats today have their Adriatic Sea, just as the Swedes have their Ikea, the Dutch their Shell, or the Germans their BMW. People are flocking to the Adriatic these days. The real estate market is charging full steam ahead; real estate agencies have quaint names like "Rock of Joy."

In their search for "the Mediterranean as it once was" many have strolled through Croatia this year: the stunning Jordanian queen Ranis, the princess of Monaco, Sharon Stone, John Malkovich, and the indispensable Ivana Trump. Cigarette boats and yachts buzz like flies around the azure Adriatic, the hotels are looking good, and the marinas look exactly like their pictures do in the tourist brochures. The crickets chirp energetically (with more energy, or so they say, than they used to chirp in communist Yugoslavia); the sun rays shine with greater potency, but the sun block creams are stronger, too. The tycoons wrangle like village dogs over what is left of the old communist workers' vacation centers (to eradicate the last traces of that "grim communist past," when workers were able to afford a vacation on the coast). There aren't any Serbs left, and that, too, is auspicious: their summer homes, with which they had "occupied" the Croatian coast, have long since been blown up, squatted in, or snapped up for a song—with offers the previous owners could not refuse—by the local inhabitants. Others are summering on the Adriatic now, the more "stable" guests: the English, Austrians, Germans, Italians, and the more generously solvent Russians.

3.

So, what connection could there be between an American doctor and Croatian tourism? None. These are parallel worlds. Our world, real and spiritual, is intersected by dense networks of parallel worlds. That is how we live our little lives. Everyone marches along his or her own path. If we were to imagine only for a moment that between the parallel worlds there are passageways, mental chaos would ensue. At least as far as mental traffic is concerned, we use metaphors. They are our defense against nightmares.

This summer I thought back to that American doctor while I was on a boat which took me on a one-day excursion from the island of Krk to the island of Goli Otok (meaning Bare or Naked Island). I happened to be with a small group of fellow writers. We had been joined by a Croat from Australia and a local painter. Our guide was a history teacher, a man who was 82 years old, a former political prisoner who had done time in the Goli Otok prison for three years. There aren't very many Cominformers like him left. The prison, too, is gone.

Goli Otok served briefly, between 1949 and 1956, as a prison for Cominformers, political prisoners who had shown greater loyalty to Stalin than to Tito. In time it became an "ordinary" prison, and was finally abandoned altogether in the 1980s. During the three decades the camp was up and running, the prisoners built a road which runs the length of the island, they planted pine trees which have grown into a thicket over time, and they raised a handful of buildings: an administrative building (dubbed the "hotel" in prison slang), prison barracks, workshops, a movie theater, a tennis court, a hospital, a dock, factories. One of the largest quarries in Yugoslavia was on the island: the prisoners literally smashed rocks. After the prison was officially closed, the inhabitants of the neighboring islands carted off whatever was not nailed down: if they had been able to roll the road up like a carpet they would have tucked it under their arm and lugged it away.

The first thing we saw as we were getting off the boat was a small improvised restaurant by the landing. It occurred to me that I should get myself a bottle of water. The professor hurried us along with him, walking at a speedy clip and out we set, obediently. I felt an irresistible urge to go back, order a cool drink, and linger by the sea for hours, but there was no getting around it. We had come to the Goli Otok prison, for God's sake, to see this horrific blemish on the conscience of Tito, the communists, and all the people of the former Yugoslavia!

4.

Drained by the heat—and my own imagination, which strained to take in the horrors the professor was relating—we could barely catch our breath. Spry and upright like a shadow, the professor paced the familiar paths: from the landing and administration buildings to the barracks and workshops, from the cement mixers to the hospital, from the hospital to the dining hall. The professor used the present tense instead of the past as he described it all. His present tense buzzed around us with a fly-like insistence.

The Goli Otok prison was a taboo topic for many years in Yugoslavia. Only in the late 1970s did there begin to be talk of it in public: the first novels appeared on Goli Otok themes, the first memoirs . . . And then, probably with the avalanche of new events as the demise of Yugoslavia proceeded, the theme vanished again. Many could, at least in this new age, have milked moral profit from Goli Otok. And yet they hadn't. I wondered why.

About four thousand people died in the "Yugoslav gulag," most of them, they say, from illness, typhus, dysentery. The Goli Otok prison was not designed as a death camp, but rather as a terrible and shameful school of mutual humiliation. Each person there was both executioner and victim. That is why the professor modestly remarked at one point that he had once struck a prisoner on the spot where we were standing. "I strike him, I must, what else can I do?" said the professor in his nagging present tense. While the professor was speaking, I noticed an old graffiti inscription left there by the prisoners: *We build the Goli Otok prison, Goli Otok builds us!*

It is victims who fight for their right to memory, not the executioners. The prisoners of Goli Otok were forced to be executioners as well. That is why, among other things, there was a conspiracy of silence among the inmates once they were released.

5.
The Australian Croat, who kept nibbling at food while he toured the island, told me:
"It is so gruesome, all this! If they'd only let me purchase one of

the cells—it wouldn't have to be the one I stayed in—you've no idea how I'd spiff the place up! Like a jewel! When I was here everything gleamed. We scrubbed each rock, you could lick the floor, it was so clean!"

It turns out that the Australian, too, had been incarcerated on Goli Otok.

"Here . . ." he said on a hill, with a sweeping view of the glistening sea, "Here I suffered . . . and all because of that bloodthirsty monster, that dictator, damn his communist mother! I even had to sing a song to him while I broke the rock . . . You know the tune!"

The Australian cleared his throat and sang out with a ringing voice . . .

"Tito marches over Romania mountain . . ."

I thought that the Australian would sing only the one line, but, impassioned, he sang us the whole song. Then he pulled out his mobile phone and explained to someone, presumably in Australia, where he was at that moment.

"What a gorgeous day . . ." I heard him say.

The Australian Croat had not been doing time because of Cominform. The Yugoslav border guards had nabbed him twice as he was trying to slip illegally across the border. He did a year for that at the Goli Otok prison. After he was released, he crossed the border illegally yet again, this time successfully, and lit out for Australia. This was the first time, after all those years, he'd been back.

The Australian moved me: because of the food he kept pulling from his backpack, because of the care he showed for the place he'd been held prisoner (I, too, found myself thinking I'd love to roll up my sleeves and scrub it all clean!), and because of his failure to demonstrate the Goli Otok humiliation. The singing in praise of the bloodthirsty monster and dictator, which had been foisted on him so many years before, got the better of him—in his own throat—with his demonstration of what was an almost physical satisfaction. Yes, *We build the Goli Otok prison, and Goli Otok builds us.*

6.

A month or so before our excursion an article had come out in the Croatian press about the filming of gay porn movies on the island of Goli Otok, in a Croatian-Hungarian co-production. There were photographs in the paper of muscular young men sporting helmets and grasping pickaxes, which lent veracity to the story.

As we walked down the hill from the prison barracks, we came upon a German movie crew making their porn movie on Goli Otok. Of the porn stars we saw only the boldest: an appealing-looking young woman in skimpy black panties who was writhing in front of the prison barracks.

The local painter, a friend of the Croatian fellow from Australia, couldn't rein in her indignation.

"Do you know where you are?" she asked the young woman in German. The cameraman stepped back quietly.

The girl responded with an indifferent shrug.

"Are you not ashamed of yourself?! You are strutting around barely dressed in a place where thousands of sufferers died!"

"Why attack her? It is hardly her fault . . ." I tried to intervene.

"What do you mean, it's not her fault! She hasn't a shred of political awareness in that head of hers!" snapped the painter. "Be ashamed!" she snarled at the young woman.

The girl shrugged again.

"You are making porn movies in a place where the bones of sufferers are buried!" the painter was unrelenting.

The scantily clad girl was finally prodded from her indifference.

"Not porn! Art!" she said so assertively that we all, for a moment, envied her remarkable degree of artistic confidence.

As if speaking of something that had had nothing to do with him, the professor detailed the methods of torture used on the prisoners with a steady voice: dripping water down a tube into the nose, nearly drowning the prisoner, piling heavy rocks on a prisoner's chest, humiliation by external control of bodily functions, and other acts, all of them so incongruous with the stunning landscape.

"I push a heavy rock there, by that hill, and here, in this place, they beat us . . ." the professor spun his sad tale.

7.

I moved away from the group at one point. I was suffering from thirst and went off toward the restaurant by the landing. Finding myself alone by the road, which looked as white as chalk in the bright sunlight, I suddenly felt an indescribable fear. I tried to move more quickly, but the terror held me back. I stepped in painful slow motion. Fear oozed out of every pore. I'd never felt anything like it. I wondered later what could have brought it on. Perhaps the silence, that particular, heavy silence. I couldn't hear my own footsteps; it was as if the road I was walking on was paved with cotton batting. The silence planted itself on my neck, lay down on top of me, pressed me, and stole my breath.

8.

Cool drinks awaited us at the restaurant, and not very fresh mackerel, which we ate with gusto. Near the place we were sitting there was a makeshift stand selling souvenirs. There were plaster figures of prisoners in prison garb lined up on the stand like old grey potatoes. Their eyes, two black holes sunken into the plaster, were meant to conjure suffering. There were also deftly fashioned cudgels, much like baseball bats (the varnished ones cost more), with the carved inscription "Greetings from the Goli Otok prison" and ashtrays with the same sentiment. I bought an ashtray and a wooden cudgel. Later I left the cudgel in my hotel room on the island of Krk, ashamed of my own compulsion to bring home an apt souvenir.

We got back onto the boat with a feeling of relief. As we pulled away from the pier my eyes were drawn by a sign on the landing: "Hunters' Society." The old fellow who ran the boat flicked on a fitting recording of Dalmatian folk singing. The Australian Croat plucked his last sack of potato chips, and a package of cookies which oozed melted chocolate, from his backpack, and he offered them around enthusiastically. The professor fell asleep in a quiet torpor.

It was late in the afternoon when we left the island, but the heat had not abated. I pinched my heart, trying to conjure fitting feelings, but, strangely, my heart stayed cold. The only sharp, clear stab I felt was when I caught sight of the Goli Otok pines. The pines had grown into a thicket thanks to the shadows cast by the prisoners. This was one of the methods of Goli Otok torture: the inmates were forced to cast shadows with their bodies so that the newly planted saplings wouldn't bake in the sun. They were saving on water. Not people.

9.

How to tame a vampire, one's own trauma? How to reconnect with the past? As my American doctor did, who had embraced the collective trauma as her own, trudging every year to the sites of the Holocaust? As the professor did who was trying to turn back "objectively" to distant inmate memories but relied on the treacherous present tense? As the Australian Croat did, who came back to the site of his trauma armed with a backpack laden with sandwiches, cookies, sacks of chips, and a mobile phone, that fragile but lifesaving connection with the outside world? Should everything be scrubbed, polished like a jewel, or left, instead, as is? How to connect the present and the past? How to communicate an old trauma so that others truly understand it? Weren't we longing to find shade and have a cool drink while we listened to the professor? And what of all we heard did we take to heart? What about me, who is passing on this story? What about my responsibility? Can I assert without a twinge of conscience that the text I am sending to its unknown recipient is merely a postcard from my vacation? How can I go forward reconciling my own past with that of the collective? Is one's own past reliable? Is the collective past reliable? And what about the "official" past, the past that is in the history books? Is that reliable?

10.

The history of the Goli Otok prison camp is, in some ways, my life story as well. I was born in 1949, and grew up with the ideology of the defiant historical "NO" with which Tito repudiated Stalin. My father, a Yugoslav, married a Bulgarian woman, my mother; Bulgarian or Russian, people didn't make much distinction, every East European foreigner was a *spy*. In that brief period of collective paranoia my mother was, I'm guessing, assumed to be a *Bulgarian spy*. My father might have been accused as a *traitor*. Luckily he wasn't. Still, my mother was not able to visit her parents for ten years. I only met my maternal grandparents in 1957, two years after the start of diplomatic relations with the countries of the Eastern block. This historical moment remains captured in a photograph that I remember. Tito, wearing his Marshal's uniform, is shaking hands with Khrushchev. While Khrushchev is bowing in a way that is almost servile, Tito is standing tall. I remember an episode from our short trip to visit my grandmother and grandfather in the city of Varna on the Black Sea. Having learned where I was from, a little Bulgarian boy my same age snarled rudely in my face:

"Your Tito is a capitalist pig!"

"Your Stalin is a pig," I retorted calmly.

11.

A person with an anthropological sensibility might well wonder how Croats (and indeed all the Balkan peoples!), who have cultivated collective obsessions for tombs and cemeteries, have not yet gotten around to making a museum, for instance, to the victims of communism in the Goli Otok prison, especially when most Croats perceive Tito's Yugoslavia as the main culprit for all their later troubles.

When the news got out that the Goli Otok prison had become a favorite destination for filming porn, the president of the society for political prisoners lodged an irate protest against the degradation of the "symbol of communist terror," adding that on Goli Otok "sacrifices were made for an independent Croatia." In saying this, the president progressed from his disgust at the real pornography, to a pornographization of history. The people incarcerated at the Goli Otok camp were, after all, "Stalinists," alleged sympathisers of Stalin and the Soviet model of communism. At that time of Yugoslav "McCarthyism," people were arrested overnight. Goli Otok was a place to be "rehabilitated" from Stalinism, in which people referred to as "hard-core communists" were supposed to be transformed into "Titoists." As far as the "Croatian martyrs" are concerned, there were those, too, but later. Many of them had fled in time, and then returned to Croatia in the early 1990s, to became, first, "Croatian heroes," and, soon thereafter, "war criminals" whose names are on the lists published by the Hague Tribunal.

Goli Otok was a site of horrific torture: people were brought here not to be put to death, but to become human wrecks. It was a place of gradual and certain dehumanization. Some preferred death, like the poor fellow, who slashed his own throat with an aluminum teaspoon, that the professor told us about. And some hastened to humiliate others, even when no one forced them to.

12.

In a country where the cemeteries and tombs were, and have remained, a key place for the struggle among the differing political options, Goli Otok—a large, sad, cemetery—awaits its symbolic destiny. Over the last ten years, Croats have been vandalizing, blowing up, urinating on, and demolishing some three thousand monuments. They had raised these monuments themselves to honor the victims of fascism. That, however, was in another life. This is a country where no one seems able to decide which historical option to embrace as official—that fifty-year, Yugoslav, anti-fascist and communist version, or the Ustasha, fascist version, harkening back to the time when Croatia was an independent state. Monuments have no staying power in a country like this. The monuments to Tito and the Partisans were blown up. New ones, of course, have been raised: monuments to Tudman, and the occasional Ustasha "hero." Even these new ones cannot count on permanence, because all it will take is an anti-fascist wink from the European Union and the Croats (and all the others waiting in line) will have to light the fuse again.

13.

Life is turning out to be a better and wiser writer than others who pretend to that role: the politicians, dictators, military leaders, historians and counterfeiters, fighters for one option or another, liars, criminals, murderers, and the writers themselves. If nothing else, life comes up with more apt metaphors, and its feel for irony is unsurpassed.

Life, bringing the metaphor full circle, drew the sex-workers of the porn industry to the (naked!) island of Goli Otok. The porn industry is currently taking advantage of the existing scenography: the abandoned quarry, the dark prison cells, the rusty skeletal remains of the prison beds that are discarded everywhere, the gray stone facades of buildings scribbled with graffiti, the history of human humiliation. Today, in the setting of the former torture chambers, the porn industry is flourishing with the clinking of dirty money, small change.

Life, I'm guessing, following the meandering of a second metaphor, may bring hunters to the Goli Otok camp. The sign that said "Hunters' Society," which caught my eye as we were pushing off, suggested just that possibility. They say that hunting tourism is quite lucrative. As part of the "Mediterranean as it once was," on the island of Krk, for instance, tourist profiteers introduced the wild boar (which had never been one of the fauna of the Mediterranean). The boar bred with a speed that outstripped the efficiency of the hunters, and now the creatures are ravaging the fields of Krk, the sheep, and the shepherds. If hunters bring game to the island of Goli Otok, a second metaphor will be brought full circle, the metaphor of "hunting people." Perhaps this will result in saving the slang the prisoners favored from oblivion, such as the *topli zec* (warm rabbit), which was the name for an initiation ritual: a newcomer to the camp was forced to run a gauntlet of prisoners who beat him with sticks or stones. The term "herring hunt" referred to the system by which prisoners informed on one another. The prisoners would taunt one another, and each would be both informer and examinee. If someone made the mistake of complaining about something, the people in charge would hear of it that instant and the prisoner would be punished. So they learned to keep quiet. They still kept quiet once they'd been released. They kept quiet for years. Many fell ill from the silence. No one, they say, succeeded in escaping the Goli Otok prison. The hunt for the occasional escapee was efficient, and nature gave the upper hand to the hunters.

There is a third option. If real estate agencies (like that one with the seductive name "Rock of Joy") take things into their own hands, the island of Goli Otok could become a paradise for tourists, for solvent Russians, for instance. Should that happen, yet another Goli Otok story would come full circle. Goli Otok was at first an Austro-Hungarian prison. Prisoners from the Eastern front were interned there during the First World War. Russians returned to Goli Otok later. These were the Russians who had come to post-war Yugoslavia as political commissars, ideological instructors, or, in today's lingo, the managers of communism. As soon as that famous quarrel with Stalin erupted, Tito arrested the Russian commissars first. The Russians were the first post-Second World War internees on Goli Otok. So if the "Rock of Joy" real estate agency takes things in hand, this could be a source of hedonistic revenge for the great-grandchildren of those Russians from the First World War and the grandchildren of the Russian political commissars. What could be sweeter!

Everyone can, and usually does, extract a profit from the past. Except the victims. The victims of the Goli Otok prison need no monument. They have raised one to themselves already, by planting those pine saplings. Behind each tree stands the invisible shadow of a former inmate of Goli Otok, shielding the tree from the baking sun and soaking the soil with their invisible sweat. The crickets chirp, the sheep wander through, leaving their droppings, a visitor passes by, stops, carves his name in the bark of a tree, but the dark pines of Goli Otok stand; they do not sway.

2006

NOBODY'S HOME

*In the more modest window of the stamp-and-seal workshop, most
of the space was taken up by enamel plates with the inscriptions
"Shut for Lunch." "Lunch hour from 2 to 3 P.M.," "Closed for the
Lunch Break," or simply "Closed," "Shop Shut," and finally a black
baseboard with gold letters—"Shut for Stocktaking."*
                              —*Ilf & Petrov,* The Golden Calf

I am standing in a bank. I am waiting for the people in front of me
in line to finish their business at the teller's window. After a while it
is my turn. I go up to the window. The young bank clerk snaps . . .

"You haven't got a number . . ."

I turn to look behind me. Nobody's there.

"Nobody's there! I don't need a number."

"First, take a number," he says coldly.

"But there is no one behind me!"

"If you do not have a number I cannot serve you," he says testily.

"The number is to prevent people from cutting in. Right now
there is nobody here but the two of us . . ."

The young man watches me with a reptilian gaze. His pupils
are rigid; he is a soldier defending the system: there is no room for
negotiation.

The essence of communist daily life—at least for the ordinary person—was not its lack of democracy; or the restriction of political,
religious, sexual, and other freedoms; fear in the face of the invisible countenance of totalitarianism; or the very visible long lines
and half-empty shops. It was the unending, everyday degradation of
ordinary human reason. The communist nightmare was comprised of

a repetitive degradation of the individual in everyday situations, the opaque mysticism of things that have been banned, the impossibility of dialogue and mediation, the everyday smashing of heads against the blind wall of the absurd. People looked like sweaty runners jogging in their life race and toting a burden twice their size. Nothing, nothing went smoothly, nothing could be accomplished without friction and anguish: doors were often closed. Signs with the inscriptions *Vyhodnoj den'* (Day Off), *Zakryto na remont* (Closed for Repairs), or simply *Zakryto* (Closed) were an essential part of the landscape of everyday communist life, and the paranoia and the profound sense of the absurd were an essential part of the other, inner, landscape.

The interchange in the bank did not, however, happen in Soviet Moscow, but at a branch of the most powerful Dutch bank in Amsterdam, in June, 2005. There was nothing remarkable about the scene: ones like it happen more and more often.

The *nummertje*, the little number, is one of the more ubiquitous of Dutch words. At the push of a button a little dispensing machine scrolls out a small piece of paper with a number on it, and this *nummertje* awaits customers at the bank, the post office, the tax office, the police office for foreigners, in shops, often in doctor's offices, and in nearly all administrative offices. A person who has had experience in both systems, capitalism and communism, cannot help but wonder whether the essentials of everyday life in communism—expunged from the countries where they ruled for decades—have sneaked illegally over to the West? What happened when the Berlin wall came own? Free flow. If that is so, then it is a logical conclusion that the flow didn't move in only one direction. It didn't flow only West to East, did it?

As far as the West-East direction goes, the nostalgic capitalist right-wingers of modest means and uncertain pensions, the disenfranchised capitalist mob who like to be reminded of the fresh taste of capitalism, are migrating eastward, to the post-communist countries. The epicenter of capitalism at this moment is in China, or so they say. But the ordinary people in Western Europe haven't the where-withal to go that far, and why should they: the brand new shiny McDonald's are here, in front of their noses, in East and Central Europe. Everyday capitalist life and its symbols are, hence, migrating eastward. In the east of Europe, in Poland, Hungary, Croatia, the barely solvent West European can afford a brief respite of dignity, a return to his oppressed individual self. The Belgian, Austrian, or German can afford to get his hair cut in the finest post-communist salon. Jura, Jacek, and Zsusza not only keep their salons open until nine in the evening, if need be, they are even prepared to come, fully equipped, to the hotel room. The weary Western Europeans from the front lines of capitalism have discovered in the former communist countries the forgotten appeal of royal treatment and full service: pedicures, hair dressers, dentists, tailors, physiotherapists, doctors, even sex. Nose jobs, work on the bags under the eyes, dental im-plants, porcelain crowns and bridges, liposuction, massage, bypasses, abortions, efficient gall bladder surgery, and treatment for gout—all of this, and much more, costs less and is done more quickly in post-communist clinics than it is further West. And the people of post-communism are courteous and eager to please. They are adept at foreign languages. The local food is healthy, varied, and inexpensive, the taxis are so much cheaper, the hotels—affordable. Everything, or at least that is how it seems from the perspective of the tourist, functions like a "Swiss watch," the symbol of capitalist precision and efficiency. Yes, the air in post-communist zones is healthy: it has the brisk fragrance of fresh money and a secure capitalist future.

Unlike the post-communist air, the air is heavy and electric, exactly as if a storm is brewing in the Western European capitalistic zones. People are nervous. They step on others, even if they haven't been stepped on themselves; they bite others even when they haven't been bitten themselves. They cannot understand why they're doing this:

after all, they live in settled, democratic, tolerant, socially sensitive societies. All their rights are safeguarded. Perhaps it is just a bit too cramped; nothing seems to work the way it should. People wait for buses longer than they used to, the trams aren't on schedule, and it is no longer certain that a traveler will be able to get from Utrecht to Amsterdam in a day. The public services are too often reduced to chaos. The bureaucracy is rigid and lethargic; oh well, it's the same everywhere, but here, aside from everything else, they are forgetful. It takes so much effort and time, traipsing from one place to another, to chase down the most ordinary of documents. Anyone normal is inclined to give up. Salespeople have become rude, and purchasing the most ordinary things can turn easily into a nightmare. The little Western European, who has been boosting his self-confidence for years by watching documentaries about Russians spending a whole day waiting in line for bananas, suddenly realizes that he has been spending his days fruitlessly chasing after services on the phone: cable television (they took the annual fee out of his bank account three times by mistake, and haven't reimbursed him yet); taxes (they sent him a tax bill that is twice the amount he earned for all of last year); the appliance store (for months he's been waiting for them to deliver him that new TV, after the first television he purchased didn't work); the hospital (they lost his test results months ago and cannot find them); the bank (it was an error: for months he has been paying off his loan at a much higher interest rate than he's supposed to); school (they refused to enroll his child in school and gave no explanation). When he finally reaches the phone number he has requested, he follows the recorded message's instructions carefully, and is greeted by a brusque recording: *Al onze medewerkers zijn op dit moment in gesprek* (All our operators are busy at this time). The message is crystal clear: everyone else in the world is at work. Only he is wasting his time pursuing his little moment of justice. The only recourse left—other than expensive lawyers or suicide—is a personal terrorist gesture (so that he, too, can get some relief!): he'll spit in someone's soup, elbow a person deliberately on the tram, terrify a pedestrian when he's cycling, jab a passerby in the ribs, give someone the runaround when issuing them a document they badly need, leave his own rubbish in front of a neighbor's door, kick in the signal light on a car.

On a day in June, 2005, I needed to find a photo shop. Amsterdam is a tourist city and there are many such shops. Two or three which I had used in the past were under renovation (*Zakryto na remont!*). Finally I found one that was working. There were two Englishmen there, obviously tourists. The saleswoman had sold them the wrong thing, and now she was reluctantly reimbursing them. The Englishmen left, and I waited. Taking no notice of me, the saleswoman tidied the shop: she stuffed a sheaf of papers vigorously into a plastic rubbish bag. Finally she looked up . . .

"What are you waiting for?"

"What do you think I am standing here and waiting for?"

The saleswoman squinted, a spurt of insult flashed across her face (I had insulted her intelligence by responding to her question with a question).

"Get out of my shop!"

This scene is more the exception than the rule, but situations which demonstrate a lack of professional courtesy and a disturbing lack of professional competence are on the rise. I was the coincidental victim of the personal terrorist gesture of an Amsterdam saleswoman: irritated, the woman had vented her rage on me. A series of flashbacks that belonged to another time and other places spun through my mind as I left the shop. They weren't real flashbacks; they were a conditioned response: I was salivating at the ringing of a bell whose sound I knew very well. The insult at the sudden and pointless humiliation floated to the surface, a legible psychogram of communist reality.

Man's liberation has happened precisely as communism had predicted it would. There is the majority, the enthusiasts, the people who take part in everything without asking themselves any questions, and there is a negligible minority, skeptics, people who pull back. The enthusiasts—who have the good fortune today to be living in a present which was dangled in front of others for years as the "glowing future"—fly on cheap flights to all destinations, clog up airports, drag their children along, elbow their way through museums, galleries, shows, pack into the Sistine Chapel giving off collective gasps of admiration, slog through the European and American MOMAs with the same energy they use to slog around the supermarket, travel in crowds, climb the Himalayas, dive in the Caribbean, kayak along the Dneiper, frequent the traveled paths, lay down new ones, buy anything and everything, gawk at their media gods and goddesses, reproduce, pay their funereal dues regularly, and die.

The skeptics slow down the tempo and gradually withdraw: they retire at forty, cancel all subscriptions, close their bank accounts, cut up their credit cards, disconnect, buy only what they need (and only with cash), move from a registered address to an *unlisted address.* At the new address they do what they can to live more "humanely," the way people lived in the communist countries in the 1960s: they visit other people, linger over coffee, chat with neighbors, make their own clothes, knit pullovers for themselves and their children, make raspberry jam (from raspberries they grew in their garden), exchange recipes, play with children, and spend their time carefully and with full awareness that they are spending the principle of their small lives. While members of the first group, the enthusiasts, are admirers of the Market and market ideology, the second, the "deserters from the working front," are quiet supporters of demarketization.

Capitalism has waded deep into communism today. The notion that work created man is profoundly communist. Today man is truly master of his own body and a "do-it-yourselfer." He does everything himself, without exploiting others. The services that other people used to do for him, today's person does alone. He makes his own travel arrangements: he selects the destination on-line, the best price, transfers the money from his account to the account of the airline, checks himself in at the airport. You can buy everything over the Internet, even the kitchen sink. At the large retail centers—designed as a place to congregate—it is difficult to find a salesperson: the buyer chooses the clothing himself. The checkout counter awaits him as he leaves the store, and he experiences that as a necessary evil of communication. There are computers on the street in America which look like cash machines. A person who gets a headache while he's out for a walk can press a button and find all he needs to know about headaches. It is possible that even the more complicated services will cease to be provided in the future: imagine a person going to the hospital, stepping into a scanner, reading off the results, and performing the operation himself with computerized guidance. Of course this will only work if everything functions smoothly, if computers don't break down the world over.

Anyone who is interested will be able to find out in museums how the world of work and exchange of labor used to look in the old days. At the museum of industrial culture, for instance, the visitor will be able to click on a screen, press a button, descend into a mineshaft, take hold of a virtual miner's pick, scrape at virtual seams of coal with the pick, and feel virtual sweat drip down his back. Once he can take no more, he pushes another button, foments a virtual revolution, and overthrows the despised exploiters. And then, leaving behind the gloom of the mineshaft, he will pause to think about how the exploiters in the old days had a face and a first and last name, and inevitably he will then begin to wonder who the exploiters are today. Today they are invisible, so perhaps that is why people seem to think there aren't any. Do they exist? Are there classes? To which class does he belong? Who are his enemies? And what is with his allies? Where are they? Could he possibly have been left alone in this world?!

Greenland has become a popular tourist destination, or so they say, over the last few years. People with frazzled nerves and deep pockets go there to watch glaciers. While they watch them with admiration in the gloom, the vast glaciers move very slowly by, gleaming magically with a milky blue glow, floating like gobs of meringue in a custard cream. The people hold their breath and gaze at the immense hunks of ice. The air is crisp, the sky scattered with countless big stars. And somewhere out there, among the stars, the Lord's answering machine is playing and replaying a message, nobody knows how old: *All our operators are currently busy . . . Al onze medewerkers zijn op dit moment in gesprek . . . Alle unsere Mitarbeiter sind zur Zeit belegt . . . Tous nos opérateurs sont momentanément occupé . . . Për momentin të tëra linjat janë t ë zëna . . . Tutti i nostri operatori sono momentaneamente occupati . . . Nygdo neni domu . . . Nobody's home . . . Nikog nema doma . . .*

June 2005

Author's Note

Every day and age has its rules. Currently, good behavior dictates that we be politically correct, evade conflicts, espouse tolerance, and make no hasty judgments. To be judgmental is viewed as one of the most reprehensible human traits. People are likely to think today that an optimist is a good person, while a pessimist is the lowest of the low. Picking your nose in public is more forgivable then being pessimistic. Pessimism and smoking go hand in hand: both of them pollute. All that would be fine, if it weren't for the fact that political correctness is most often a mask for human hypocrisy, that conflict avoidance masks cowardice, tolerance masks indifference, a lack of a critical faculty masks brownnosing, and optimism trumps loyalty on every occasion and under every system. We live in a time that urges us to behave as if we are in paradise. Yet the world we live in is no paradise. This book breaks the rules of good behavior, because it bickers.

My eyes are often drawn by "lunatics," those nutty passersby who mutter to themselves, shout, gripe, carp, protest, argue with invisible opponents. These people are not panhandlers; in fact, they hardly see us. They trudge through the world, grumbling. When I see them on the street, I am struck by the poetic thought that these "lunatics" are inscribing a vast, invisible book of complaints in the air. There are certain advantages to being a writer: as a writer you can carp in public and no one says you're crazy. Furthermore, a newspaper sometimes offers you a bit of space and a little honorarium for doing so. That space is called a column.

Nobody's Home appeared in its British edition in the fall of 2007. The book was already in bookstore displays when I stumbled on a quote of Virginia Woolf's, which I had once come across but had since forgotten: *As a woman I have no country. As a woman I want no country. As a woman my country is the whole world.* The manifest power of the statement took my breath away. If someone were to ask me to sum up the substance of my book in a few sentences, I would choose these words, though I have no hope of measuring up to Virginia Woolf's woman of the world.

Most of the short feuilletons in the first part of the book were written between 1998 and 2000 as a column for the Swiss newspaper *Die Weltwoche.* The editors set only one condition: each piece should be no longer than eight hundred words. The feuilleton is a particular genre of journalism, an exercise in brevity, a sort of commissioned diary. There are many incidental themes which I never would have put on paper had it not been for this sweet commitment. I say all this because some readers may be startled by the fragmented brevity of these pieces. There is no need to waste time counting the words (I confess transgressing the limits many times), but rather decide whether I used them well.

Some of the longer essays in the second part of the book also came from literary commissions. For instance, the essay "What is European about European Literature?" is part of a project in which some thirty European writers mused on an assigned theme. The essay "Europa, Europa" was written on a train in which I traveled with another hundred writers from one side of Europe to the other for forty-five days. The essay "The Alibi of Cultural Differences, or: How I Got the Picture" was written for a thematic issue of *Neue Zuricher Zeitung* dedicated to the "problematic" ex-Yugoslav refugees who live in Switzerland. The essay "Amsterdam, Amsterdam" was published in Dutch as a slim separate volume.

The essays in the book more or less follow the chronology they were written in. I care more about thematic rhythm than I do about chronology, so for the American edition, at the last moment, I decided to add several recent essays, a few of which appeared in a column I have been writing for the Polish newspaper *Gazeta Wyborcza*, and a couple more which appeared in the British quarterly *The Drawbridge*. All the essays in the fourth part of the book were written in 2007. As I write this author's note, an essay for the Polish paper, which I still need to finish and send, is on the desk in front of me. In other words, only the book ends here. The column goes on.

And one more thing. The reader may wonder why I have introduced so many quotes from the novel *The Golden Calf*. Let me explain. I feel that every writer should pay some sort of symbolic literary "tax," because writing is not the humblest of vocations. A tax, hence, on narcissism.

Nearly all my books contain references to other works of literature. This is a way to pay my symbolic tax and, more importantly, to remind readers that literature is a vast cultural system. If the structure of the chosen genre, or the book itself, does not allow more subtle ways to pay homage to my literary predecessors (or contemporaries) as is the case with this book, then I use quotes. I do this in hopes that the reader will decide to read unduly neglected or underrated books. The *Golden Calf* by Ilf and Petrov is one such book.

Amsterdam, October 2007

Dubravka Ugresic is
Museum of Uncond
essay collections, most re
broke out in the former Yu
and was proclaimed a "tra
posed to harsh and persist
in 1993 and currently lives

Ellen Elias-Bursać has translated works by several Yugoslavian writers, including David Albahari's *Götz and Meyer*, for which she was awarded the ALTA National Translation Award in 2006. She also received the AATSEEL Award in 1998 for her translation of Albahari's *Words Are Something Else.*

Open Letter—the University of Rochester's nonprofit, literary translation press—is one of only a handful of publishing houses dedicated to increasing access to world literature for English readers. Publishing twelve titles in translation each year, Open Letter searches for works that are extraordinary and influential, works that we hope will become the classics of tomorrow.

Making world literature available in English is crucial to opening our cultural borders, and its availability plays a vital role in maintaining a healthy and vibrant book culture. Open Letter strives to cultivate an audience for these works by helping readers discover imaginative, stunning works of fiction and by creating a constellation of international writing that is engaging, stimulating, and enduring.

Current and forthcoming titles from Open Letter include works from France, Norway, Brazil, Lithuania, Iceland, and numerous other countries.

www.openletterbooks.org